As They Slept

A Year in the

CW00881934

Dedicated to Sophie Louise Leeks.

Foreword

As Andy greets me to discuss this 'book', he follows my opening pleasantry with the phrase "I'm absolutely knackered".

Given that the 'inspiration' for this tree waster was a Facebook row where he suggested people who sleep on trains are wasting their lives, there is more than a whiff of self righteousness in my nostrils.

Andy and I go back almost a decade, during which one of us has forged a career as a respectable mortgage broker, (with very reasonable rates by the way) and the other has become a sour-faced cretin, desperate to win a petty Facebook argument.

To my mind this is a pointless book - as ill conceived as his lifelong dedication to Watford football club.

So it's your call - you can inflate his ego and endure this nonsense, or you can just put it back in the bargain bin where you found it.

Whether you read on or not is up to you; just don't say I didn't warn you.

Dean Mason

Wednesday 19th September 2012

On Tuesday 18th September 2012, I posted a status on Facebook.

I was on the 07:51 train into London and everyone around me was asleep.

The status read:

"Maybe I'm in the minority here, but it really annoys me when commuters sleep on trains, especially on the morning leg. They've just had a whole night's sleep! You can get so much done on your commute – it's criminal to sleep through it."

Some of my friends totally disagreed. Well, I say friends, but this was Facebook, so it's probably more accurate to say that some people I barely knew disagreed. Apparently I was wrong to assume people had enjoyed a whole night's sleep, and there were doubtless many factors contributing to why they were sleeping. Many things could be responsible for their tiredness, such as work stress or restless children.

I honestly didn't doubt for one second that these people had busy lives and that for them sleep was often at a premium; I was just making the point that using the commute to sleep was a waste of potentially valuable time. I then decided to list all of the things which could be done during their nap time. "You could pay some bills, research a recipe, get in touch with an old friend, catch up on the news, do some online shopping, enter a competition or even do some creative writing," I asserted.

By the time I'd got to the last two, I had run out of ideas and my brain was clearly running on empty. It's for this reason and this reason only that I then followed it up with the perhaps foolhardy promise: ".....In fact, I'll prove how much time you're wasting by sleeping – I'm going to write something on every commute for a year!"

And just like that, 'As They Slept – A Year in the Life of a London Commuter' was born. A challenge laid down to myself – to prove to all of those narcoleptic commuters just what could be done in those lost sleepy hours. At the time, I had no idea what to write about, and the content of the book was as much a mystery to me as to you, but I realised that was what made it truly exciting. I've always enjoyed a challenge, but this was the first time I had ever actually set one for myself. Normally there's a friend involved, and almost always alcohol to blame and/or a woman to impress. This time there was no alcohol, no woman to impress and, as Facebook was involved, there were certainly no friends involved.

I then set out a series of rules and guidelines that I would try to adhere to. Firstly, and most importantly, the book would only be written while commuting. Put simply, that means if I'm not commuting, I'm not writing. Every day that I commuted to work, I promised to add a chapter to this book. I was adamant that I wouldn't be spending my workdays, evenings or weekends writing. I have a day job to do and a family to keep happy. You'll see as you go through the book that every chapter is titled with the date that it was written. From time to time there will be gaps in the dates and this will be because I was either ill, working from home or on holiday.

Some days I imagine you will get some news, some days maybe a little story or anecdote, but almost every other day I expect I'll be moaning about the fat bastard in the seat opposite, listening to his rubbish music, with a Tesco carrier bag between his feet, a can of Stella in his hand and an almost certain tragic early death ahead of him.

I kid you not - he has managed to down four cans of Stella in the time it has taken me to write this first entry! That's four cans in the time it has taken to get from London Cannon Street to Tonbridge. Four cans in 45 miles. That's a can every 11.25 miles. I hope this guy never travels long distance, it just might kill him. What if he tried to keep his can to mile ratio up on his holiday this year? Benidorm is 895 miles away, so that would be just short of 80 cans. Looking at him, I think he could give it a bloody good go.

The whole point of this book is to show what can be done while commuting, and hope-fully to prove once and for all that sleeping on trains really is a complete waste of time.

Friday 21st September 2012

The new school term was recently upon us, and the few weeks over the summer where the train was devoid of hormonal offspring was a pleasant and enjoyable time for me. That said, in some ways it's nice to have them back. They're so fresh-faced and innocent and their worries seem so trivial.

I've spent the last couple of days dealing with my inner demons, determined not to put the heating on until October the 1st. "Just another few days" I tell myself as I hop about, shivering in the early morning darkness. School children, however, have worries of a different kind. "I'm not sure if Olivia is talking to me, she didn't text me back after PE!" "Jack was on Facebook last night and he ignored my live chat request!" Depressing really, when you consider that school-children's worries and woes these days seem to revolve around social issues and very rarely actually involve school itself.

It was refreshing then this morning when I heard three girls debating which day was their favourite. "I like Mondays because we have double Maths, followed by P.E and R.S" said one "I like Wednesdays as we have Double French, followed by History and Art" followed the other. It was easy to see that these girls were new to the school and therefore the timetable. They had the telltale signs – they had the clean blazers, the new bags, the shiny shoes and smiles on their faces. It probably won't be long before they are discussing their least favourite day and then I suppose it's a gradual slide towards the inevitable question, "Is Olivia talking to me?"

It would be nice if commuters talked about their days in the same way. "Tuesday's my worst day – it starts with a morning commute where I contemplate suicide, followed by small talk with the world's most boring receptionist, and finished off by a meeting with a room-full of arrogant arse-holes."

The great thing about school, and what children truly don't realise and unfortunately won't realise until it's too late, is that it is a lot of fun. It's a lot of fun because it offers a lot of variety. I remember one particular day at school where I had eight single lessons. Most days we had four double periods or a mixture of double and singles, but Wednesday was fun because we had eight different lessons. I can't remember exactly what we had on Wednesdays, but it was something like Maths, followed by English, followed by Geography, followed by P.E, followed by Science, followed by Art, followed by I.T, followed by French. Ok, it was a terrible way to end the day, but where else were we going to learn some foreign swear words? (And Miss Kleine was possibly the best looking teacher that I ever encountered).

Just think though – what if we could incorporate that kind of variety into our working lives today? How great would it be to do a spot of Accounting, followed by Building, followed by Catering, followed by Bus Driving? Maybe that's the solution. No one would leave their job through boredom and it would be difficult to get the sack. Agreed, there would be a few things to iron out on the admin and logistical side, but I honestly think it could work.

Monday 24th September 2012

We had a birthday in the household this weekend as my wife turned 35, or as she likes to call it, her 30th birthday, plus 5. She is adamant she remains in her early to mid-thirties and will only cross over to her mid-thirties when she turns 36. At 37 and 38 she will still be in her mid-thirties, and finally at 39 she will then, and only then, and for one year only, be in her late thirties. We have not discussed what she will be when she turns 40, maybe she will be in her really late thirties or maybe she will be 30 plus 10.

Birthdays are strange things. Growing up, we never made a huge thing of birthdays. I can't really remember any parties being thrown and I distinctly remember the first time presents were replaced by vouchers and money. Birthdays are, after all, a lot of effort. If we're being honest, a birthday is simply a celebration of the day you were born. A day that is then celebrated year after year after year until you die. Here's the hard truth, people – enjoy your birthdays when you are young, because by the time you turn 21, you will have had all of the birthday excitement that you are ever going to get.

Year 22 and upwards will be a succession of disappointment for you and stress for your loved ones as you try and fail to drop hints about what you like and they in turn try and fail to spot interests and hobbies which never existed in the first place.

"I got you this because you mentioned once, when drunk, six years ago, that you'd like to try drawing with charcoal!"

"Thanks," you say as you try to decide whether it would be better off in the shed or the spare room, eventually deciding on the shed as that's where the other flammable items are kept.

I think it's right to have a big party when you're 21. You are celebrating finally becoming an adult. Sure, turning 18 gives you the right to poison your body with cigarettes and alcohol, but turning 21 gives you the maturity to deal with it. For instance, when you're 18, you'll go out and get irresponsibly drunk, mixing drinks, talking to strangers in kebab shops and throwing up over the dog. When you're 21 you will still go out and get irresponsibly drunk, mixing drinks, talking to strangers in kebab shops and throwing up over the dog, but you'll take a glass of water to bed.

What I suggest is to keep the 18th and 21st birthday parties, but introduce a new major celebration – the 22nd birthday party. This is where you gather all of your friends and family, (the advantage of this being that at 22 you still have plenty of both) and you have one big final party which represents all of the birthdays that you will ever have in your lifetime. It's brilliant, because you can go through all of the emotions as you drunkenly celebrate your last ever birthday party.

You'll be sober at the start of the party and that will represent your sensible years, where people buy you a special pen for work, or a desk toy, or a new wallet. You'd then have a few drinks and be merry; this would represent your early twenties, with all of the hope and wonder, your life still ahead of you, a career to forge and a relationship to nurture. After a few more you might get a bit silly; this would represent the time that you decide to have a career change and go from being a solicitor to a bus driver, or when you decide to leave your wife for the boss's daughter.

After a drink or two more you will become emotional. This represents the time, approximately two years later, when you're driving that bus or having an argument with your new lover, when you sit down and think "What have I done with my life?" Eventually, at the end of the party, you'll be unconscious on the floor in a pool of your own sick and I don't need to tell you the years which this represents.

So there we have it. No more awkward gatherings, no more tedious meals out, no more surprise parties and no more birthday stress. If none of that is reason enough to introduce the 22nd birthday party, just think of the savings you'd make on candles.

Tuesday 25th September 2012

We have a two and a half year-old daughter and when she was about two and a half days old, we decided we needed to get a baby monitor. Ever the gadget man, and to my wife's initial horror, I walked in with a bit of kit that wouldn't have looked out of place in a police command centre.

It was a video baby monitor, but not just any old video baby monitor. It had a remotely controllable camera that allowed you to see any part of the room, and it had night-vision. The sort of night-vision that they use in those ghost-hunting programmes. Everything can be seen clearly in ghostly whites and greys and eyes show up as a weird kind of black.

To my surprise my wife grew to love it. She loved that she could not only hear what was going on, she could see it with her own eyes, without having to go into the room and turn on lights and disturb the baby. Suddenly, if there was a bump or a rustle, a quick check on the video monitor was all that was needed to see that the baby was safe and well. The only problem with this fancy bit of kit, however, is that we are now reliant on it.

A few weeks ago, one of the leads which charge the parent unit decided to die. It meant that we had to use the lead to the camera unit to charge the parent unit when it wasn't in use. Not ideal. In fact it was a complete pain in the arse. We checked online and there was no way of replacing the lead, and the product was no longer under warranty, but instead of buying a new monitor we carried on. We did so for two main reasons. Firstly, video monitors are relatively expensive, and secondly, we could not bring ourselves to buy an ordinary sound-only monitor – we had seen the other side. So our ridiculous routine went like this.

We'd wake up, unplug the camera unit and plug in the parent unit. For her afternoon sleep, we then had to unplug the parent unit and plug in the camera, now relying on the internal battery. When the baby woke up we unplugged the camera and plug in the parent unit. For the night-time sleep we'd have to unplug the parent unit and plug in the camera, once again relying on the internal battery. The problem was, however, that the internal battery only lasted six hours a best, so an hour before we went to bed, we unplugged the camera, plugged in the parent unit, opened baby's door and turned down the TV after an hour. That gave us just enough charge to see us through until morning and then the whole thing would start again. What I didn't mention is that as we always had to rely on the internal battery and the battery life was so poor, we had to conserve energy by putting it on power-save mode, which meant that it was being used as a sound-only monitor for 99% of the time! We would often hear a noise, look at the battery indicator and weigh up whether it was worth taking a look.

Eventually we decided we needed to invest in a new monitor and of course, it had to be a video one. To my delight I found a monitor that had been reduced and instead of £150 it was being sold for £75. It was a reputable name and it was a reputable high street shop, so I purchased it without hesitation. (I have tried very hard to protect the shop that sold it to me, so I will not name it in any way and I hope that I can tell my story without you being able to correctly identify the shop).

To cut a long story short we got it home, tore off the protective packaging and set it up, and it was absolutely rubbish. It just didn't offer any sort of peace of mind because the video function was useless. It effectively provided us with a rectangle of grey. Fantastic if you like the colour grey and even better if your favourite shape is the rectangle, but in terms of providing us with a reassuring picture of our baby, it was absolutely pointless.

The next morning, I packed up all of the parts and put them neatly into the box that they came in. I then put the box in the blue bag that it came in and made sure I had the receipt stating my collection point. I got back to the shop, flicked through the catalogue, chose a replacement model, (that was nearly double the price) filled in the seven digit code with my little blue pen and then strode up to the customer services desk.

"I'd like to return this please." I said.

"Sure sir, what is wrong with it?" he asked.

"It's rubbish; this is the first time I have used this brand of monitor and it is not as good as our last one, it doesn't provide us with any sort of security – the picture is very poor." I said.

"No problem sir!" he said.

He then proceeded to check the returned item and asked where the protective packaging was. I explained that if he was talking about the small plastic bags that were sealed around the screen and camera, they were in the bin.

"Why is that?" he asked.

"Because they were torn" I said.

"In order to return an unwanted item sir, it needs to be returned in the same condition it was bought in…" he said.

"I understand that" I said, "but in order to open the item I needed to take it out of its packaging and it was sealed, so I needed to rip it to open it, and once ripped it's useless so I threw it away."

"But sir, how do you expect us to be able to sell this to another customer without its protective packaging? You wouldn't be happy to buy an item without the packaging would you sir?" he asked.

After five minutes or so we came to a stalemate. He wasn't going to give me a refund, irrespective of the fact that I did in fact want to spend more money on a more expensive item, and I wasn't going to leave the shop without either a full refund or a part-exchange for a better item. Finally he said "Look sir, there is nothing I can do. If I allow this item to be returned to us in this condition I could lose my job as it will have my name on the return; it just cannot go back into stock in that condition, and it's not faulty, so there is nothing I can do!"

What did he say........? It's not faulty, so there's nothing he can do. So that therefore means that if it were faulty, there would be something he could do.

"That's fine" I said, "but the problem is, that it doesn't actually work! I can't make out any picture on the video monitor, so unfortunately I am returning this item as it is faulty."

"Really?" he asked. "But you said you weren't happy with it…"

"That's right" I said, "I'm not happy that it doesn't bloody work!"

Five minutes later, I had my part-exchange and the unnamed shop in question had a "Faulty" item on their hands that wasn't actually faulty, it was just unbelievably crap!

So there we have a lesson in life. Be honest. Be really honest. Failing that, lie.

Wednesday 26th September 2012

Last night it finally happened. We were hoping to hold out until 1st October, but there was no escaping it – the heating had to go on. I dread putting the heating on for the first time. It's the final nail in the coffin for summer, the bills will be rising, and you have to deal with that awful smell when the radiators kick in and burn off all of the dust and old spiders that have collected over the summer.

So, depressingly, the heating is on and Christmas is approaching. (Yes I know it's only September, but already there are adverts on the TV and special displays in the shops). Ladies and Gentlemen, it's time for my annual cut-back.

Every year, around this time, I like to look at what I'm spending and attempt to cut back, in the vain hope that we'll make some savings that we can put towards the winter bills and Christmas, only for me to forget about it a week later and then revive the idea again when the heating gets turned on next year.

I thought I would start as I meant to go on, so first things first, I decided against buying a coffee this morning. I have a long commute and a hot coffee just about gets me through it intact. Ever since I gave up alcohol, (I'm sure that will feature in a fun-packed entry in the future) I have become more dependent on another drug – caffeine.

A morning coffee costs me £2.20. Let's work out what that would cost me over the year. I religiously buy a coffee every day. I don't always commute five times a week, however, as I often work from home on Thursdays (and we need to consider the bank holidays). So lets say, on average, I buy 4.5 coffees a week. I get 28 days holiday, but I only ever take around 20 days a year, (sad but true) so let's take 4 weeks off the 52-week year.

So 4.5 x 48 = 216 coffees. That's a lot of coffee. Next we need to find out the annual cost of that coffee. 216 x £2.20 = £475.20. So, if I cut out the coffee, I can save just under £500 a year. That's amazing. Well actually, I need to get real here. £475.20 is actually a good price to pay for the enjoyment I get out of it. I need to consider that without the morning warmth and buzz that I get from my coffee, I would be miserable. I would inevitably turn up to work in a mood, have an argument with my boss and lose my job. Drastic, yes, but entirely possible. That is why this morning I searched the kitchen cupboards for an unused present from 2008. My trusty travel mug!

This morning I made a coffee at home and brought it with me, and it's actually not too bad. Ok, it's not anywhere near as good, it's not as hot, I have to carry it with me everywhere and I have to wash it up every day, but it doesn't cost me £2.20. Although, in order to work out the true savings I would make in a year, I need to work out the cost of the home-made coffee and deduct that from the £475.20.

When drinking the instant variety, I drink Kenco Rich Roast. (Don't judge me, people) It costs £4.68 for 150 grams. Thanks to some quick research on the internet, and some people that are even sadder than me, I have found out that I can get 74 teaspoons out of 150 grams of coffee. I like my coffee strong, so I use one and a half teaspoons per cup, which totals 49.3, but for the purposes of this, let's call it 50. So a £4.68 jar will buy me 50 coffees. That's not bad. That's amazing actually – it works out at just 9.3p per cup. Except it doesn't. While I've never bothered with sugar, I do like milk, and a very quick calculation gets me to 3p per cup. So, 216 coffees x 12.3p = £26.56. I then deduct £26.56 from £475.20 to get my total net saving of £448.64.

Ok, that's a lot of work to come up with a figure, and £475 would have done as a rough estimate, but it is nice to know exactly what you could save by just making a small tweak to your daily routine. That £448.64 would probably pay my gas bill over the winter. It's certainly food for thought, and talking about food, that was my next natural step.

I aim to take in some lunch from home every day, but it doesn't quite work out like that and I probably buy lunch at least three times a week. Lunch these days in London costs around £5. For me it consists of a sandwich, wrap or salad, a drink and an accompaniment, whether that be crisps, a granola bar or a piece of fruit. Depending on where I go it could be more or it could be less, but let's say it averages out at £5. So £5 x 3 days x 48 weeks = £720 a year. Without going into the same detail as above, I could make my own lunch each day and it would cost around £1 per day. So £1 x 3 days x 48 weeks = £144. The net saving would be £576.

So in total, this year, I could make two very simple changes to my daily routine and I could save over a thousand pounds per year. That would pay for my winter bills and a good chunk of Christmas. So why am I not that excited about this revelation? Because you know as well as me that this time tomorrow I will be sipping on a shop-bought latte debating whether to buy lunch from M&S or Pret.

Friday 28th September 2012

We have a coffee morning at work this morning. I've been guilty in the past of sniggering at those who partake. I've always assumed it's something that the Women's Institute or the local bowls club get up to. I've always been polite enough to buy a piece of cake and coo and gasp at how light the sponge is or ask just how they got that filling so creamy, because behind all of the pleasantries the main reason for a coffee morning is to raise money, and in most cases, that money goes to charity. Today's coffee morning at work is in aid of the Macmillan nurses, an organisation that really earns its crust.

Put simply, without this organisation hundreds of thousands of people would suffer an extremely painful and lonely death from cancer. Macmillan nurses are there to give cancer patients the home care that they need while suffering their awful illness. I know because right now a family member has terminal cancer and is in their care.

So today, not only have I brought my spare change, I've brought a cake. Yes, brought, not bought! A cake! An actual cake! A cake that I made!

I'm sorry that that last paragraph featured so many short sentences and exclamation marks, but I don't know how else to make clear how remarkable it is that I made a cake! Whilst I enjoy cooking and all of the pleasure that cooking and eating brings, I despise baking. It's all so precise. 150 grams of this, 225 grams of that and if you're one gram out, or if you don't mix the ingredients until both of your arms fall off, you end up with a pancake. (Ironically, one of the few sweet things I actually can make) This time, however, the problem is not the cake itself – it's how to get it to the office. It's a delicate item – you can't just wrap it up in tin foil and chuck it in a carrier bag. Actually, it turns out you can, as that is exactly what I resorted to after trying and failing to find a container that would fit.

So today I have a bag with me, a carrier bag. I hate having bags. Normally I take four items with me each day. Train pass, wallet, keys and phone. Four items, four pockets, zero bags. The reason I don't like bags is not down to the bag itself, it's down to my own lack of confidence. I don't trust myself to remember that I have it with me and spend the whole journey paranoid that I'll forget it. I joined a gym a few years back and I spent more money replacing my gym kit than I did on the membership itself. What I could never work out was how my property never actually found its way to lost property. Who are the people keeping hold of sweaty and smelly gym clothes? Who thinks to himself "Ok, it's minging now, but I reckon, after a wash, that will go lovely with my black cords."

So right now I am panicking. Partly about the cake, and whether it meets my high standards, but mainly about the bag and the possibility that I might leave it on the train.

I'm not exactly sure how women cope in this situation. They have lots of bags. Lots and lots of bags. I remember when women just had one bag. The rule seemed to be one bag, but no limit on size. The bags got bigger and bigger until one day, I started to see other bags creeping in. Suddenly, there wasn't just a handbag – there was a bag for life, a cotton bag, a little brown bag and every so often, when really desperate, a carrier bag. Not content with this, they went further and we now have rucksacks, normally with the name of a gym on the back, and pull-along cases on wheels. I'm certain that a lot of women carry around more stuff on their morning commute than I would on a six-month round-the-world trip.

In their defence, women do get a rough deal. Women's clothes often don't have pockets and if they do, they look unflattering when filled. Women often wear shoes that are incredibly uncomfortable to walk long distances in, so it is sensible to bring an extra pair, sometimes two, if a gym visit is required. Long hair can be a pain, so there are brushes, lotions, bobbles, bands and hair-ties that need to be considered. Then there's make up – it's not just a case of a bit of powder and mascara, its far more complicated than that – there are toners and moisturisers and bronzers, as well as cotton wool and wipes to consider. I'm a new age man – I understand all of the things a woman needs to consider when coming to work. The thing is, I've also seen a woman's desk and I know that scattered across that desk you will see all of the above. Check under the desk and you will see at least two pairs of shoes. Check the cloakroom or the clothes rack and you will see spare coats, cardigans, dresses and umbrellas.

So I've got an idea. All of those women and, come to think of it, men who come to work like Baa Baa Black sheep, (three bags full) should today clear their desks of all of their old junk. Chuck it away. Put all of the stuff you do carry around with you on, in and under your desk. You are now free of your bags. The trains will be able to take more passengers and suddenly we have solved the problem of lost property.

Speaking of which, if anyone did find a Reebok rucksack containing a sweaty t-shirt and shorts on the 18:12 from Euston in the spring of 2007, it was mine; contact details are at the back of the book.

Monday 1st October 2012

My daughter is now of the age where she can make decisions. They are not always sensible, in fact sometimes they don't make any sense, but she now has the requisite brainpower to think and, consequently, decide. Most weekends, we ask her what she wants to do and she thinks for a moment and then says something like "I'd like to go to the baker's", or "I'd like to wash the car". While practical and, particularly in the case of the latter, necessary, they don't exactly make for a fun-filled afternoon out.

What usually happens in this situation is that we say, "Shall we go to the farm instead?" or "Would you prefer to go to the park?" and she jumps about, gets excited, we get our things and off to the farm or park we go. Not this weekend. This weekend we asked our daughter what she would like to do and she said five words which, even now, send shivers down my spine.

"I'd like to go swimming", she said.

"Shall we go to the farm instead?" I asked.

"No, swimming", she said.

"Would you prefer to go to the park?" I asked.

"No, I'd like to go swimming, Daddy."

This was the first time she had ever come up with a sensible suggestion, and certainly the first time she had decided she wanted to go swimming. For the first 18 months of her life my wife took her to swimming lessons where she spent the whole 30 minutes either crying, pooing or sleeping and amazingly, every so often, a combination of all three. While I wanted my daughter to be able to swim and at the very least be confident in the water, I couldn't help but feel slightly pleased that I wouldn't ever have to take her swimming.

You might think I'm being a misery, but I hate going swimming. Before we start, I'd best clarify what I mean by 'going swimming'.

Actual swimming, I love. I enjoy the feeling of the water trickling through my fingers as I glide along. I love the feeling of weightlessness. I love the fact that when you go underwater, the world stops for a moment, your vision is blurred and your hearing is reduced to muffled noises; it's just so quiet and peaceful. Swimming on holiday is fantastic – it's generally done in the open air, you have the sun on your back and there's an endless supply of ice cream nearby – what's not to love about swimming?

'Going swimming' is very different. On holiday you tend to do other things, and the swimming happens naturally in between all of the other stuff. It's the filler. It's the staple. To use an analogy, if you were looking at a plate of food, swimming on holiday would be the humble potato. It's readily available, not wildly exciting, but you'd miss it if you didn't have it.

So 'going swimming' for me while not on holiday is like being force-fed a huge plate of potato, but as if that's not enough, I have to eat it in front of strangers, while sitting in my underpants.

I woke up on Saturday morning with visions of fluffy bunny rabbits, cute sheep and a dog called Barney. That to me is fun. Throwing on an old jumper and going down to the farm to feed the animals. Watching the children's faces as they stroke the animals. As soon as it starts to rain, off to the shop for coffee and cake. But not this time. Instead I get to see people called Dawn and Tony, 90% naked, shouting and smacking their offspring. I get to watch a dysfunctional family play out their sorry lives in front of me, like a very wet episode of Jeremy Kyle. I'd like to say that it's all worth it, that seeing the smile on my wonderful daughter's face makes everything ok, but it doesn't, because her smile is hidden by the snot that is streaming from her nose.

To make matters worse, we went to a 'splash pool'. Essentially, what this means is you can do everything, except swim. There are floats, flumes, slides, whirlpools and rapids. Every twenty minutes an alarm goes off, which when I was a child meant that Smelly Simon had just proved once again how he got his nickname, but apparently nowadays it signals the start of a tsunami. Wave after wave comes tumbling towards the shallow end, knocking over every toddler and pregnant lady that stands in its path. Unfortunately my final destination is near and so I haven't got time to share with you the baffling parking system, the awful changing-room experience, the pre-pubescent lifeguards or the science experiment that they call food.

I'm glad my daughter had fun on Saturday and I'm truly glad that she got to choose what she wanted to do. Next week, she will be choosing again. She will be choosing between the farm and the park.

Tuesday 2nd October 2012

As a commuter, I have my routines. All commuters have their routines. They generally take the same route to the station, at the same time, buy the same coffee, get the same paper, stand in the same place and sit in the same seat.

I'm lucky enough to get a seat every time on the morning leg of my commute, no doubt to the frustration of other commuters. What they have to remember, however, is that my commute is longer than theirs and therefore far more expensive. I would actually far rather stand all the way for a journey half as long and a ticket that costs half as much. That said, I chose to live as far out as I do and so can't really complain.

When I started writing this book, however, I found that I had to change one of my own routines. I had to change where I sat. Choosing your seat on a train is a delicate operation and there are many things that need to be factored in to the decision. You have to weigh up the fact that the front of the train will be busier, but you'll be first off the train and therefore first out of the station. The back of the train will be quieter, but on a 12-car train, it's a hell of a walk at the other end. I therefore decided on the middle of the train as it is moderately busy and has a moderate walk at the destination point; the only real downside was the fact that the toilets were so close. You might think that being near toilets is a good thing, but being within 200 metres of train toilets is not a good thing, it's a danger to your health.

My usual seat of choice was a table seat, by the window in the middle of the train. The table offers a flat surface on which to read a paper or use the iPad. When I started to write this book I noticed I had a problem, as people were reading what I was writing. You might think "What's the big deal?" but it is incredibly off-putting. Can you imagine trying to write a dissertation with a total stranger reading every word over your shoulder? I also had the problem that my 'dissertation' could well feature said stranger, and if that were the case, it wouldn't be congratulating them on their good hygiene or their exemplary manners. So essentially, I had to move. It was a difficult thing to do and an even more difficult choice to make. I needed a seat that meant I wasn't overlooked, but also meant it wasn't too busy or too far to walk. I eventually found the perfect seat. Well, almost perfect.

There is a seat in most trains that sits alone. It has plenty of leg-room, a giant window and zero chance of anyone looking over your shoulder. The seat I am sitting on right now is effectively in a corridor where people can secure their bikes. No major problem there you might think, but it is also right next to the toilet. Now I'm not wishing to be dramatic here, but I need to explain exactly how close to the toilet I am. I am close enough that I can open the door without getting up. People often assume I am the toilet attendant. People come out of the toilet and the slightest bump or jolt sends them sprawling across my lap. I am so close that I can't just smell the fumes, I can taste them.

Strangely though, I love my new seat. I love watching people's toilet habits and find them fascinating. I've become something of a toilet expert. "You need to press the yellow one that's flashing to open the doors, you then need to press the green one inside to close the door, and don't forget to press the red one to lock it." When there's a queue, I seem to have become the conductor, explaining to people approximately how long the wait is and giving them insights into the noises that are coming from inside. "That's the flush just gone there, and that's the sound of the hand dryer; shouldn't be long now." Every so often, when the toilets are out of order, I get abuse too. Not directly, but when I politely explain that there is no point in waiting because the toilet isn't working, I often get a barrage of swear-words thrown in my direction.

One thing I have noticed and had never realised is that people actually do poo on trains. Now I know I mentioned about the smell earlier, but I had always assumed the smell was down to the fact that these trains run late into the night and often have to cope with inebriated travellers and perhaps are just poorly maintained, but no, some commuters actually use train toilets to have their morning poo. I haven't managed to find anyone that's established this as part of their morning routine, but it seems there are plenty who have absolutely no qualms with taking in the morning paper and doing their business.

I have always had a fear of using public toilets and to this day, I'm still not able to do 'number twos' in a public loo. On the rare occasion that I have had no choice, I am ashamed to say I have had to use the disabled toilet. I need to be locked away in my own room. I'm sorry to be blunt here, but I cannot stand the sound, let alone the smell, of other people shitting and I would hate other people to be subjected to my business too.

To me, it's a very personal thing – it is certainly not a public outing. Public cubicles in my mind should all have a sign reading "Absolute Emergency Only". They should have a spring loaded door, so that they only open if people are charging through them at more than 30 mph. Routine pooers should be banned. Those that look at their watch and think "Oh, it's 11 o'clock – I'd best empty my bowels." No sir, wait until you get home and do it in private, I want neither to hear it nor smell it.

I know that a lot of people must feel the same as me because at work, there are the people that I've nicknamed 'the cats'. These are people who come down from other floors to crap in our toilets. They are clearly embarrassed and don't want to be recognised. It is often said that cats don't crap on their own doorstep, often preferring to poo in other people's gardens. Generally, it is accepted that this is because they are clean animals and they don't want to live in their own mess. I think it's because, like me, they are disgusted and embarrassed by the whole thing and they just want a bit of bloody privacy.

Wednesday 3rd October 2012

This morning I woke up late. I'm not exactly sure how I managed it, considering the alarm was set for the same time as every other day this year, and of course the time on the clock itself is set 20 minutes fast in the vain hope that it will trick me into thinking it's later than it actually is. Why do I still persevere with that ridiculous tactic? All it does is cause more confusion than is necessary at that time in the morning. This morning I woke up late because of a condition that I have. I suffer from sleep snoozing. Somehow, in my sleep, I manage to hit that big black button on the top of the alarm clock, without any knowledge of doing it. Those that suffer from sleep walking have my sympathy, but spare a thought for those, like me, that sleep snooze. Those that sleep walk may suffer once every few weeks. I suffer eight or nine times a day and there are only nine minutes or so between each of my episodes. Who on earth came up with the nine minute snooze setting? Which boffin was scratching his head one day thinking, "Eight minutes, that's barely a nap. Ten minutes, no, that's a full-on sleep. Nine minutes, now that's a snooze!"?

I hate being late. I'm one of these people who aren't late, ever. Even, like today, when I get up late, I'm able to make up the time and get to my destination on time. The only time I am ever late is when the situation is completely out of my control, and that is usually down to someone jumping under the train I'm on, or 100,000 other people being on the same road as me. Not content with just not being late, I have to be early. I'm always early. Even my bloody hair has fallen out early.

When travelling, the trickier the journey, the earlier I tend to leave. I've adopted a strange rule that seems to be to leave 15 minutes earlier for every stage of the journey. If going by car, every motorway will have 15 minutes added for traffic. If travelling by train, 15 minutes added for each change. I went up to Inverness last year which involved getting six different trains. I ended up getting to Inverness before the train did.

Being early can have its advantages. If you turn up early to a gig, you can generally stand nearer the front. Turn up early to a food buffet and you are guaranteed the freshly cooked stuff. There are other situations where being early completely sucks though. Turn up early for an appointment and you have a hell of a wait. An early death can have obvious disadvantages. Book your holiday early and you'll spend most of it on the verge of suicide as every other holidaymaker tells you just how cheap their holiday was because of how late they booked it. Turning up early to a pub is an extremely unpleasant experience. There is nothing that shouts "Loser" more than rocking up on your own, ordering your sad little drink and getting on with the crossword.

So it's an awful shame that I have spent the last fifteen years turning up early to pubs. All of my friends, every single one of them, have spent fifteen years turning up late. When you turn up early and the people you are meeting turn up late, a potential twenty minute wait turns into forty. A long time to wait in most environments, even longer in a pub, but longer still in a pub when England are playing and you are trying to hold eight front-row seats. There is only so long that one person can hold onto eight seats in a busy pub, but when you combine that with England and a World Cup, that time diminishes rapidly. When the football isn't on, I would say it's around thirty minutes. When the football is on, it could be as little as ten.

Firstly, a group of people will enquire as to whether the seats are free; I will state that my friends will be along in a minute, knowing full well it will be at least forty. I then spend five minutes spreading all of my possessions around the table. Nothing is wasted. The Evening Standard gets spread out across the table and if I'm lucky, I might have a supplement too. I'll then hang my coat on the chair next to me; my jumper on the one opposite and even my pen will be tactically placed.

What happens next is like a scene from a wildlife documentary, where the cackle of hyenas team up to prize away the lions' latest kill. The only thing worse than having to watch the game from the car park is having to keep bumping into the bullies every time I go to the bar or the toilet. Even the poor old lion doesn't have to put up with the indignity of facing the hyenas every time they go for a piss.

It's often said that it's better to be late in this world than early in the next, and while I agree with the sentiment, I won't be changing my habits. Being early has its down-sides while booking holidays or attending appointments, but being early can also be absolutely bloody spectacular. I urge you, some day soon, to set the alarm, get down to the coast, or failing that somewhere high up, and watch the beauty of the sunrise. It's something that those who are late will always be missing out on.

Friday 5th October 2012

While it's true that I don't believe in superstitions, I do try wherever possible to avoid walking under ladders. But this is on the grounds of safety, rather than any possible bad luck. However, since becoming a father, I suppose I have become a little more superstitious. There are times when our little girl is sleeping well and I will attempt to mention it to my wife and she will say "Ssshhhh, don't say it!" The belief is that if you mention it, you will 'jinx' it and suddenly, without warning the thing you want to happen, suddenly won't, or the thing you don't want to happen, suddenly will, or in this case, the thing that actually is happening, suddenly won't be. It's amazing really just how sophisticated this superstition is.

Thanks largely to my wife I now employ this utterly ridiculous tactic in almost every aspect of my life. When on the motorway, I sometimes start to think how wonderfully traffic free the road is, but then I hear my wife's words in my head – "Ssshhhh, you'll jinx it!" When my football team of choice are winning, I start to think how great the three points will be and exactly where that might put us in the table, when suddenly I hear my wife's words once again, loud and clear.

The problem with this ridiculous superstition is that by not saying it, you actually make things worse for yourself because instead of saying it and moving on, you are left with this thought that is bouncing around in your head, desperate to get out. Thoughts have a natural outlet – it's called speech. Thoughts are generally created in the brain and leave via the mouth, normally via some sort of an 'embarrassment filter' – a filter that can process the thought and work out whether it should be shared in the current company. This filter is quite sensitive, however, and is often impaired by alcohol, stupidity or both.

On Wednesday it's fair to say that I 'jinxed' myself. I made the bold statement that I am never late.

Today, I am late.

It was, however, completely out of my control. On Fridays my mother-in-law looks after our daughter, and every Friday she drives at 83mph down winding country lanes in order to arrive on our driveway approximately three to four minutes late. It's normally nothing a little jog to the station can't fix.

Today however she was fifteen minutes late and it wasn't down to the traffic or the car; it was down to the weather. The relentless wind and rain through the night had managed to uproot a tree and deposit it across the main road that links her house to ours.

I couldn't work out what was more annoying, as I lightly jogged down the road to the station. Was it the litres of water that were being splashed up my leg every time so much as a milk float passed me by, or was it the conkers that were flying towards me at both head and groin height? My decision was made easy in the end, as I crossed the road and a bus roared passed to ensure I was soaked evenly on both sides. As a pedestrian, I think October has got to be one of the most dangerous months. Sure January and February can get slippery, but in October we have to deal with flying conkers, crazy umbrella owners and the tricky job of walking on slippery leaves and spent conker shells. This morning I feel like those two burglars in Home Alone.

Eventually I got to the station, bought a coffee and stood at my normal place on the platform. I hadn't realised that as I was on a later train and there are fewer people to accommodate, the train has fewer carriages. (The train people like to dress it up and say the train is a 'shorter formation'). The end of the train was now thirty metres to my left and I had to run to make sure that I got on. Running for me is never going to come naturally, but running with a coffee in one hand and an inside-out umbrella in the other is a skill that even the greatest monks have yet to master.

So now, finally, I'm on a train and I'm dry. I just hope we don't get delayed!

Bugger, I think I've just 'jinxed' it…

Monday 8th October 2012

This weekend I decided to make a complaint.

This may sound innocuous to you, run-of-the-mill even, but for me this is genuine progress. I have ambled through the last 33 years on this planet, totally unable to complain. No matter what a shoddy experience I might have, or what terrible service I might receive, I'll smile politely, keep quiet and pay the bill. As soon as I'm in the car, my wife, family or friends will then get a full run-down of exactly what was wrong and exactly how they should improve.

I am a closet complainant, happy to moan, but doing so behind closed doors and out of earshot. Cold food? Sloppy service? Rude staff? Boy, are they going to get it in the car on the way home. I'm not sure why I'm like this. I'm quite confident in normal every day life. Sometimes too confident for my own good. A celebrity only needs to be within five square miles and I'll be able to seek them out for a little chat about what they're up to and what they have in the pipeline.

You sometimes hear celebrities say things like "Oh no, people are very respectful, I rarely get people just walking up to me in the street." Maybe I didn't get the memo. I can count at least ten times in the past where I have just introduced myself, said I was a fan of their work and then gone on to have a lovely chat. I have a rule of not disturbing them if they are chatting with others, or if they are eating, but if they are just sitting there or standing there, then that's fair game. My most recent chat was with Dame Kelly Holmes on this very train. She sat down opposite me and we got off the train together, so I wasn't going to turn down that opportunity. We actually had some common ground too, in the very broadest sense. It was leading up to the 2012 Olympics and she was obviously heavily involved and so was I. Well, sort of. I was a 'Gamesmaker' for the Olympics and during our chat she seemed genuinely excited and proud of the volunteers and she wished me luck for the games. If I'm honest, it seemed a bit surreal that a Dame and double gold-medallist was wishing me good luck for the upcoming Olympic Games.

There was another time that I approached a couple of celebrities and I realise now, looking back, that the celebrities in question must have been terrified. Firstly, I was under the influence of alcohol. I wasn't drunk; I was just very well lubricated. Secondly, it was dark. Thirdly, they were in a blacked-out Range Rover. (Thinking back, I've no idea how I spotted them given those three factors). And lastly, because I wasn't 100% sure it was them; I circled the car four times.

So, picture the scene. It's a dark, cold, winter's night. Two celebrities are parked up at the side of the road in a blacked-out vehicle and a scruffy drunk is circling the car. (It was also a Friday and dress-down day involved me not only relaxing my dress code, but my facial hair too).

Suddenly, the scruffy drunk approaches the car and knocks on the passenger-side window. After a lengthy discussion between the two and a second knock from the scruffy drunk, the electric motor kicks in and the window is slowly lowered and in a broad Geordie accent, Dec from Ant and Dec asks if he can help me, with Ant from Ant and Dec looking on.

I had spent so long trying to figure out if it was them and building up the courage to speak to them that when it came to actually saying something, I had completely dried up. After what seemed like ten minutes I finally managed to say something, and to this day I still go bright red at the thought of it. "So you really are friends outside of work then."

That was it!

I had knocked on the window of a blacked-out car and disturbed two celebrities, (who were both chatting and eating, thus breaking both of my own silly rules) in order to state that these two very nice gentlemen are indeed friends. Thinking back now, I'm annoyed I didn't make reference to the fact that, even in a car, Ant was on the left and Dec was on the right!

Annoyingly, my encounter with the pint-sized Geordie duo wasn't my most embarrassing celebrity moment. A year or two later I was walking hand-in-hand with my wife through Camden when I spotted TV's Stephen Mangan, and proceeded to confidently smile, wave and say hello. Well, that's how it now goes in my head as I try desperately to erase the memory of pointing at him and saying "Look, it's him, off of........" as he politely smiled and waved and said "Yes, it's me, off of ......" and continued walking. He knew that I couldn't think where I knew him from, but he just rolled with it. He wasn't embarrassed at all.

Stephen Mangan is in that awkward category where he is famous, but not really famous. I imagine people point or stare, trying to work out where they know him from. Is he famous? Did I work with him once? Is he a friend of Stan's? For those of you that have now Googled Stephen Mangan, yes, he is that bloke that was in Green Wing, Alan Partridge and Episodes. And yes, he is a bit strange looking.

So, we've established I'm confident and stupid in equal measure, but still unable to complain, until this weekend that is. We visited some friends of ours and went to a beautiful park. The park has gardens, a museum and a lovely restaurant. After spending a good while in the children's play-park, watching our children swing, slide and climb their way to exhaustion, we retired to the restaurant for some much-needed refreshment.

It was rustic, home-cooked food and the hand-made burger and chunky chips fitted the bill perfectly. Mine was fantastic. It was hot, tasty and completely devoid of sharp plastic objects. My wife's burger on the other hand managed the first two, but failed on the last. The object in question was extremely hard and sharp. It was by pure luck that my wife managed to pluck it from her mouth before it did any real damage. Who knows what it was or how it got in there, but it was certainly time for me to man up in front of my friends. I told them that it wasn't right and we should complain. They agreed. We should speak to either the manager or the chef. They agreed.

To my surprise one of our friends Nic, took the initiative and asked the waitress if the chef could please come out to speak to us. That's fine, I thought. She's taken care of the admin; it's time for me to take care of the business. Ten minutes later there was no chef and no manager. I now had an issue. I was already highly stressed about having to complain, but now, there is a second complaint that needs discussing. I've now got to complain about the wait to speak to the manager as well as the original complaint. This is like asking someone who is afraid of flying to board a plane and then, halfway through, telling them that it's their turn to fly it.

Ten minutes later and we still had not been visited by either the chef or the manager. It is at this point that my daughter asked to go to the toilet and as she is only two and a half, she needed some assistance. I am ashamed to admit that I took the bait. I've never been so happy to accompany my daughter to the loo.

"I'll go!" I shouted, as I grabbed her hand and skipped off to the toilet. Needless to say, by the time I got back, the situation had been resolved. Our good friend Jay managed to explain, very articulately, I'm told, exactly what they needed to do in terms of improving their customer care. The sharp, plastic item was presented to the manager and he apologised accordingly. We later received free coffee and cake by way of apology and everyone seemed to be happy. Everyone except me. My coffee was cold and my cake was stale.

Boy, did they hear about that in the car on the way home!

Tuesday 9th October 2012

Since I started this book I have had to get used to establishing a new routine. I am someone who generally welcomes change with open arms. I think my attitude towards change is down to my school days, where I constantly had to deal with it. Firstly, while at school you have to deal with your body going through changes. I had to deal with my voice getting lower, my face getting spottier, my legs getting longer and my body getting hairier.

Changing teachers meant that I had to get used to a new set of rules, new guidelines and boundaries. The things that made you good or bad in one teacher's eyes were not the same for another. I was a well-behaved child at school, but never a top achiever. I was always in the top set, but I generally achieved average results. I never misbehaved, but I often got bored, so my time in the classroom was often spent trying to make other people laugh, with varying degrees of success. Often, in order to split up a group of chatty children, the teacher would move you around and sit you next to other people. This didn't really work in my case, as it just gave me a new audience to try my material out on.

School days provided an endless stream of change; every other day you would change best friends, every few weeks you would change your underwear, every few months you would change hairstyle and every few years you would have to up sticks and change schools.

And then in order to write this book I had to make a change. Instead of reading the paper or listening to a podcast, I started to write. It's extremely enjoyable and I'm annoyed that I didn't do it sooner. I find that I am more creative and ideas are far more free-flowing in the morning, so my routine tends to be to write on the morning commute and then, after a long day's work, I spend the evening commute going over what I have written and editing it where necessary. I have found that the nine-hour gap in between writing and re-reading gives me sufficient time to make judgements on whether something is unnecessary, boring or simply doesn't work.

The one problem with this new routine is that it means I can no longer catch up with the news. No more morning paper, no more Evening Standard on the way home, and no more podcasts. A few years ago I couldn't get enough news, but now, with a young daughter, news is harder to come by as time is very precious. I tend to spend my daughter's waking hours keeping her happy. That will generally involve going to the park, playing with wooden kitchen items or watching Peppa Pig. No chance of catching up with the news there. I then spend her sleeping hours doing mundane things like cooking, eating and tidying up after her. In terms of this book, having a lack of knowledge of the news is actually quite good. It would be far too easy to comment on the news each day, but I have two main reasons for not doing that.

Firstly, that's what journalists are there for, and even if I did try to put a comical slant on it, that space is currently filled by comedians and I am neither a journalist nor a comedian. (as I'm sure you'll agree)

Secondly, by commenting on the news, I will be dating this book. Who wants to read this book in ten years' time and read about some boring politician who was having an affair with his wife's sister's yoga instructor?

This morning, however, I did manage to catch five minutes of news. On a Monday and Tuesday, it's my job to get our daughter ready and take her to the child-minder. Most mornings, while eating breakfast, and in an attempt to keep her still while trying to put her shoes on with one hand and brush her hair with the other, we watch some child-friendly telly. This morning, my daughter spotted my iPad. Now, sorry to dispel the magic, people, I don't use a fancy laptop or Mac and I don't use any fancy word processing software, I simply use my iPad and the application called Notes. (For those of you reading this in the year 2020, an iPad was a small touch-screen device. Yes, we had to touch the screen with our fingers! How terribly old-fashioned!).

After spotting the iPad my daughter insisted that she wanted to play with it. A few days earlier, in an effort to keep her happy while eating out with friends, I had downloaded a game called Peppa Pig's Party Time. Initially, I was unwilling, due to the proximity of the milk, but I soon realised that if she were playing the game, then the telly would be free for me to take in some much-needed news.

After just two minutes I wished I hadn't. What I didn't realise is that the last few weeks haven't just been news-free for me, they have been bad news free, and that is a good thing. The last few weeks have proved once and for all that no news is definitely good news! How often have we turned on the news, only to be subjected to a seemingly endless barrage of depressing stories?

I think they should rename the news and call it 'Bad News'. To counter that, they should also create a totally new programme and call it 'Good News'. They could run one after the other and so the viewer would have the choice of watching just the good news, just the bad news, or both.

Now I know what these pesky broadcasters are like with their viewing figures, so I can't see the 'Bad News' format getting past the executives, but I think it could work. What if the world of news broadcasting finally found its way to the 21st-Century viewer and introduced an interactive element to the start of each broadcast?

Red buttons at the ready, everyone. What would you like first, the good news or the bad?

Wednesday 10th October 2012

This morning I noticed the first hat and the first pair of gloves of this winter. Officially it's still autumn, but this morning it feels incredibly wintry as there's a crisp frost underfoot and plumes of steam escaping from the mouths of all of the commuters.

It marked a special occasion for me, as I have added my first layer since spring. For the last few weeks, everyone else at the station has been wearing a combination of jumpers, jackets, blazers and coats; I have continued to wear nothing but a thin cotton shirt. Ok, it might be polyester, but let's move on. I hate wearing layers and avoid it whenever possible. The problem with wearing layers when you commute is that it's essentially extra baggage that needs carrying around, whether on your back, in your arms or stuffed in your bag. Trains have become relatively advanced in recent years, with the welcome inclusion of air-conditioning for the summer and heating for the winter.

Air-conditioning during the summer is fantastic. You arrive at the train hot and bothered, board the train and within a few minutes you start to cool down, genuinely appreciative of the cooling facilities on offer. The problem with trains in the winter is that there only seem to be two heat settings, and they tend to be 'Off' and 'Surface of the Sun'. Today it's been set to the latter.

As everyone boards the train, hats, gloves, coats, jumpers, blazers and jackets are removed in unison in an attempt to acclimatise to the train's ridiculously high heat setting. There really doesn't seem any point in having heating on trains. People have dressed warmly for the weather and are generally rather snug in their chosen extra layers. Even with no heating at all, the train would be far warmer than the outside temperature due to the body heat of the passengers, and people could just regulate their own temperature by layering and de-layering accordingly.

Banning heating on trains would almost certainly save money on electricity or fuel and I'm certain that lost property would be reduced as people would tend to de-layer less often, therefore keeping their possessions about their person. I'm certain I've made up the word de-layer, but having used it three times in the last three sentences I'm warming to it, (pun definitely not intended) so it's staying.

As I've said, I'm not a fan of bringing unnecessary items, like warm clothes, to work and I try to travel as light as possible. I'm normally able to go until late October, sometimes early November, without the addition of so much as a jumper. I'm aware of how ridiculous this is and I'm reminded just what a fool I am on those mornings when my skin ends up matching the colour of the sky-blue shirt that I'm wearing.

On mornings when it's extremely cold, I tend to jog in an effort to get to my destination a little quicker and to raise my body temperature just a little. So, with a coffee spilling and splashing about due to a combination of the motion of the jogging and the slipping and sliding on the leaves and conkers under foot, I get to the station both layer-less, (another new layer-based word) and coffee-less.

October the 10th is extremely early for me to be adding a jumper to my morning commute and I am still likely to use the jogging technique from time to time, until it's time to upgrade to the winter coat. Like a seasoned explorer, I like to use nature as my guide. When the last tree has shed its last leaf, it's time. Even my winter coat is a fairly light affair. It finishes at the waist, has no hood and has relatively little padding. It's effectively a zip-up jumper with pockets.

Having written that last sentence, I'm annoyed to realise that a zip-up jumper with pockets is effectively a fleece, and with two or three fleeces in my possession, I could have been using them all along, thus saving money on the purchase of a coat and the extra few grams of weight on my back.

As I look down the train, I can see passengers starting to stand up and commence the process of layering; we must be close to our destination, and that is my cue to finish today's chapter.

It looks a beautiful morning in London. If only I didn't have my jumper, I'd quite fancy a light morning jog.

Friday 12th October 2012

Today the tables have turned; the roles have been reversed; we have indeed come full circle. Today I am taking my Dad to the football. I've been to the football plenty of times *with* my Dad, but I've always been of the opinion that he is taking me. Even well into adulthood, and with me able to pay my own way, it was my Dad that was taking me to the football, rather than the other way around.

I've always had a close relationship with my Dad and as I grew up to love sport and then, later on, alcohol, we grew closer and closer. My Mum has always said that while my brother inherited my Dad's humour and looks, I inherited his love for sport and his temper. Thanks Dad.

My Dad spent quite a lot of time trying and failing to convert my brother to sport. My brother was into his music and sport just didn't interest him. When you look back through family albums you invariably get at least one photo in either a school sports kit or some sort of fake football top from the market, but not in my brother's case. It was just an endless succession of jeans and Iron Maiden t-shirts. The nearest my brother got to school sports was when he had to run for the bus in the morning, and even then the long hair, the ankle-length trench-coat and the smoke-filled lungs managed to slow him down to a light jog.

As soon as I was old enough to make my own decisions, and with the pressure off, I naturally fell into sport. I got into most of the school sports teams, never being the star, but able to hold my own, and I could see that my Dad was proud.

One of my happiest childhood memories, which I still play back in my mind now, is when I scored my first goal in front of my Dad. I remember it so clearly. We were playing against Francis Coombe, which, in a strange twist is where my Dad used to go to school. Francis Coombe were the worst team in the district at the time, closely followed by us, so it was an opportunity to score a rare goal. The team sheet had gone up the day before and my Dad had confirmed that he was coming along to watch; I couldn't wait.

Twenty minutes into the game and Dad still hadn't arrived; I had already hit the post and I was sure that he had forgotten. Hitting the post was an impressive achievement on our school pitch as they tended to move in the wind and had the diameter of a toothpick.

My stomach was churning and I spent longer looking at the entrance to the school field than I did at the ball. Finally, I saw him coming down the path and, in an amazing piece of timing, he arrived behind the goal at the same time that I got put through, one-on-one with the keeper. My legs were like jelly, I had no idea what to do, so I just smashed it. The keeper went down early and the ball rifled into the middle of the goal. My Dad isn't one for emotions, but the nod and the thumbs-up told me that he was proud. A very happy memory for me.

When playing football for your school team, there is a certain pressure to support a good football team. When I was at school, Manchester United were just becoming popular again due to them winning the league for the first time in twenty-six years, and Liverpool had a rich history, so most kids went for one or the other. I however, was happy to be a Watford fan. To me, it was an easy choice to make. I lived in Watford, my Dad supported Watford, so a Watford fan I became. The advantage of supporting a local team is that you can actually go and watch them play; the disadvantages are the food-poisoning and pneumonia. I remember coming in on Monday mornings and telling and my friends about the games. I loved seeing the envy on their faces. Of course, being kids, they didn't say, "Wow, it sounds great, nice one!", they simply said "Watford are shit, you gaylord."

So today, my Dad and I are going to the football, but this time not to see Watford, to see England. I received an email a few weeks ago, inviting me to buy tickets for the price of £20.12. A strange price you might think, but as I had been involved as a volunteer at the recent Olympics, the email explained that "As a show of our appreciation, we would like to offer you tickets at this special price." I took them up on the offer and, having read Wednesday's Evening Standard, so did 7,999 others. The Standard wrote "The London 2012 Olympic 'Games Makers' have again been offered tickets at the promotional price of £20.12, with 8,000 volunteers taking up the offer."

The story also confirmed that tonight's game is a sell-out, which is impressive considering the opposition is San Marino, one of the lowest-ranked teams in the world. To be fair San Marino has a population of just over 30,000. That's the same population as Hitchin, a small town in Hertfordshire. Hardly fair is it – England versus Hitchin?

I'm really looking forward to tonight – a game of football, a catch-up with Dad, a bout of food-poisoning and a touch of pneumonia. Perfect. Just like the good old days, with the welcome exclusion of people claiming that England are shit and that I am a gaylord.

Monday 15th October 2012

I managed to travel on the train this weekend without writing a chapter of this book. I was unsure as to whether I should, as my promise was to write something on every train journey, but as this journey was for pleasure and not business, and I promised to write on my commute, I decided that it didn't qualify.

Instead I bought a paper. It's the first time in a month that I've been able to enjoy a morning paper. After about thirty minutes, I came to the conclusion that I wasn't missing much as, once again, story after story seemed to concentrate on murders, abductions and general political incompetence. The only really interesting thing in the paper was the write-up about England and how they had performed against San Marino and that was the one thing I didn't need updating on as I was there to witness it.

I really do think that with the technology available to us nowadays, they should stop printing papers. It's old-fashioned, it's bad for the environment, and on the tube it's downright annoying.

I personally think papers should only exist in the virtual world and be solely downloadable on the various handheld phones and tablets that are available. The name would have to change as you couldn't call them papers anymore; they would probably have to be called 'Downloads' or 'News Updates'. I admit that there are a few things we would need to iron out as not everyone has the ability to access these digital downloads, but I think that gives us an opportunity to kill two birds with one stone.

Every time I see a politician on the telly, they go on about two things: the current financial crisis and the environment. By banning papers we could help both. Banning papers would reduce both emissions from the production and the landfill from the waste. We could also help ease the financial crisis, as it would mean everyone without a suitable device would be tempted to buy one, thus boosting the economy. It's a win-win. The only true losers are the cute fluffy rabbits, who will no longer have anything to line their hutches.

Obviously these digital downloads already exist, but the quality is varied and the fact that only a certain percentage of people use them means that they are not the top priority for the news corporations. Banning papers would ensure that all of the money and effort went into producing the best possible content.

I also think that it should be possible to do a 'pick and mix' and effectively create your own news. The problem with a paper is that many pages go unread, as they try to target everyone with one paper. Is a sixteen year-old student going to be interested in the same things as a sixty year-old accountant? Ok, maybe if that student is studying accountancy, but you understand the point I'm trying to make. By doing a 'pick and mix' you can choose the news that interests you. So I, for instance, wouldn't have to read the stories about fashion or music. Never again would I be told what is 'On Point', and never again would I utter the words "What's the point?"

Newspapers often do giveaways such as CDs, and even this could be carried over to the digital version. Once you have bought the digital download, you could qualify to download the latest single from Plan C, Nemo or Kanye East. Never again, when selling a car, would you have to clear the glove-box of cardboard sleeves with titles like 'Lazy Sunday' or 'The ultimate chill-out'.

The paper I read this weekend had a giveaway, one that I actually may use. Jamie Oliver is releasing a new book and there were two recipe cards enclosed. Last Christmas I received Jamie's latest cookery book and I was genuinely impressed with it. I used it quite a few times and still do now, in fact the only thing that is wrong with it is the title. It's called 'Jamie's 30 Minute Meals', whereas in fact it should be titled 'Jamie's 50 Minute Meals', or more accurately, 'Jamie's Meals in Just Under an Hour'. There are some excellent recipes that are simple and tasty, but you not only have to factor in the extra time it takes to cook, you always have to make an extra trip to the shops in order to find those essential puy lentils or mung beans.

So, Christmas is on its way and Jamie has a new book out and who can blame him, the boy's got to eat. It's called 'Jamie's 15 Minute Meals', or as I've decided to call it, 'Jamie's Meals in about Half an Hour, but You Have to Factor in the Extra Time to Get to the Shops and Back, so Let's Call it an Hour'.

Not as snappy, but far more accurate.

Tuesday 16th October 2012

Last night I happened to catch an advert for the latest iPhone and it annoyed me. In case you are unfamiliar with the iPhone adverts, they essentially walk you through a few features, or sometimes they show you what can be done when you download certain apps. Want to tumble-dry your washing while riding a bike? There's an app for that..... That kind of thing.

Yesterday's advert centred on the headphones and it went something like this: "Everyone's ears are different; none of them are round, why would anyone possibly think of manufacturing round earphones? Look at ours – aren't they great? They're ear-shaped."

A brilliant idea. Ear-shaped earphones. Well done, Apple. The thing is, before they came up with the ear-shaped earphone, they were selling their products complete with the terribly old-fashioned round earphones. So effectively their new marketing campaign is saying: "I know we were lazy before, pedalling our product with inferior spherical accessories, but look, we've finally bothered to look at the issue and we think we've sorted it out."

Strange, isn't it, that they are quite happy to create a marketing campaign that effectively points out that they got it wrong before? You only have to look at how washing powders have evolved over the last ten years to see this in action. It used to be quite simple – you made your choice based on price, and every product simply claimed to be able to wash your clothes better than the others.

Nowadays, every few months, a different brand comes up with a different claim. Firstly there was the temperature debate. "Washing at fifty degrees? Our product works at forty!" Then the following week another company would say: "Forty? No no no, with ours you can wash at thirty." At this rate it won't be long before our washing machines resemble Slush Puppy dispensers.

It's not just temperature – it's the endless claims they make with strange-sounding phrases such as 'actilift', 'anti-bobble' and 'colour care'. If they thought they could get away with it, I'm sure they would happily sneak on preposterous claims such as 'with cancer-curing properties' or 'complete with anti-ageing effect'.

With food, you often see the words 'New and Improved' quoted either on the advert or by the person voicing the advert. I am certain that in 99% of the cases, nothing is new and nothing has been improved, it's just exactly the same as before. All that has happened is they have managed to save up enough money to create another ad campaign, to make yet another failed bid to gain that tiny extra little bit of market-share, and without a new product to hook us in they tell us it's both new and improved.

Even if they aren't lying, and it is both new and improved, new could simply mean a new label, and improved could mean that instead of tasting like dog excrement, it's now been upgraded to taste more like cat.

Advertising and marketing exists solely to create the idea that you are missing out, and without product X Y Z, life is simply not worth living. That's a really easy job when talking about things that conjure up emotions – things such as holidays or food. People can easily picture themselves lying on the beach or tucking into that tasty joint of roast beef.

It's not so easy when talking about kitchen tongs or garden furniture. In order to sell these products, they use things called shopping channels. If you are ever feeling a bit down-in-the-dumps, I urge you to watch twenty minutes of any given shopping channel. Suddenly life feels a little bit better. In my opinion shopping channels are second only to Jeremy Kyle when it comes to making you feeling better about yourself. Doctors should stop prescribing anti-depressants and start prescribing QVC or, in really bad cases, Bid Up TV.

The strange thing about shopping channels is that they actually seem to work. There are actually people not only watching these channels, but phoning in and buying the products. Some even have a little chat with the presenter. "That's right, Simon, I was just sitting here flicking through the channels thinking, if only I could get my hands on a set of purple feng shui cat ornaments!"

The frustrating thing about all of this is that while writing today's chapter, I haven't been able to truly concentrate on the job in hand. All I've been able to think about is why my stupid earphones are round and not ear-shaped.

Wednesday 17th October 2012

Today I decided to re-write this chapter. I had followed my usual morning routine and settled down in my usual seat and begun tapping away. It was an ok piece. It didn't really need re-writing.

This book and the chapters within are never pre-planned and the process of writing is an organic one. Things happen and then they get written about.

I received a call about half an hour ago from my Mum. The call was expected, but it didn't make it any easier to deal with. My dear old Gramps had passed away, two weeks after his 86th birthday. Without going into too much detail, he had been ill for a long time. In a previous chapter I talked about helping raise money for the McMillan nurses, for it was my Gramps who was in their care. Gramps had always been an active man and continued to play bowls right up until his body decided he shouldn't anymore. Within months of giving up bowls and driving the car, he began to lose his sight.

Gramps suffered from a rare condition that rendered him completely blind and it was this that frustrated him more than the lack of mobility. "At least I could live a normal life in a wheelchair", he would say. "I'd rather lose both my legs than both my eyes", he'd often proclaim. What upset him more than anything was that he would never see his newborn great-grandchildren. His memory was fading, but at least he had a vague picture of the older family members. With the new additions he couldn't, and babies don't take kindly to being poked and prodded by tobacco-stained fingers.

In the last year or so Gramps had been struggling with stomach pains and, after a lot of persuasion, he visited the hospital, to be given the news that he had terminal bowel cancer. Gramps was well-known for being the pessimistic type, and when Victor Meldrew graced our screens in the early nineties even he could see the similarity. Given the awful news, Gramps could have been forgiven for uttering Victor's famous line, but he didn't. He simply said "It is what it is and it will happen when it happens."

The last few months were tough for Gramps, and in a way even tougher for my Nan, who at 83 was having to do everything for him, even carrying him up and down the stairs. As a family we did all that we could, but we needed some extra help and that's where the McMillan nurses come in. I've never seen the nurses myself, but I've been told what a wonderful job they do. They remind me of the story of the elves and the shoemaker, where they sneak in unseen at the hour of need and sneak out again when it's time to say thank you.

Gramps was a simple man. Give him a roast dinner, a packet of chocolate brazils and a black and white film on the telly and he was a happy man. There was a longer list of things he didn't like than things he did. Loud music, cold food and drunk people were high on his list of dislikes, so parties with Gramps were always a barrel of laughs.

Gramps was a proud man and loved talking about his adventures during the war. I'm really going to miss that. I was extremely lucky to have had him in my life and I hope that he is in a happy, comfortable, peaceful place right now.

I'm sorry for the lack of humour today, but I'm sure you understand in the circumstances. It's a shame because the stuff I wrote this morning was bloody hilarious!

Dedicated to Albert Leeks, 03/10/1926 – 17/10/2012.

Friday 19th October 2012

Over the last couple of years our daughter has been suffering from various colds and viruses and, as a result, has always struggled to breath through her nose. It's a fairly minor thing, but it does disturb her sleep as it causes her to snore and it also affects her eating as she can only breathe through her mouth and her taste and smell are affected.

After many trips to the doctors she was referred to the hospital, and in late September we went to see an ENT specialist in Maidstone who confirmed that our daughter should have an adenoidectomy. After a puzzled look from me, the doctor confirmed that this was removal of the adenoids. A further puzzled look required the doctor to explain what the adenoids are and what they do.

Apparently they are small lumps of tissue, located above the tonsils, which help fight off infections and viruses. Hers have been overworked and they are now swollen and inflamed and unable to carry out their job. Her adenoids obviously felt overworked and undervalued and decided to go on strike. Only they haven't just gone on strike, they are actively making things worse. It would be like a fireman not only refusing to go to work, but going around town starting fires. Or like a soldier crossing enemy lines and opening fire upon his erstwhile comrades. What we are taking about here is a traitor. A Judas. Our daughter is having to deal with a traitor within. That's a lot for a three year-old to have to deal with.

The doctor explained that we should receive a letter confirming when the operation and the pre-operation assessment would take place.

"It could take up to three months", he said.

"Wow, I know Royal Mail are slow, but......"

"The date of the operation," the doctor interrupted, "Not the letter, the letter should be with you in the next week or so."

As promised, the letter arrived a week later; it confirmed that our daughter's operation was booked for the 29th October and her pre-operation assessment was to be on the 18th October. We were both impressed and delighted with the news. You see, three months would have meant our daughter having an operation near Christmas – not the best time for any child to be feeling under the weather, but as our daughter's birthday is on New Year's Eve, it really would have been a double whammy.

We were also happy because we were told by the doctor that she would need a week at home to recover during which she wasn't to go out, which meant that one of us would have to stay home. The 29th October is the first day of the school holidays and with my wife being a teacher it works out perfectly.

People complain about the NHS all of the time and I'm sure often with good reason. It isn't perfect and I'm sure they get things wrong a lot of the time, but my issue with that is that you never hear about the times when they get it right. Today I am going to tell you about how they got it right.

Obviously, the first positive thing for us was the speed with which our daughter received her operation date. It could have taken three months, it took just one. Yesterday, we drove over to the hospital, a different one to where she had had the referral. It's a fairly new hospital and it was very impressive. There was ample parking, which for once had a sensible tariff. The first half an hour was free and then it went up in sensible amounts after that. Watford General Hospital (and yes, I am happy to name and shame them) have a ridiculous parking policy. They have a minimum charge of £4, so even if you are back within ten minutes, it will still cost you £4! Every three hours, it will cost you another £4. When our daughter was born there, I spent over £40 on parking.

The reception area of the hospital was also impressive. It was a large, open, welcoming space. There were about ten 'Check In' terminals, where you scan in the barcode of your letter and it confirms your arrival and lets you know where to go and wait. Within two minutes we were in a large waiting room which once again felt open, spacious and welcoming. There were plenty of toys for the children and reading materials for the adults. There were also two huge flat-screen monitors that would flash up a name every few seconds directing each patient to their consultation room. So far there has been no contact with a human. You might think this is bad, but I don't. You might think that back in the 'good old days' you would have been checked in by a receptionist, and beckoned into your room by a nurse, and that the introduction of a computerised system has rendered them jobless and on the scrapheap, but it hasn't. The receptionists and nurses are still there, it's just that now they can do other, more important tasks, such as writing up notes, filing reports and fetching test results.

The way I look at it is if a job can be done more efficiently by a computerised system, then go ahead and computerise it. Why settle for second best? The system that the hospital uses to check people in and send them to their consultation rooms is better than a human because it does a better job. It never calls in sick, it never needs a lunch break and it is never caught flirting with Dr Thomas. On top of all that it can speak over 200 languages. By employing a computerised system to check people in and move them around the hospital, they can spend money on other crucial employees that often get overlooked, like the porters and the cleaners. No computer system in the world is going to be able to move a bed from one ward to another or a rubbish bag from the ward to the incinerator.

I was hugely impressed with the whole operation. The staff seemed happy and well-organised and the patients looked comfortable and at ease. We were seen five minutes earlier than our appointment time – another advantage of a computerised system, as it can spot gaps and prioritise accordingly, dealing with hundreds of patients at a time. We were in and out in less than forty minutes and we even found time to visit the coffee shop situated within the hospital.

Our visit was completely stress-free, which was in stark contrast to the visit I made to another hospital on Tuesday evening to see my dear old Gramps. It is really refreshing to see that new technology is not only being embraced, it's making a real difference.

Monday 22nd October 2012

This morning I have to make an admission. It's finally time for me to be honest and admit that I drink too much. This weekend was the worst I have been for a long time. I'm not sure whether it's the stress of bereavement, the stress of work or the general stress of family life, but I just couldn't seem to stop myself this weekend. Even more worrying was that I mixed my drinks. I got to the stage where it didn't matter what it was, so long as it was coffee.

That's right, coffee. Over the course of one weekend I managed to drink about fifteen cups of coffee in various forms, whether it be instant, filter, americano or latte. I even had a slice of coffee cake!

Ever since I gave up alcohol, nearly three years ago, I have become a coffee freak. I seem to crave coffee more than I ever did alcohol. I've given up one drug and replaced it with another.

I gave up drinking by accident. I never intended to give up. I went to the doctor's one day with a relatively minor ailment that needed treating with antibiotics. In order for the antibiotics to work I had to make sure that I didn't drink any alcohol for seven days. Seven days might not sound a lot, but for me back then it was. I used to drink regularly, and by that I mean most days. I always seemed to have a reason; sometimes I would find a reason to celebrate; sometimes it was a bad day at work; sometimes it was simply a stressful commute. Strange, isn't it, that alcohol can treat so many moods?

I never considered myself to be an alcoholic. Alcoholics roamed parks and congregated on park benches; they didn't have a job and have a cheeky few after work.

When I think about it now, I realise that I did have a drink problem. Whenever I met up with friends I would arrive early and have a couple of drinks before they arrived, sometimes I would even have a couple at home before going out. Suddenly, instead of having a few beers at the football with my friends, I started to watch it on the telly at home with only the beer to keep me company. Soon I had moved from having a glass of wine with dinner to having a few glasses, and the quick beer after work turned into a few. It wasn't long before every day seemed to be a 'stressful day'.

Looking back now, I was an alcoholic, pure and simple. There tend to be three accepted 'stages' or 'forms' of alcoholism, depending on which information you read. They are hazardous, harmful and dependant. I would say that I was firmly in the dependant stage, slowly working my way towards harmful. No, I didn't swig from brown paper bags, I didn't ever drink during the day, but I did get to the point where a drink was the only thing that could relax me after a hard day.

It was quite hard for me to write that last sentence, but it's easy for me to write the next one. Giving up alcohol was best thing I ever did. If I was being dramatic, or maybe if I was American, I would probably say it saved my life.

So, the doctor told me I needed to take some tablets and I wasn't allowed to drink alcohol for a week. A week later and my ailment was treated, my blood pressure had gone down and I had lost nine pounds in weight. (Four kilos in new money).

Bloody hell! Those tablets must have been good!

I knew then that while the tablets may have helped, it was the absence of alcohol that had really made the difference. I actually think that the ailment itself was a warning mechanism within me to get me to the doctor, like the warning light on a car. It was time for this old banger to see the mechanic.

So many people get that warning light, but how many people do anything about it? Here is a question for you. What is the best way of dealing with the warning light in a car?

Is it:

A) Find out what the problem is and fix it. The mechanic confirms that it's the oil light, so you give him the go-ahead to top up the oil.

Or is it:

B) Who knows what it is? Let's just unscrew the bulb. No more warning light, no more problem!

As you probably know, solution A will result in a healthy car, solution B will result in a trip to the scrap-yard. I honestly believe that there are hundreds of thousands, if not millions, of people who are happily selecting option B and unscrewing the bulb when it comes to their health. Doctors and patients alike are happy to treat the effect, flagrantly ignoring the cause.

You might be expecting me to say that giving up alcohol was hard, but it wasn't. It was easy. The easiest thing I have ever done. I didn't go cold turkey; I didn't spend months in a dark room craving alcohol; I didn't go to any meetings; I didn't feel sorry for myself. I simply used the most powerful tool available to me.

I used my brain.

It may sound simplistic, but I simply told myself that I didn't need to drink any more. Cravings are easy to deal with if you know how. Every time I had a craving for alcohol, I turned that negative, sad and empty feeling into a positive, happy and fulfilled feeling. Instead of feeling sad that I no longer drank alcohol, I was able to flip that emotion on its head, immediately feeling happy that I didn't.

It's very similar to how you would think about your ex-boyfriend or girlfriend, the one that cheated on you. I'm sure that when things were going well, you couldn't get enough of them, and every time you thought about them you had that warm, happy and contented feeling. Skip forward, six months later, to when you found out that they had cheated on you with your best friend. I'm sure very different emotions surface, such as sadness, anger and hatred. It's the same memory; you are just able to attach a different emotion.

My visit to the doctor not only confirmed that alcohol had cheated on me with my best friend, it confirmed that it had been controlling my life and was now threatening to kill me.

Some friend alcohol turned out to be.

My new friend coffee treats me much better but there are times, like at three o'clock this morning, where I lie there, wide awake, thinking to myself "Why did coffee have to become my new friend?"

Tuesday 23rd October 2012

I've been asked to write the eulogy for my Gramps. I'd already decided that I wanted to, and I was really glad when my Nan said that she'd like me to do it.

I'm extremely proud to be doing it, but there's also a lot of pressure. Chiefly there's the pressure of writing it. I've got to sum up my Gramps' life in about five minutes. The bits about his childhood in the East End of London and the bit about joining the army and fighting in World War II take up fifteen minutes alone. I've decided that I'm going to speak about Gramps from a Grandchild's perspective. I'm going to talk about all of the things we used to enjoy doing with him, and all of the happy memories that I have of that time. I've decided that the best way to sum this up is in a poem.

I'm not sure if this is a sensible decision. I've tried writing poetry many times before. Firstly, with catastrophic results, as a 10 year-old schoolboy. One of my first crushes was on a girl called Sonja. Yes, that's how she spelled it. I liked Sonja, but Sonja didn't like me. She was very good friends with Laura and, to complicate matters, Laura had a crush on me, but of course I didn't have a crush on her. We had this weird triangle where Laura had a crush on me, I had a crush on Sonja, and Sonja had a crush on neither of us. It was not so much a love-triangle, more of a love-cul-de-sac.

It was going nowhere, so I decided that poetry was the best way forward. I can't remember exactly what I wrote, but it was around the theme of 'Roses are Red; Violets are Blue', as it was popular at the time. The boys used to shout it out in class towards the girls they disliked, with the finishing lines inevitably being something like "I hate you 'coz you smell of poo!"

I was sure I had written a poetic masterpiece. I was sure it was going to win Sonja over. My only issue was how to get it to Sonja. I decided that the best person to deliver this masterpiece was Laura.

Big mistake.

Laura kept her promise. She delivered my masterpiece, only she didn't just deliver it to Sonja, she delivered it, out loud, to the whole class. I was mortified. It took weeks to get over, and it was years before I would write any poetry again.

I've decided I need to practice. If I am going to write the eulogy in the form of a poem, I need some practice at writing poems first. I've decided that the best platform is this book. I have a book to write and I have a eulogy to write, so why not combine both?

It's far too late to change the past; there's nothing I could do

It all just seemed to change so fast; trouble seemed to brew

I hadn't felt his lips for weeks, that's just how it started

I felt just like an old antique, shattered, broken hearted

A newer model appeared one day, tall and sleek from China

What was wrong, he didn't say, the details seemed so finer

Washed up thoughts fade to black, he left me out to dry

Even when I began to crack, I never thought I'd cry

He picked me up; he put me down, tears a little closer

The final, awful, painful sound, her settling on his coaster

So that's my story, time is up; I really need a hug

Now he's got his china cup, he doesn't need a mug.

I'm not sure that it's up to the standard of the poem I wrote for Sonja, but I enjoyed writing it and it's given me the confidence to write the eulogy now. The only thing I am worried about now is delivering it.

I'm a confident guy, and talking to large groups of people does not worry me, but talking to large groups of people while crying and wiping away snot does. There will be people who are upset, myself included, and the most important thing for me is to try to hold it together. I've been able to practise writing the poem, but I won't be able to practise reading it. Sure, I can read it in front of a mirror a thousand times, but I will never be able to replicate the day itself. I just hope I can hold it together.

The last thing I want is for someone else to read out one of my poems again.

Wednesday 24th October 2012

Dreams are strange, aren't they? Last night I decided to watch two programmes, back-to-back, all about the vile man that was Jimmy Savile. The true extent of this man's evil is yet to be fully uncovered, but I would hope that the whole truth will be available by the time this book is printed. The two programmes had been recorded from the previous night.

There was a Newsnight programme, hosted by Jeremy Paxman, which essentially slated the editor of the programme and then proceeded to interview the programme's own journalists, reaffirming the point that Newsnight's editor was an idiot. It was a Newsnight special, about Newsnight; very strange indeed. It would be like a private investigator hiring himself to investigate his own private life.

The second programme was Panorama, which also focused on the same issues, but went into more detail about Savile himself and how he could have possibly got away with it for so long. It finished by questioning whether senior bosses at the BBC, including the director general, were involved in a cover up. Two BBC programmes, aired at the same time, one on BBC 1, the other on BBC 2, both primarily concerned with criticising the BBC.

Whatever you think about the BBC, you have got to admire their balls.

So having watched both of these programmes back-to-back, relatively late last night, I inevitably started to dream about it. Last night I became the lead investigator in the case and it was down to me to get to the truth. I spent the whole night conducting interviews with BBC staff, including journalists, presenters, editors, producers and even the bloody security guard on the gate. I interviewed victims, witnesses, family members; I held press conferences, spoke to MPs and even took advice from the queen. This morning I am exhausted.

I'd like to say that I cracked the case, but of course I didn't. While interviewing the staff at the BBC, the office I was in suddenly became a circus tent, the person I was speaking to suddenly turned into an orange, and the paper I was writing on turned into a paper plane and flew away.

One minute I was interviewing the director general at BBC headquarters, the next I was interviewing a bloody orange in a circus tent. In truth, it really hindered my investigation, but, as always in dreams, I never questioned it for a second. I was determined to get to the truth and if it had to come from a tangerine, then so be it.

Of course, like all dreams, it was just a jumbled-up mess and none of it made any sense. I still woke up, tired and confused, convinced that I'd made some inroads and some of the leads were worth following up. I often have the dream where I've won the lottery and I'm convinced that I'll be able to recall at least some of the numbers.

"I'm sure there was a six... Or was it a nine? I remember the number one... Or was it eleven...?"

The worst dream is the one about work. I have a recurring dream where I spend the whole night dreaming about work. Tossing and turning all night long, work work work, only to wake up and have to do it all again, only for bloody real. Twenty four hours of non-stop bloody work. So unfair.

The other dream I have regularly is the one where I'm convinced I can remember it all, but can in fact remember nothing. I'll say to my wife:

"I had a dream about us last night where we were in Paris."

"Really? What happened?" she'll ask.

"Well you were there, only it wasn't you, it was someone else... And we went to Paris, only it wasn't Paris, it was somewhere else..."

Twenty minutes later and I am still trying to explain the 'vivid' dream that I had, with the only recalled details being that my wife was there but she wasn't, and we went to Paris but we didn't.

Popular dreams tend to focus on fantasy, so guys will often dream about playing up-front for their favourite football team, and girls will often dream about being a princess and marrying a prince. I've always wondered what footballers and princesses dream about. Maybe they dream about driving a van or working in a shop.

Dreams offer an alternative reality, and I think they're a good thing, even if that means I have to wake up every so often wondering why my doctor is the new Prime Minister.

As Gabrielle once famously sang, "Dreams can come true", so if you'll excuse me, I have some crucial leads to follow up on.

Tuesday 30th October 2012

You may have noticed that it has been six days since my last chapter. Unfortunately I had to attend my Gramps' funeral on Friday and yesterday I had to spend the day in hospital. When I originally booked the Friday and Monday off, a colleague in HR asked if I was up to anything nice.

"Funeral on the Friday, day in hospital looking after my ill daughter on the Monday." I replied.

"Oh," she said. "Enjoy!"

Enjoy?

To be honest, I'm not sure what I would have said if I was put in that same situation. Good luck is about the only response which fits both occasions, although I've never liked wishing people luck. It's essentially saying "Look buddy, you're on your own. I can't help you and neither can anyone else, the only thing that will get you through this is a massive stroke of luck."

There are times when it's right to wish someone good luck. If someone enters a raffle, go ahead and wish them luck. Everybody has the same chance (assuming everyone has just one ticket, let's not get technical here). If someone enters the X Factor it wouldn't be right to wish them luck, as luck has nothing to do with it. It would be down to their talent and exactly how strong their particular sob-story was, nothing to do with luck at all. You should simply say "I hope you sing well", or "I hope you manage to cry in all of the close-ups".

When someone goes for a job interview the stock response is "good luck", but again, luck has nothing to do with it. You should simply say "I hope you give interesting and insightful answers and that you are able to accurately communicate your ability to work independently or as part of a team." Or if you were being especially honest, you would say "I hope you don't bore them to death with your stories of how misunderstood you are, how unlucky in love you are and why you can't understand why no-one else has been willing to offer you a job."

Anyway, I can honestly say, even though the two events were separated by a weekend, I still feel absolutely shattered. I feel both emotionally and physically exhausted. On Friday I had to say goodbye to my Gramps and I was honoured when I was asked to do the eulogy. I always thought that I'd be preparing a best man speech way before being asked to prepare a eulogy, but life is rarely straightforward. I managed to write a poem that summed up my Gramps and I delivered it with what I would describe as 'controlled emotion'.

There were pauses, and at times my voice cracked and wobbled. At one point I produced a noise that I am unfamiliar with, and I think only dogs would be able to decipher, but I managed to compose myself and finish the poem. Many people came up to me afterwards and said how nice the poem was, and one person said that having watched what I did they would be changing their funeral plans and would be asking one of their Grandchildren to do the same.

Poor bastards! I really feel for them!

Wednesday 31st October 2012

Today is Halloween and, with it falling on a Wednesday, I have had to put up with seeing photos of fully grown adults dressed up as ghosts, goblins and mummies since last Friday. As it has fallen mid-week, I will have to put up with it right up until this Sunday. Nine days of watching adults behave like children. I've never had anything against Halloween but it does frustrate me that it is annoyingly close to Bonfire Night.

It's like Christmas and New Year. Two celebrations that are annoyingly close. Ok, it works well in the sense that we get an extended Christmas break, but then we have to wait another three or four months until Easter arrives.

We should move a couple of our celebration days so that they are sensibly spaced out throughout the year. Christmas should stay where it is, because it makes sense that it should be cold at Christmas. Reindeers work well in the cold, Santa is always suitably dressed, and who wants to eat a Christmas pudding in August?

Easter should stay in where it is too. We should move Halloween to June, have the New Year in August and Bonfire Night should stay where it is in November. By doing this, there is a suitable gap between all of the celebrations and people can enjoy each one on its own merit.

Halloween in June would have its challenges, but none that could not be overcome. It's lighter in the evenings for a start, so although it wouldn't have the same spooky feel, children would inevitably be safer. Pumpkins are not ready for harvest in June, so people would have to be a little more creative, but I think that's a good thing – people have been far too lazy for far too long. Let's see what people can create from onions, broad beans, beetroot, cabbage, asparagus and strawberries. I can already picture far more intricate vegetable-based doorstep lanterns.

Having the New Year in August also makes perfect sense. Ok, there's some work to do on the calendar side of things, but it's a lovely month to go out and celebrate something. My birthday is in August and I can vouch for it being a good party month. It is well before Christmas, so money will be less of an issue, and it's relatively warm, so you wouldn't have to worry about getting frostbite when you decided to walk home because there were no taxis.

Now, going back to the calendar, it would seem a bit weird to have the New Year on the 31st August, so we would probably have to rename the months. So August would now be called December, September would be January, and so on.

This would cause a lot of confusion, I agree, but it would all be worth it in the end. So, Christmas would be on 25th April, (but it would still be cold, don't worry) Easter, confusingly, would be in July, because although it is normally in April, next year it falls at the end of March, so with my new calendar it would fall in July and not August. To really confuse matters, even though I've just moved Halloween to June, with my new calendar, Halloween would now be back in October. Of course, we'd have the added complication of the Winter as we know it becoming Spring, the Spring becoming Summer, Summer becoming Autumn and Autumn becoming Winter, so I've decided to summarise things below.

31st December (New Year's Eve) – I've moved the date to 31st August, but then moved the calendar so that it still falls at the end of December.

5th March (Bonfire Night) – I've kept the date the same, the dates have just changed due to the calendar shift.

25th April (Christmas Day) – Same as above.

29th July (Good Friday) – Same as above, but of course the Easter dates change every year.

31st October (Halloween) – I've moved the date to the 30th June (as June only has 30 days, not 31), but then moved the calendar, which means that June has become October again, so I've moved the date back to the 31st.

Why this simple solution has not been put forward before, I will never know!

Friday 2nd November 2012

This morning I feel like a teenager again. I don't mean it in the same way as when middle-aged people say it to try to explain how they feel when they finally meet someone who wants to have sex with them. No, I feel like a teenager again because I have woken up with a massive spot on my nose.

I feel that I need to explain exactly how big this spot is. You are probably picturing a red mark, a relatively small, insignificant mark that any adult could easily get on with. Stop picturing that small red mark. This is not a small red mark. This is not a spot, a blemish or a pimple. This is a huge embarrassing zit.

It's so big that it seems to have its own pulse. It's in that awkward place where I can actually see it out of the corner of my eye. I can't even just try to forget about it, as every time I look down I think I've smeared jam on my face.

I would honestly rather have a black eye or a busted nose than have to deal with this spot. I would rather people assume that I have a drink problem or that I am the victim of domestic abuse than have them looking at my spot and questioning my facial hygiene.

When I think about it, I probably have neglected my face when it comes to pampering. I watch my wife do things to her face that I thought were only carried out at spas. When I say spas, I mean the things that used to be called health-farms before fat people started going, not the chain of tired old convenience-stores where fat people have always been going.

I've been reliably informed in the past that my wife washes, tones, cleanses and moisturises, although I will never know in which order they happen. If she were a car, she would be selecting the Platinum Wash and if I were a car, I would simply be using a bucket and sponge, probably bought from Spa.

As a man in his thirties, I feel woefully exposed, without any excuses to cling to or make-up to hide behind. If I were a teenager, or for that matter a woman, it could easily be excused as something to do with hormones, diet or stress, or a combination of all three; but I'm not – I'm a balding bloke in his thirties.

I've decided that I'm going to have to try to cover it up; it is just too big to ignore. If I left it, it wouldn't just be the elephant in the room, it would be the mammoth in the broom-cupboard. People would be talking to me, thinking "Don't mention the zit", and I would be thinking "He's noticed the zit and now I've put him in the awkward position of having to tell himself not to mention the zit".

As soon as this train pulls in to the station I'm going to make my way to Boots to buy some plasters. I will select the smallest one and place it over the bridge of my nose. There are three ways to play this.

Option 1. Stroll confidently into work, plaster on nose, and say nothing. A risky strategy which will almost certainly result in whispers and strange looks, but I might just be able to get through the day unscathed.

Option 2. Stroll confidently into work, plaster on nose, and say that they were not wrong about these nasal breathing strips – that was the best night's sleep I've had in ages. Another risky strategy, as I might have to explain the pros and cons of a product that I have neither used, nor intend to use.

Option 3. Stroll confidently into work, plaster on nose, and say "Look everyone, I have a huge spot on my nose, and I can't face you having to look at this disgusting scab on my face all day, so I've done the best I could in a bad situation. It's covered up, I know it looks stupid, but can we all just get on with the day? I'll make the coffee, and let's all just concentrate on the fact that it's the weekend in nine hours' time."

Against my better judgment, I'm going to go for option three. I'll be completely honest about why it's there, while not brave enough to actually show why it's there.

Honesty over bravery. The wimp's way out.

Never take me to war; the enemy would have me blurting out secrets before they had a chance to strap me to the chair.

Monday 5th November 2012

This morning I spent ten minutes searching for some old work-trousers. This happens from time to time when I realise that my preferred pairs are either in the wash or still scrunched up on the floor behind the wash basket.

Today it happened for a different reason.

Today it happened because I can no longer fit into them. I have two pairs of trousers in my current waist size which I alternate. Suddenly, neither pair fit me. How can that happen? One weekend of careless eating and suddenly it's impossible to do either pair up. Surely they must have shrunk in the wash. Surely someone is playing a practical joke and altering my clothes in my sleep. Surely someone has switched them for another size. Surely!

Looking back, the warning signs have been there for a while. Last week I was forced to change my penny/split ratio. This is a complex ratio between the value of coin that I am prepared to pick up, compared to the potential risk of my trousers splitting. It's always hovered around 5 pence, but I've recently had to increase it to 20. I've also found myself emptying my pockets before I sit down. Sitting down with a phone and keys in my pocket will either result in the items being buried so deeply into my legs it would take four of the country's most gifted surgeons fourteen hours to remove, or, depending on the fabric, the trousers will simply explode under the pressure. An office full of men in tight trousers with full pockets could easily turn into a warzone as buttons fly across the office and shrapnel-like wounds are created by the trousers that have held fast. If you ever see a man emptying his pockets before sitting down, it's not because he needs to use his mobile, it's because he's deeply worried about the onset of this chaos.

I have to be honest and admit that it has not just been one weekend of careless eating; it has been many weekends combined with many weekdays too. I've slowly been putting on weight for the last couple of months and unlike most people, who like to blame stress or glands, I simply need to blame myself. You see, in my case it's rebound. I lost almost six stone two years ago. (That's 84 pounds to any Americans reading and 38 kilos to everyone else. Why we Brits continue to weigh in stones, I will never know!).

How did I do it? Very simple indeed. I started eating the right food in the right quantities at the right times. I also started exercising more. That's it. There isn't any secret formula, you simply need to want to do it in the first place and then have the mental strength to carry it out. I cut down my portion sizes, cut out all of the unnecessary snacks and started to walk everywhere. I didn't go on any fancy diet that involved me counting points or having red or green days, I simply questioned what went in my mouth every time I ate. If I really wanted something, I had it. It's about moderation, and trusting yourself to make the right choices. I never felt unhappy or deprived while using this self-taught method of losing weight. If you make your goal achievable and hold it in high-enough regard, then I'm certain this method will work perfectly for anyone.

So what went wrong? I started to ignore the rules! I was still questioning what I ate, so the alarm system was still functioning perfectly, but my inner security guard seemed intent on ignoring the alarm-bells, the guard-dogs, the searchlights and even the bloody CCTV. Every time I ate something bad, the alarm would ring, the dogs would bark, the searchlight would kick in and the CCTV would be filming the crime taking place, but the security guard would just shrug, turn the page of his book and take another bite of his pizza.

When I was losing weight, the single most satisfying thing about the whole process was purchasing new clothes. Now I'm putting some weight back on, I realise that the single most depressing thing is having to rummage through the cupboard and pull out the saggy old discarded clothes from before.

So today I'm going to recruit a new security guard. One who cares. One who jumps to his feet even before the dog starts barking. One who patrols the perimeter gate. One who's armed with a truncheon and not afraid to use it.

This book was born from a self-imposed challenge and now I am going to use it to set myself another. I'm going to set myself the challenge of losing twenty pounds by the 14th December. That's just over nine kilos in just under six weeks. Twenty pounds, as that is how much weight I have put on, and the 14th December as that is the date that I had set myself to release the first part of this book on Kindle.

I've always set myself challenges and, while I've not always succeeded, I've always given it my best. If I don't succeed this time, I'll be completely honest, and I'll know exactly whom to blame. That lazy, bone-headed, good-for-nothing security guard.

Tuesday 6th November 2012

While standing in the queue at a mini-supermarket yesterday lunchtime, I noticed that they had hidden all of their tobacco products behind a sliding door, and the notice on the front of it read something like "If you are buying tobacco products please let a member of staff know and we will assist you".

I knew that there was a rule coming into place meaning this step had to be taken, but wasn't aware that it had come into force, as I normally do my food shopping online. Apparently, according to ex-health minister Anne Milton, "Banning these displays will help young people resist the pressure to start smoking and help thousands of adults in England who are currently trying to quit".

Really? The law only requires shops of a certain size to take this step, so the only establishments currently obeying this ludicrous rule are supermarkets. How many children pop into the supermarket on their way home from school? How many children ignore the corner-shop in favour of the out-of-town supermarket?

Let's look at the second part of that statement – "help thousands of adults in England who are currently trying to quit". How will this help the thousands who are trying to quit? How is hiding tobacco products in supermarkets going to truly help anyone addicted to nicotine? If anyone happened to be struggling with nicotine addiction and needed a quick fix, I doubt they would jump in their car and head to the nearest supermarket; they would almost certainly do what anyone would do with any addiction, and go to the nearest possible place to get their fix. That place is the same place that children get their sweets – the local shop.

Even if they did, do you really think that once they got to the supermarket and failed to find the tobacco products, they would just give up and say "Oh well, looks like they've sold out, silly me, what a fool I've been, let that be a lesson to me"? No, they would do what any of us would do in the same situation, and ask someone. Instead of a spotty fourteen year-old having to explain to an octogenarian why they have moved the tinfoil to the crisp aisle, you now have the situation where a spotty fourteen year-old is having to explain to a grown adult that they have in fact hidden them, and for their own good.

In order for this stupid law to have any hope of working, it needs to be employed by everyone. That's not going to happen, and rightly so; why should shopkeepers throughout the country have to bear such a huge cost to undertake such a stupid idea? I don't know the solution, but I do know that hiding products from view in a small percentage of outlets is a stupid idea. It would be like telling the supermarkets to cordon off their cakes, and then releasing a statement saying "Look, we're helping fatties to get thinner!"

As I stood in the supermarket queue, it wasn't just the sliding door covering the tobacco products that annoyed me; the automatic queue-caller annoyed me too. I don't know what else to call it, but it's that annoying voice that says "Till number 3 is now available". Its monotone, featureless, automaton voice was already quite high on the "What could be the most annoying sound in the universe?" scale, but then it suddenly started switching voices, alternating between male and female.

"Ah, but we don't want to come across as sexist", someone in a suit presumably thought. And no, you don't come across as sexist; you just come across as stupid. Even worse than that, in your desperate attempt to come across as all politically correct, you in fact seem to have assumed that your customers are all stupid. Without the inclusion of both a male and female voice, you seem to think that we will be marching down equality street, pitchforks in hand, headed for the equality street police station. It's a bloody recorded voice. It can be male or female, and no-one would care either way. Chill out, Mr PC, and take a look at the other parts of your store which actually do need looking at.

Instead of adding to the obesity epidemic, why don't you stop offering "Buy one get one free", and start offering 50% off like you used to, before you started messing around with robot voices. Why don't you look at the fact that your fruit and veg has an even bigger carbon footprint than your vastly overpaid managing director. Why don't you stop trying to pull the wool over our eyes by claiming that products are "Tasty" and "Nutritious" when they are about as tasty and nutritious as a turd dipped in chocolate.

As much as I hate shopping online, at least I don't have to put up with hermaphrodite robots and pointless games of hide-and-seek.

Wednesday 7th November 2012

It annoys me that I have to shave. My hair stopped growing some time ago now, and only requires a token trim around the back and sides every few months. If I'm totally honest, that particular cut, which I carry out by myself, is more of an excuse to keep the neck and ear hair under control than it is to keep any actual head hair in check. My face has no such problems; in fact, since the hair stopped growing on my head, my face seems to have taken on the extra responsibility by growing hair faster than ever before.

My head and face is like a village with two bakers, both of them happily going about their business, neither of them overworked, both happily making a living, until suddenly baker number one, let's call him Mr Baker, dies. Now baker number two, let's not call him Mr Baker, let's just call him Bob, is left inundated, having to serve the whole of the village. Bob (my face) has taken it upon himself, out of respect for Mr Baker, (my head hair) to bridge the gap and serve the whole of the village (grow more hair). That is possibly the most stupid analogy I have ever come up with, but I like referring to my stubble as Bob and my bald head as Mr Baker, so it's staying.

I found out to my horror a few years ago that as you get older, the hair that you want to grow doesn't and the hair that you don't want to grow does. It's a weird thing the body decides to do as you advance in years. I see it as a punishment for getting older and therefore having less to worry about. I've long since stopped worrying about females, friends and fashion, so my body's replaced that with worries about ear, nose and back hair. Thank you, body, thank you very much.

Hair in general has many functions, but the hair on your head is there primarily for warmth and protection. Surely then, when you get to the time of your life where you spend half of your time buying blankets and the other half falling over, you should be growing more hair on your head, not less? I reckon that if it weren't for flat caps the average life-expectancy for a man would be somewhere around 55.

Tuesday 13th November 2012

My wife and I have a fairly good system. I take care of the finances, the cooking and the food-shopping, and she takes care of the cleaning, washing and diary-management. Both of us know our roles, so it's very rare that we argue over who should do what. Obviously there are cross-over points where there is too much work for one, so if we are hosting a dinner party my wife will put on her apron, and if there's a spring-clean to be done I'll ask my mother-in-law round for coffee.

I have to admit that I have it fairly easy. Looking after the finances is an easy-enough job because that's what I do for a day job, and the cooking provides enjoyment and relaxation from the stresses of commuting and working in London. This weekend we had the in-laws round, and I decided to do a couple of courses. The weather has turned very cold and wet, so I thought I'd go for two winter favourites: soup followed by a roast. What had seemed a fairly simple meal actually turned into a whole weekend of cooking, which went as follows:

The soup that I settled on was pea and ham, and I decided to cook it on Saturday, meaning we could enjoy it for lunch on Saturday and then have it for starters on Sunday too.

As I wasn't following a recipe, I had no idea how many peas to buy, so I bought a couple of kilos. Similarly, I had no idea how much ham to buy, so I asked the butcher if I could have some cooked ham that would go well in a pea and ham soup, and he sold me the end piece from a huge joint of ham.

"How about this piece?" he asked as he held it up.

"Perfect." I said, as I weighted up in my mind whether I actually needed that much ham and how much such a big piece would cost.

"That'll be a pound." he said.

I was astonished. One pound for what was clearly more than a pound (in weight) of prime pork. At first I thought that maybe he had given me a special deal because I had already spent £15 on a joint of pork but, having thought about it more, I think he is actually just a good businessman. If he had said £4 or £5, I might have said "No that's fine, I don't need the whole piece." He then would have been left with a piece of ham which would have been very difficult to sell, and he might even have ended up having to throw it away. I imagine one of the most frustrating things about being a retailer is throwing things away.

Retailers who sell fresh goods must hate throwing away stock that doesn't sell. Someone who runs a toy shop can simply run a sale of their old stock. There is no time frame as to when it needs to be sold by, and they would certainly not have to throw away any of their stock. Selling food must be extremely stressful as every fresh item is effectively a ticking time-bomb.

I made a decent job of the pea and ham soup, but I had enough to feed the whole village. The plan was to make it on Saturday so that we could have it for lunch, but there was enough to have it for breakfast, lunch and dinner for a whole week. It didn't go to waste, however, as we had it on Saturday and Sunday and our neighbours came round to have some too.

After making the soup I was left with some beautiful vegetable stock and, having learnt from the butcher, I decided not to throw it away. After racking my brain and raiding the cupboard, I decided on a risotto and set about whipping it up for our evening meal on Saturday.

On Sunday we had to be out by ten o'clock, because we were walking into the village to watch the remembrance service and pay our respects to soldiers past and present, so it meant starting on dinner at nine o'clock in the morning. Rather than doing a traditional roast I had decided to do 'pulled pork', which requires the pork to be slow-roasted for five to six hours. Once back from the service I set about preparing the potatoes and vegetables, while also reheating the soup. Lunch was a success, but once again there were plenty of leftovers. I decided that with so much pork left over, I had to make some apple sauce, so that we could enjoy a pork roll in the evening and also for sandwiches the following day.

The total time that I spent in the kitchen this weekend was twelve hours, but I'm not complaining, as I know I still have it easy when it comes to the household chores. That message was hammered home at around nice o'clock last night as I watched my wife sort through the washing basket, picking through my dirty pants, one by one.

Wednesday 14th November 2012

Today it was announced that there's a car being made by a French manufacturer which can be driven at the age of 16. It has a 400cc diesel engine, has a top speed of 28 mph, and weighs less than 350 kg. Due to these vehicular vital statistics it qualifies as a 'light quadricycle', but that is the only thing that can be described as light, as it will cost around £10,000 and likely cost any 16 year-old around £2,200 per year in tax.

A statement from the manufacturer said "We believe that the young rider market for scooters and mopeds has been contracting lately". Yes, because no-one can even afford a scooter these days, let alone a £10,000 quadricycle. They back up their point by saying that "This is due to the difficulty in convincing parents of the safety issues surrounding mopeds and scooters. This will offer a safer method of transport".

I don't think it's issues of safety stopping parents allowing their 16 year-old ASBO-owners to ride these death-machines, I think it's more to do with the fact that in the current financial climate, the parents of these children are finding that their benefits don't stretch as far anymore. These poor parents can barely afford their Rothmans and Carling, and they've had to tell their drug-dealer to only pop round once every fortnight, so something had to give. It isn't just sales of mopeds and scooters that are in decline though. What about Reebok Classics, string vests and pitbulls? Spare a thought if you will for establishments such as McDonald's, Sports Direct and Elizabeth Duke.

Those parents who do have the disposable income to afford such a car, and the insurance that goes with it, would simply not consider buying it. Precious Peter would be picked up by Mummy, or perhaps Tarquin's Mummy. This would carry on until Peter or Tarquin were old enough to drive their own proper car, at which point they would each buy a Citroen Saxo, spray-paint it lime-green, lower it, put a bass box in the boot and race it up and down Southend sea-front.

So who will buy a £10,000 quadricycle? There are people out there who buy another type of scooter, sales of which are most definitely on the up. Ladies and gentlemen, I give you the mobility-scooter. About ten years ago, the only people allowed on our pavements on four wheels were the disabled. Since then we have had an influx of mobility-scooters, carrying a range of elderly and obese people. These people don't need insurance, a licence or even a brain – they can simply spend £300 at Fatties R Us and go about causing misery for all who come into contact with them. There seem to be two types of mobility-scooter: ones that don't have any brakes and cause the person in charge of them to be rendered both blind and stupid, and ones that have a top speed of 2mph and cannot negotiate a gradient of more than 2%.

I would make it the law that all mobility-scooter users had to buy one of these new cars instead (and I am not including disabled people here, because they ride their motorised wheelchairs perfectly capably). Some might say that the danger would just be moved from the pavements to the roads, but I think it's a risk worth taking. All they ever seem to do is go to the shops and back, either to draw out their pension or buy chicken nuggets, so the total mileage would be negligible, meaning the actual risk to others on the road would be minimal.

Just close your eyes and imagine a pavement you can walk along, without fear of having your ankle crushed, or your toes squashed. We all know that the NHS is constantly struggling with their budgets and trying to find a way of cutting costs. Just think how much they would save in minor injuries admissions.

Friday 16th November 2012

We have the auditors in at work at the moment, and it's always a very strange time to be around the place. There are a team of people sitting in a small side-office going through all of our work in minute detail. It's like being back at school, waiting for your teacher to return your homework, only you can actually see them marking it, via the wonders of flexi-glass.

I remember one time at school when I had done a pretty good job on a Geography assignment and was looking forward to handing it in. Geography was one of my favourite subjects and, although I wasn't top of the class, I was in the top set and got on really well with the teacher. The lesson was in the afternoon, and Amit Patel came up to me and asked if I had completed the assignment and I said that I had. He asked if he could check mine over as he was unhappy with his and wanted to see what I had come up with, in order to get some ideas. Those weren't his exact words, but I imagine that's pretty much how it went down.

Amit was a star pupil; he had moved to the UK from Kenya the previous year and had gone straight into the top set for every subject. He was well-spoken, had rich relatives and was a bloody good cricketer to boot. In fact, he was so good that he became captain straight away, and in his second game for us got into the local papers for scoring 100 runs in a 20-over match; pretty good going for a 14 year-old.

Needless to say I was extremely proud and somewhat honoured when he asked to check my assignment for ideas and inspiration, so I gave it to him without a moment's hesitation. It seems that he was so inspired by my work that he decided to copy it, word for word.

Now the problem with copying homework is that, in order for it to work, you need to be clever in how you copy. I should know – I was an A-grade student when it came to copying. Essentially you copy the theme but change words and sentence structures. If there's an example, use a similar one, but make sure it's slightly different. I always made sure I wrote the last sentence myself and summarised it in my own way, often coming up with a different conclusion. This works in everything but Maths. Do that in Maths and you'll be advanced to the bottom set quicker than you can say "Amit Patel is a bastard".

Amit did a stupid thing by copying me word-for-word, but he was clever at the same time. He had worked out that he didn't need to change anything because he was regarded as cleverer than me, so when two identical pieces landed on the teacher's desk, it was me that was going to carry the can. That's exactly how it played out. Mrs Brambley, in big red biro, had written:

"Andrew, you have copied this word-for-word from Amit Patel. This is not acceptable. See me after class."

Amit ended up with an A-, and I ended up with a detention. The most frustrating thing about the whole thing is that he never admitted it. To this day that assignment was written by Amit Patel, and Mrs Brambley thinks I am a cheat. Still, he did get bowled for a duck in the next match we played together, so every cloud...

Anyway, auditors are generally very nice people and they do a very important job. Why is it then that I feel compelled to poison their coffee every time they say yes to a hot drink? They're just so bloody pedantic. Every single statistic, report and spreadsheet is checked in minute detail. They will come up to you with questions on things that you did eleven months ago. I often forget what I did eleven minutes ago, so eleven months is a real challenge. The only way around it is to do it again and provide them with a detailed run-through of how you got to where you did. Can you imagine doing that in any other occupation? Imagine asking a lorry-driver how many traffic lights he went through on his journey from Sheffield to Hull on the 10th December 2011, and then asking him to take the journey again when he couldn't come up with the answer.

I've come to the conclusion that auditors are the brainy cousins of personal trainers. They exist for the greater good, and the end-result of their work is always immensely satisfying, but they can be real arseholes along the way.

Tuesday 20th November 2012

I stopped going to the barber's about ten years ago. It was a forced retirement. I was devastated – I was in my early twenties and my hair had already stopped growing. The financial benefits didn't outweigh the stress it was causing, so I continued going for a lot longer than was strictly necessary. It was an embarrassing experience for both me and my barber, as we lightly danced around the elephant that wasn't only in the room, it was in the chair behind me, glancing up and waving every time I looked into the mirror. To be fair to the barber, he dragged it out as long as he could, snipping at imaginary bits of hair, brushing and combing bare bits of scalp and he did a fantastic job of angling the mirror at the end so that the light didn't bounce back and blind me.

What I hadn't realised at the time was that there was another benefit of not going to the barbers. I would never have to experience small-talk ever again. Why would an overweight man in his fifties, with a dodgy taste in shirts and a tan to rival David Dickinson's, want to know if I was going on holiday? My Mum always told me never to talk to strange men, but not only am I talking to them, I'm giving them dates and times of my whereabouts.

The fact is that the barber feels as awkward as the customer when he's reeling off the classic one-liners such as "Going anywhere nice this year?" "How's life treating you?" and "What is it you do for a living?" but he feels compelled to do so, because he thinks that the dead space needs to be filled with talking. I honestly don't think it does. It's a noisy world out there and I actually think a lot of people would genuinely enjoy the experience of having their hair cut in silence.

Since I stopped going iPods and iPhones have taken off, so maybe these days kids just go in, pop one earphone out, tell the barber what they're after and then pop it back in. It would get a bit tricky around the ears with the various wires, but I'm sure the barbers would rather that than suffer the ridiculous charade that is small-talk.

If I were a barber I would sit the customer in the chair and as I am raising or lowering it, would simply say "Look, I'm not one for small-talk, you're probably uncomfortable telling strangers your intimate secrets and to be completely truthful, I'm not at all interested." Ok, it's not the friendliest opening gambit, but it's honest, and customers like honesty.

If I were a barber I would give my 'small-talk-free' customers the choice of silence or a quiz. A quiz is the perfect thing to get strangers talking, and most guys love a good quiz. You could have different subjects and difficulties based on the appearance of each customer. As soon as you saw a string vest you could be ready with the Jeremy Kyle quiz, and a pair of cords would see you scrabbling for the geography questions. I wouldn't suggest introducing this idea to beauty-salons though, as it is a fundamental requirement for the person asking the questions to be able to read.

This weekend I had to put up with a barrage of small-talk from a host of fifteen year-old girls. No, I wasn't at a One Direction gig – I had simply gone Christmas shopping. Now, while a fifty year-old man questioning a twenty-two year-old guy about his holiday plans might seem slightly sinister, a thirty-three year-old man telling a fifteen year-old girl that yes, he is looking forward to seeing Santa, is just wrong, no matter how you dress it up.

A fifteen year-old girl does not want to know about a thirty-three year-old man's plans for Christmas. She wants to know whether her mate Charlie got off with Jason who works at Clinton's.

I think all shop staff should be taught the basics in terms of customer service, ensuring that they are polite and friendly while never engaging in small-talk. Small-talk should never take place over a till. It is too short a transaction to give a proper response. I was genuinely tempted to go off on a long ramble about Aunty Julie not being able to get down this year because of her swollen ankles and the fact that Uncle Kevin might struggle because he hasn't had confirmation of his release date, but that would just have been cruel. I said what everyone else would say in the same situation, through gritted teeth. "Oh, I can't wait, it'll be lovely. It'll all be over soon though eh? Ha ha. Hee hee." etc, etc.

When I thought it was all over and I could finally escape the small-talk hell, I was met with a barrage of questions. It seems that the shops have already gone ahead with my earlier idea – they've gone down the quiz route!

"Would you like a bag with that?"

"Do you need help packing your bags?"

"Would you like the receipt in the bag?"

"Is this a present? Would you like it wrapped?"

"Have you thought about taking out a store-card?"

Questions, questions, questions.

Needless to say, I'll be doing the rest of my Christmas shopping online.

Bah humbug.

Wednesday 21st November 2012

My daughter loves to sing, and as we settled down to read a story before bed last night she launched into a rendition of "I love you", which is a sweet but irritating song sung by a huge purple dinosaur called Barney.

The lyrics are:

I love you.

You love me.

We're a happy family.

With a great big hug and a kiss from me to you,

Won't you say you love me too?

As I said, sweet, but it is infuriatingly American, and by that I mean annoying. If there are any Americans reading, please don't take offence, I mean it in a very British way. By that I mean that I can't apologise enough! My daughter sang it with gusto, and it was only the second time around that I realised that she was getting the third line completely wrong. Instead of "We're a happy family", she was singing "We're a happy found a leaf".

I thought it was pretty cute and innocent, and I imagine it made perfect sense to her. To be fair, she often gets distracted, so I can imagine her thinking "We're a happy– oh look, I've found a leaf!" She perhaps just thought Barney was someone who was easily distracted.

She is three years old so she can be excused, but it did remind me of all the misheard lyrics I, and my friends, have been guilty of in the past. I remember being told off when I was young for singing "Now bring us some friggin' pudding" when singing "We wish you a Merry Christmas", and being exceptionally confused when corrected. Even now I don't really know what figgy pudding is, and only know of its existence through the song.

When I was about twelve Nirvana were pretty big and Smells Like Teen Spirit was a big anthem at the time, and a friend of mine misheard the lyric "Here we are now, entertain us", and instead used to sing "Here we are now, in containers".

The stupid thing is that we often don't question it; we just assume that the artist may have indulged in a few illegal remedies that day. With Kurt Cobain, that was almost a certainty.

My favourite misheard lyric was from a friend called Ben. He had just learned to drive and Bon Jovi's Crossroads album was constantly in the tape-deck. The song was Living on a Prayer, and the lyric was "It doesn't make a difference if we make it or not". He managed to hear it as "It doesn't make a difference if we're naked or not".

Now, most of the time, misheard lyrics don't make any sense, but this particular one kind of worked. The line before says that "we gotta hold on to what we got", and with the next few lines stating that they are "halfway there", that they will "give it a shot", and together they will "make it or not", it starts to paint a far steamier picture than the artist no doubt intended.

I seem to mishear lyrics all of the time, but not just in songs. Announcements always seem to say the strangest of things. I used to think "mind the gap" was "mind the bat". I actually thought the underground network was inundated with bats, and required regular announcements to warn us of their presence.

Even now, when the train I am currently sitting on announces that it will stop at Headcorn, I hear "Bed Porn". This is incredibly stupid of me. Why?

Because I live in Headcorn.

Friday 23rd November 2012

As a commuter, I experience delays and cancellations on a regular basis. The railway network is huge, and there's a lot that can go wrong. After ten years of commuting, I've finally learned to accept this. In the last couple of years, however, I have noticed an increase in information and I'm not sure that I like it.

It was only a few years ago that the train would stop for no apparent reason. It would sit there for half an hour and then slowly hobble into platform number 76, and not a word would be said. If you dared to ask someone what had caused the delay, you would be met with nothing but a shrug and a blank stare. I'm not sure whether the new system of telling everybody everything is an order from the top, or whether the conductors are all just free-styling. Maybe they're all frustrated DJs.

I've counted more than fourteen announcements so far on my journey today. In my mind, that's about thirteen more than is actually necessary. The problem is that at every station we stop at, more people get on, so that is more people who need to be updated. Today I have heard the following: "Apologies for the delay this morning, this is due to a cancelled train and congestion", which was swiftly followed by "Apologies for the earlier announcement which didn't fully explain the delay, and someone rightly pointed out that a cancelled train shouldn't cause congestion, but the train was cancelled due to an electrical fault and as it was stuck on the track, trains are having to be diverted around it, which is causing congestion."

We then had various versions of that message, together with confirmation of how late we were each time, which started off in five-minute increments and then increased to fifteen. We then had announcements as to how the trains behind us are getting on, followed by an announcement on how best to get to stations that this train isn't going to, owing to the cancellation of the earlier train. The final announcement told us how we could claim a refund on our journey as we were now over half an hour late.

I'm fully expecting the conductor to announce that there is a taxi outside in the name of Wilkins and that the next song is dedicated to Sheila and Brian, who after 40 years of marriage are retiring and moving to Spain.

Everyone around me seems quite relaxed about it and I know why that is; it's because we are on the way in to work. If this had happened on the way home from work, we would have a mutiny on our hands. There would be passengers relaying stories of how much they pay to be treated like cattle, there would be others detailing the exact dates and times of previous delays, and there would be lots and lots of shrugging, head-shaking and swearing under people's breath. All we have now is people frantically tapping on their Blackberries and laptops, and the odd muted sound of someone saying "Christine, can you let Paul know that I won't be able to make the 9:30; we'll have to reschedule".

I'm picking up two different vibes as I look around the train – one of frustration, and one of acceptance. This more or less correlates to those that are standing up and those that are seated. I've decided I'm going to give the lady in front of me a break and offer her my seat; she's most definitely in the frustrated camp. She's currently juggling two phones, a huge folder and a handbag that Mary Poppins would be proud of. She seems stressed, and is not only struggling to remain calm – she's struggling to stay on her feet.

Step forward the hero of the hour – the knight in shining armour!

Well that went down rather well. She very much appreciated me offering my seat and she is now able to spread her folder across her lap whilst carrying on with her phone call.

I would have liked to have ended the chapter there, as a proud hero, doing something selfless in someone's hour of need. But as I write this, one-handed, swaying about the train, struggling to piece together the last few sentences, she sits back, opens her handbag and begins to apply her make-up! Hour of need indeed.

Andy Leeks, what a bloody hero!

Tuesday 27th November 2012

As weekends go, the weekend just gone was pretty miserable. It rained the whole weekend, our daughter came down with a horrible cold, and I received an email from the gas and electricity company telling us our quarterly bills are due. In fact, the misery continues, as it is still raining, my daughter is still ill and I've still yet to pay those pesky bills. Oh and as if my misery weren't already complete, my train has just been cancelled and I'll now have to take a later train which will be twice as busy.

So here I am on a later train, squashed into a corner, soaked through and tired from a night of nursing my daughter, and I've got to find the inner strength to come up with something informative, thought-provoking or witty. The problem is, however, that I have just found out that the train I'm on does not stop where I need it to, meaning I have a choice between changing at the next stop and walking a long way in the rain. I've come to the conclusion that I can't be any more miserable than I currently am, so an extra walk in the rain can't hurt. Anyway, if I get off the train I might not be able to finish this chapter, which would be a plus-point for you, dear reader, believe me, but a definite failure on my part.

I'm aware that I'm moaning about trivial things and it is easy to forget that there are people with far greater worries out there. I know there are people who are starving, people living in poverty and people who are being exploited and abused. But those people don't have to put up with last-minute cancellations and constant delays, do they? I'm joking of course, but it is very easy to forget that our problems are tiny in comparison to others.

A few years ago Ashley Cole notoriously decided to include in his autobiography a chapter which detailed his anger at being offered only £55,000 a week instead of £60,000 while playing for Arsenal. The book was aimed at those who didn't earn that much in a year. That would be like me writing a cook-book for the starving.

It's a shorter chapter than usual today as I've had to write it with just one hand (my other one is trapped under either a person or a person's luggage, I'm not sure which, but either way, I'm pretty handicapped).

I'm hoping normal service will resume tomorrow, in terms of both trains and content.

Wednesday 28th November 2012

I love my neighbours. When I say that, I don't mean the Australian soap, I mean the people who live in the house attached to our house. We are extremely lucky to have such nice neighbours. I often hear of arguments and even fights between neighbours and it always seems to be down to car-parking or noise.

We are lucky enough to each have our own drive and, by living in an Edwardian house, we are also blessed with thick walls. Maybe that's it; maybe I've just stumbled across the magic ingredients for nationwide neighbour harmony. Never mind the 'Big Society', Mr Prime Minister; never mind 'Hug a Hoodie'. Let's tarmac everyone's drive and thicken everyone's walls. Imagine how nice it would be if everyone actually did 'love thy neighbour'. It would be like the 'Olympic Fever' all over again, only the feel-good factor would actually last longer than it took Jessica Ennis to complete her lap of honour.

If I'm honest, you could have the biggest drive in the world and the thickest possible walls, but if your neighbours are inconsiderate arseholes, there's really nothing you can do. They say to keep your friends close and your enemies closer, but being neighbours with your enemy is frankly ridiculous. Having to live next to a neighbour you hate would be like being forced to live with your ex, minus the knowledge of what they look like naked, hopefully. Although, saying that, a friend of mine used to regularly see his neighbour, a fifty-something widow, lying naked in the garden.

The reason we get on so well with our neighbours is that they are genuinely lovely people. They're kind, considerate, generous, funny, interesting and happy people, and not once have they been naked in the garden. We have only known them for seven months, but I already know that we have a friendship that will last years, if not a lifetime. It started off as a friendship out of circumstance; we decided to move and live out our lives three feet to one side of them, but very quickly it turned into a genuine friendship that had nothing to do with the proximity of our houses.

When you think about it, getting to know and then getting to like your neighbours is rather convenient. We have friends all over the place and often have to travel huge distances to meet up with them. If everyone became good friends with their neighbours, no-one would need to travel anywhere and we would solve global warming quicker than you can say "Can I borrow a cup of sugar, please?"

Yesterday, my wife found out that she needed to attend an important meeting at work and therefore couldn't take our daughter to nursery. Unfortunately I also had important engagements at work, so we were left in an awkward position. Step forward our lovely neighbours. Not only did they offer to drop our daughter off at nursery, they offered to look after her for a couple of hours first, even giving her breakfast, and ensuring we could both get to work in plenty of time.

As the famous line from the soap says, "Neighbours, everybody needs good neighbours!"

Friday 30th November 2012

I don't know what's happened to me this morning. Today is one of the busiest and most stressful days of the year for me. Today I have to finalise some very important figures, and these figures determine a lot of people's bonuses. It's a very sensitive time, especially this close to Christmas.

But instead of feeling stressed and apprehensive, I feel completely relaxed and content. This morning I was struck by the beauty of the planet that we live on, and it has left me feeling strangely humble and peaceful. No, I haven't gone mad and I haven't been drinking, I've just been noticing things this morning that I wouldn't normally notice.

When I first drew the curtains, I was greeted by a beautiful blackbird, sitting no more than three feet from my window. His feathers were plumped up, protecting him from the morning chill as the sun glistened and reflected off of his jet-black plumage. I was mesmerised by his beauty and needed the sound of the snoozed alarm-clock to bring me back from my trance.

As I trudged up the garden path and passed under the tree that housed my morning friend, I was met with a full moon and it stopped me in my tracks. The night before we had been blessed with a full moon that lit up the sky like a flare and I hadn't expected to see it again so soon. It was on the opposite side of the sky to the night before, and its silvery glow had been replaced by a wispy, cloud-like white. It was elegant and beautiful, silent and stunning.

As I sit here now, on the train, describing the sights which have humbled me, I can see vast, rolling hills covered in a blanket of white frost. There is smoke rising from the chimneys of distant cottages and church towers peeping into view, partially hidden by the hills before them. The last of the autumn leaves are floating gently to the ground as the trails from long-gone planes leave a lattice of white stripes overhead.

As I lose myself in the beauty which sits outside my window, I am interrupted by a loud crackle, followed by an announcement. "Ladies and gentlemen, we are now approaching London Bridge; please remember to take all of your belongings with you."

It's on days like these that I wish the conductors would go off-piste, forget about lost property and bomb-threats and do what pilots do so well. Describe the beauty sitting outside the window.

"Ladies and gentlemen, it's 7:54 am, we should be arriving into London by 8:40. If you look outside the window to your left you will see the beautiful parish church of Smarden. The current church was built between 1325 and 1350 of local Kentish ragstone and Bethersden marble quarried at nearby Tuesnoad. Now if you look to your right......"

Monday 3rd December 2012

Today marks twenty years since the first text message was sent and received. I suppose that is an important point – the fact that it was also actually received. I imagine that anyone could claim to have sent the first text. There could have been thousands of texts sent over the last hundred years or so, but they just weren't being received.

"Shit, just heard that J F K got shot!"

"Who would have thought it, a woman for a Prime Minister?!"

"Apparently there's gonna be a big storm tomorrow. Don't worry though – Michael Fish said it will all be alright, lol"

"Just heard that some guy called Hitler has invaded Poland"

"OMG, the Titanic has sunk"

The person who actually sent the first text was a guy called Neil Papworth, a 22 year-old telecom engineer who worked for a company developing text communication on behalf of Vodafone. He sent it to one of the directors, who was at a Christmas party, and the message simply read "Merry Christmas". That's a lovely story and a great quiz question, but surely they should have thought of something better than that.

This was a groundbreaking moment and they surely would have known that at the time. Why didn't he send something like:

"If this works, I want a pay rise"

Or

"Just think before you have that next glass of red, we're meeting Bob from Vodafone tomorrow"

Or

"Can you please not leave me on the dressing table tonight? I deserve to be on your bedside table, with your glasses and your crossword"?

I'm not a massive fan of text messaging. The only time I find it acceptable is when asking and answering simple questions.

"What time will you be home?"

"8pm"

As soon as it goes beyond this simple function, I find it infuriating to use. The problem with the written word, and the written word in the form of mobile texting in particular, is that it's often misunderstood and taken out of context. A polite request can suddenly seem rude, or a simple question can come across as an invasion of privacy. I spend so long re-writing texts so they cannot be misunderstood, that it's always quicker to call. The problem for me is that I also hate calling people. I'm always worried that I'm disturbing them, so I tend not to bother to text or phone anyone if I can help it.

I know it's old fashioned, but I actually like the process of sending and receiving letters. Ok, it's an incredibly slow and expensive way of communicating, but people always seem genuinely pleased to receive a letter. Can you imagine receiving a personal letter through the door and thinking "Oh, it's him again, what does he want this time?"

(Famous people with stalkers don't have to answer that last question)

You can be completely honest in a letter and you will never cause any upset. The fact that someone has taken the time to write something and physically post it means they will almost always be let off the hook. Every now and then there are situations where you need to be honest. These situations tend to manifest themselves as your best friend asking your opinion on his latest haircut, or deciding to go through that phase of thinking that dungarees are cool. A letter is genuinely the only way of dealing with this type of awkward situation. I've lost count of the letters I have sent to ex-girlfriends saying "Yes your arse does look fat in that", or "It wasn't you, it was me".

It was also reported today that, for the first time, texts are actually in decline. I was initially optimistic, thinking that letters might be making a comeback, but I'm disappointed to report that texts are just being replaced by social networking sites and free messaging apps.

So unfortunately, we will have to go on living in a world where dodgy haircuts are the norm, where dungarees are still being purchased by adults, and where arses continue to look fat in things.

Tuesday 4th December 2012

I'm writing this while standing up today. I've never minded standing up while commuting, even though my journey takes well over an hour. My theory is that I sit down all day, so standing up for an hour isn't exactly a hardship. There are people who have to stand all day in order to do their job, so it's they who deserve a seat.

I would actually be happy if the train companies announced that they were going to introduce priority passes for those who work in upright professions. In fact, thinking about it, wouldn't it make it simpler if you were issued a pass based on your personal circumstances? There should be a priority sit-down pass for anyone who works in an upright profession, anyone with a disability, anyone over sixty and anyone who is pregnant. Everyone else is issued with a non-priority pass, meaning they have to give up their seat once someone with a priority pass asks to sit down.

I would actually go one stage further and introduce three differently coloured passes – a green one for those who qualify to sit down at any time, an orange one for those who don't qualify, and a red one for those who actively opt out of sitting down altogether and elect to stand up. Those going for a red pass would maybe even qualify for some kind of discount.

I'm sure this system would create harmony amongst travellers as there would be less squabbling for seats, and it would mean those in the upright professions can get more rest and therefore do a better job. I can't see many negatives here. The only real negative is the one I'm experiencing right now, in that I have to type this with one hand.

The reason I'm currently standing is that I gave up my seat to a young mother and child. As I've mentioned before, I sit by the toilets, but it is also the area for wheelchairs and pushchairs. I have actually given up my seat for this same lady a number of times, and she is always very appreciative. It seems to be Tuesdays and Fridays that she has the child with her, and I am effectively responsible for keeping her seat warm.

You may ask why I continue to sit in the seat, knowing full well that I will end up having to move, but I do it for a very good reason. If I didn't give up my seat it is highly likely that she and her young daughter would have to stand for the whole journey. It is amazing how many young, male professionals seem to get a little bit sleepy, or suddenly find an article about coastal erosion absolutely fascinating as soon as she steps on board.

I've often given up my seat to people who wouldn't normally come under the 'Priority' category. I genuinely don't care whether I sit down or not, so when I see someone upset at having to stand, I will invariably offer my seat. It doesn't matter whether they are old, female, pregnant, or none of the above; if they would prefer to sit down and I'm not bothered, then I'll offer them my seat.

It's a very simple form of charity, and it has made me realise that I don't do enough in that respect. When I look around my house there is plenty of stuff I no longer want or need, and there are people less fortunate than me who could either use it, or use the money raised from it. With Christmas coming up, there is no better time to clear out the spare room and take a trip down to the charity-shop.

When I started writing this book, I saw it as an opportunity to be creative and share my view on the world around me, but it's turning into more of a voyage of self-discovery and enlightenment. Ok, maybe that's going a bit far, but I'm definitely going to clear out all the crap in the spare room, so I've got this book to thank for that!

Wednesday 5th December 2012

The train is delayed again this morning, but there are no broken-down trains, no staff shortages, no engineering works and no-one has committed suicide. Today we have delays because of "poor rail conditions".

Have the rails caught an illness? Have they suddenly deteriorated overnight? No. We have poor rail conditions because approximately twenty minutes ago we had a light flurry of snowfall, which lasted about three minutes.

I don't like to moan about the trains because in general, I think we enjoy a good service, but on days like today I am left scratching my head. There can't be more than a millimetre of snow on the tracks at the present time – how can this delay a five thousand-tonne train?

Do trains experience delays in the snow because the tracks are slippery? If that's the case then surely a simple fix would be to heat the rails or introduce some sort of a modification to the wheels where a button can be pressed and extra grip can be generated. I'm assuming the reason we don't have these features available to us is the cost. I get a cold sweat every time I receive a gas bill for my house, so I would hate to see what the bill would be to heat a whole network of rails. Cars have traction control and ABS, though; surely trains can have that too?

Apparently it's not always down to the simple fact that the rails get a bit slippery, there are a whole number of contributing factors. Points start to freeze up, equipment starts to fail and train staff find it difficult to get to work. Add all of this to "poor rail conditions" and you start to get a knock-on effect where delays turn into cancellations, and cancellations mean sweary commuters.

I have an idea to combat the weather issues. There will never be any problems with snow and there will never be any issues with leaves on the track. How about, now I know this might sound crazy, but how about we build a network of rails... underground?

We could call it the 'Underground', and as all of the equipment would be underground, nothing would break or fail, and there would be no issues with staff getting to work, meaning there would never be any delays and everyone would be happy with the service.

Next week, I'll be suggesting an extra lane to completely eradicate congestion on the M25, and a coalition government to finally sort out the political malaise.

Friday 7th December 2012

Train etiquette is very much like bus or toilet etiquette. There is an unspoken rule that everyone adheres to. You must head for the areas that are sparsely populated. This means that once on a bus or train, you must look for empty seats in clusters of two and men in a public toilet should always look for a cluster of three, as it guarantees a space either side. This unspoken rule is completely instinctive. It doesn't have to be taught or handed down generation after generation, it is just good old human nature.

Would I rather sit next to the guy reading Carp of the Week and with breakfast down his chin or would I rather just sit on my own. Would I rather stand within four inches of another mans penis while emptying my bladder, or would I rather just pee in peace. (I was nervous when deciding on the distance to go with in that last sentence, using inches and penis in the same sentence is always tricky. I went for four inches because no-one likes a show off).

On busy days of course, this theory goes out of the window and it is every man, woman and child for themselves. This is accepted and this is fine. So long as you follow the basic principles up until the point where there are more people than clusters of two's and three's then you won't be labelled a weirdo.

The weirdo got onto the train about ten minutes ago.

I'm staring at him now.

He seems quite normal really; his hair is neat and tidy, he looks presentable, he's not reading Carp of the Week and there are no visible signs of his breakfast. Why then, when there are many clusters of empty seats, has he sat next to someone? Initially, I thought he knew the other person, but if they know each other, they clearly don't like each other because they are not talking. Stranger still, he didn't just slide in next to him, he had to ask him to move so he could sit down by the window.

Hang on, they're talking, maybe they do know each other after all.

Ok, I have an update.

After an awkward silence and a fair bit of huffing and puffing from the rightly disgruntled passenger, our weirdo has explained that he likes to sit by the window, facing forward and this was the only seat that was free that fitted that description. He then went on to say that he liked to see where he was going. What, just in case the driver takes a wrong turn and takes us to Margate for the day? What is he expecting to see today that he didn't see yesterday? I would absolutely love to kick off my shoes and put my feet up while travelling, but I don't because firstly, I am considerate to the other passengers and secondly I am not a weirdo.

Please, everyone reading; don't be a weirdo and just follow the simple rules of train etiquette.

Thank you

Monday 10th December 2012

Real or fake, that seems to be the main debate at the moment. Fake ones look great and they never droop, but they just don't feel the same, do they?

I'm talking about Christmas trees of course and this weekend saw us buying our annual 8 foot tree before cutting it down to six, so that it fits. Real Christmas trees tend to get a bad press. Like naughty teenagers they are often charged with being temperamental and messy. Well, like teenagers, if you get the right one, they can be totally worth the effort. Ok, our Christmas trees have never tidied up after themselves or made us a cup of tea after a hard day, but they do tend to stay fairly mess free and they always produce a pleasant smell; far nicer than the dusty aroma that I associate with a fake one.

People often say "It's just such an effort! Going out, choosing one, bringing it back, dragging it through the house, getting pine needles everywhere....." That sounds a lovely day out compared to the rigmarole involved with setting up our old fake tree. My Mum and Dad have never got around to installing a proper loft ladder. Not the crime of the century you might think, but they never got around to buying more than a four foot step ladder either. The loft hatch in my Mum and Dads house hovers dangerously over the stairs and only a highly trained acrobat from the Moscow State Circus would attempt an entry via the step ladder. Every year however, my Dad would come back from the pub and announce that it was time for the tree to come down. This happened every year until my brother was old enough / tall enough to take over and he had two main advantages over my Dad in that he was 20 years younger in age and 20 units lighter in alcohol.

On a slight digression, while talking about my Dad insisting on doing things while under the influence, I remember one year where my Mum had gone Christmas food shopping. She had gone out in the morning and come back late in the afternoon and the car was full of festive food. Dad had been to the pub to meet a few old friends and had consumed, shall we say "A festive few."

My Mum had spent ages trying to rearrange our freezer to fit in all of the frozen food, but it wasn't any good, it just wasn't fitting in. It was one of those combination fridge/freezers that stood about six foot tall, with the freezer compartment at the bottom and the fridge on top. She had noticed that the freezer was thick with ice and if it could be defrosted, she would be able to fit in all of the food.

Step forward my Dad, with a hammer in one hand and a pallet knife in the other. The reason that he had a hammer just lying around was simple. Dad always put all of the decorations up with a hammer. I am certain that we were the only family that had no use for blue-tac at Christmas. The tree was hammered together with a mallet and everything else from lights to stockings were attached to the wall with a hammer and nail.

We heard a combination of banging and swearing for just under an hour before it all went quiet. After a few minutes, we decided to go and check to see if everything was ok and what we witnessed was like a scene from a Laurel and Hardy movie. My Dad was sitting on the floor holding his head, completely dazed, while our dog was running around the kitchen gobbling up a floor full of pickled onions.

It didn't need Colombo to work out that while Dad was getting to work with the bottom compartment of the freezer, the catering sized jar of pickled onions on top of the fridge/freezer was slowly making it's way towards his head. The thought of my Dad being nursed by my Mum; who was holding up a combination of fingers while the dog gagged in the background still makes me laugh today.

So our Christmas tree is up and the decorations are in place and I haven't once had to use any carpentry tools or acrobatics. I just need to make sure that I defrost the freezer before the food shopping arrives.

Tuesday 11th December 2012

Today is the last chapter of the year for me. It marks an interesting and emotional three months where I have blathered on about a variety of things, such as introducing a 22nd birthday, lying when returning unwanted gifts, introducing an interactive news show, moving Halloween to June, banning mobility carts, why I can't complain, why I hate small talk and why my Dad uses a hammer to put up Christmas decorations.

It hasn't all been a load of rambling nonsense, there have been times of sadness, where I had to say goodbye to my dear old Gramps; there have been times of reflection, where I decided I needed to put other people first and there have been times of realisation; where I saw the beauty of the world around me and was humbled by it's elegance and simplicity. There are also times where I moaned about my zits and explained why I couldn't poo in public, so let's not pretend that these are the works of Chaucer.

As it is the last chapter of the year, it is the perfect time to tie up a few of the loose ends. Early on in the book, I mentioned that I would start bringing my own coffee to work in a flask. I decided that it would be a real money saver, possibly saving as much as £448.64 in a year. This idea was fantastic in principle, but I quickly learned that it is a false economy. My workings only accounted for one flask. The problem is that I keep leaving them on the train, meaning I have to keep buying new flasks. I'm on the 5th or 6th one since I started the book, so I reckon I'm probably just about even.

On the 5th of November I challenged myself to lose twenty pounds in just under six weeks. This was all very well at the time, but what I hadn't factored in was that effectively, the Christmas season starts on the 1st of December and ever since then, I have been gorging on mince pies and chocolates. I'm happy to announce that I am currently wearing my old work trousers and I have lost around a stone in weight, but I didn't manage to lose the twenty pounds I had hoped.

Oh and maybe I am being too honest here, but I never did manage to get down the charity shop, but I promise I will do before Christmas.

So that is it for this year, a strange three months that started with an argument on Facebook and ended with me listing my many failings.

Wednesday 2nd January 2013

So that's it, Christmas is over and the New Year is upon us. I get the same feeling going back to work after Christmas as I do when boarding a plane home after a relaxing holiday. I worry about how much money I have spent, how much weight I have put on, and how much work I have to go back to.

In fact the only real difference between the two is that I come back from holiday with new sandals, and Christmas with new socks. Maybe that's how the whole 'wearing sandals with socks' cliché started. Someone, somewhere went to visit their family in a hot country over Christmas, bought themselves some new sandals while they were there, and then found the inevitable pack of five (Size 8-12) under the Christmas tree.

I always enjoy Christmas but it seems to throw up lots of unanswerable questions.

Why do I always end up sitting on the chair from the garage?

Why do toys now require a toolbox just to remove them from their packaging?

Why do we continue to buy nuts in shells when we have never owned a nutcracker, and always have to resort to a tea towel and rolling pin?

Why do Ferrero Rocher make it impossible to open their boxes, meaning we have to resort to a tea towel and rolling pin?

Why do we always buy a 25lb turkey, only to end up throwing 15lb away?

How do foxes get into wheelie bins?

How do foxes eat 15lb of turkey in one sitting?

Why do foxes make so much mess?

Why did they ban fox hunting?

Christmas and the New Year come very close together, but when you look at the two celebrations, that's the only thing they have in common. Christmas is all about family traditions, gorging on food and forgetting about the leaky tap. New Year is the complete opposite – it's all about resolutions, change, diets and promises. The New Year is all about fixing that leaky bloody tap.

It makes perfect sense; for every heavy drinking session there is a hangover, for every shopping spree there is a credit card bill, and for every bit of consensual marital sex there is an even bigger credit card bill. New Year is the Christmas payback. The yin to the yang, the chalk to the cheese, the Prince William to the Prince Harry.

So after a busy few months Thornton's will now be empty until Easter, while LA Fitness will be printing membership cards quicker than the Bank of England can print money.

Why hasn't anyone thought of going into flexible retail? I know there are shops and department stores that cater for the seasons and various trends, but I'm talking about opening a shop that constantly changes all of its stock, based on the time of year.

Mine would look like this.

January - March - Half Gym, half DIY shop.

March - June – Mother's Day gifts and cards, Father's Day gifts and cards, and Easter Eggs.

July - September - Ice creams, sunglasses, beachwear and 'back to school' items.

October - December - Halloween, fireworks and Christmas items.

Of course, you would always have to leave space by the till for those essential personalised key rings. It's never the wrong time of year to buy a key ring informing people that Angelica means 'lactose intolerant' in Ancient Greek.

Thursday 3rd January 2013

There are times when I love Facebook and there are times when I hate it. I hate Facebook when I get constant updates from people asking me to play tedious online games, and when people upload pictures of their food. I hate Facebook when people leave statuses that are clearly designed to invite a response. You know the ones I mean, there's probably at least one sitting in your news feed right now. "Why do I bother", "I can't believe he's done it again", "Is it really supposed to double in size" – that kind of thing. People are lured into responding, not because they care about the person, but just because they're plain nosey!

There are also times when I love Facebook, and the period around Christmas and New Year is when I fall back in love with it. Christmas is great because there is so much positivity and everyone just seems happy to be off of work and relaxing with family and friends. The New Year is even better, because in the twenty-four hours either side of midnight you often get to see the very best of people and the very worst of them. As I scrolled through my news feed leading up to and then entering the New Year, it was a perfect mix of hope and excitement, followed by the dawning of realisation.

As this book was born from an argument on Facebook, I have decided to dedicate this chapter to it, and I've created a poem made up solely from status updates on my news feed in a twenty-four hour period, over New Year's Eve and New Year's Day.

Overworked and underpaid,

Congratulations on getting engaged.

Ok I'm drunk, I confess!

Work tomorrow, so depressed!

Think it's time to clear out the loft,

Watching season 5 of Lost!

Housework done, time for beer,

Look out people, this is my year.

Surely it's got to be gin o'clock?

Chris would like to play lucky slots.

Sorry about my drunken post,

Looking forward to a big fat roast.

Wake me up when it's all over,

It's 2 in the morning and I'm still sober.

Chips are ready! Ketchup or Gravy?

Kim and Kanye are having a baby.

Time to lose my Christmas gut!

Anyone know what time Tesco shuts?

Haven't been this drunk in a while,

Time to party Gangnam style.

Time to lose the Movember 'tash,

Mosie would like to play Bingo bash.

Oh my god I look like a goth,

2012 can piss right off.

Time to weigh in,

I'm laying off gin.

Lovely weather!

Yeah whatever.

Ouch my head,

Time for bed.

Here come the tears,

Happy New Year.

Friday 4th January 2013

Since I started this book in September I have had precious little time to read the newspaper while commuting, but thanks to the overrunning engineering works in New Cross, leading to numerous cancellations, delays and platform alterations, there has been ample opportunity today for me to catch up with the news.

In the last three days alone, I have been delayed by just over six hours. How do the train companies compensate us? With another 'above inflation' price rise, that's how. Merry Christmas and a Happy New Year to you too!

As annoying as these price rises are, we have known about them since last August. It was a very clever move, but while we were watching Jessica Ennis run, jump, throw and smile her way to Olympic glory, the train companies quietly announced their latest rises. So although it is infuriating to be paying more, we knew it was coming. It's like being annoyed about the fact that it gets cold in winter, or that the grass needs cutting in the summer, or that I'll forget my anniversary next year. We know it's going to happen, so let's just make the best of it.

But inevitably, one of the lead stories in the papers this week has been the recent price rises across the railway network. To me this is lazy journalism. This story is four months old. This isn't 'news', this is 'olds'.

If the news agencies were really bothered about it, why didn't they do more back in August? If they had attacked the story with the same amount of ferocity back in August, something might have actually been done about it. Instead, the papers are littered with lazy stories, written by bored journalists just before they clocked off for Christmas. All that's left to do is to send out the office junior to pick up a few commuter quotations and they have themselves a story. Well, Andy, 33, from Headcorn, says "You are a bunch of lazy arseholes".

But journalists haven't just been lazy this week, they have been irresponsible. One newspaper today announced that it had taken out an advert in an Argentinian newspaper in response to an open letter sent by the Argentine president, calling for the Falkland Islands to come under their sovereignty. So our newspaper decided to take out an advert, basically telling Argentina to keep its hands off. Our Prime Minister had already reacted in a mature and sensible manner and announced that the islanders should decide. Why do certain newspapers feel obliged to constantly get involved in matters that don't concern them? It's irresponsible at best. We've seen examples in the past where articles, and in some cases cartoons, have resulted in violent retaliation.

I find it strange when journalists go out of their way to breach security and then go ahead and write about it in the paper, leaving us all feeling dangerously exposed. I've seen numerous reports about security breaches in airports and train stations, and most recently there was a breach at the Olympics that made the headlines. Of course, you could argue that it is in the public interest, and that by highlighting the matter publicly they are in fact ensuring that something gets done about it, but that doesn't stop me sitting on a plane, sweating, thinking "Shit, I hope no-one read that article last week about how to smuggle explosives under your finger nails", and then looking accusingly at anyone wearing gloves.

Monday 7th January 2013

Today marks a special anniversary and, in an interesting twist, it's one that I remembered and one that I don't have to buy a card for. Today marks ten years since I joined the company I work for.

Ten years is a long time. It's longer than my wife and I have been together, and if I forget another anniversary it's likely to be longer than we will ever be together. There are many friends of ours who have been together far longer than we have and I've often heard the jocular analogy that they would have "got less time for murder!"

It's a good line. There aren't many one-liners that include the word murder and get a good laugh. The problem in my case is that we have been together only nine years, and the same joke just doesn't work. Try joking with your friends that you'd have got a shorter sentence for grievous bodily harm or sexual assault. Even better, try it with strangers at a party and see how long it takes them to move on. My record is twelve seconds.

I work in accounts, so naturally I like numbers, and getting to double figures is a good feeling. There are not many things I have stuck at for ten years, so I should be very proud. Now that I think of it, aside from bodily functions, there aren't many things that I have done for more than ten years. I've only had a mortgage for seven years, been married for six and I've only been driving for four. And then there are things that only lasted days, like the Tamagotchi I received on Christmas Day in 1996 and had killed by New Year's Day 1997, and things that lasted hours, like the money I received for Christmas a year later and promptly lost just four hours later while walking the dog.

I'm sure at this point my wife would have liked to chip in with the things that only lasted seconds, but luckily for me she doesn't get a say, and this isn't that kind of book.

Tuesday 8th January 2013

I saw an advert at a bus stop yesterday and it really made me smile. It didn't have a catchy slogan or a raunchy theme; it simply had a picture of the product in question.

The product in question was a KFC 'Bargain Bucket' meal, and I smiled because of the bottle of Pepsi Max standing awkwardly to one side, looking almost embarrassed to be a part of it all.

You've got to admire KFC. It's January – probably the worst month to try to promote a high calorie deep-fried meal, but instead of saving up the budget for Easter, when people have given up eating free-range eggs in favour of Cadbury ones, they decided to push ahead with the campaign.

I assume someone somewhere said "Let's try to even it up a bit and put a low calorie drink on the advert", but the problem is that it just looks a bit silly. It looks like they are trying too hard to be responsible. It's reminiscent of children's TV programmes in the 80s when TV executives started introducing black characters, because they thought it was the right thing to do. The problem is, however, that they ended up insulting everyone as the characters were given bemusing accents and were always terribly stereotyped.

KFC have opted for Pepsi Max and I think it's a predictable choice. It's the safe bet. Everyone knows that, Pepsi Max or Coca-Cola, the 'Bargain Bucket' is a high calorie meal. We also know that out of all the 'Diet' drinks, Pepsi Max shouldn't be first choice. It's like deciding to hire a David Beckham impersonator instead of going for Mr Beckham himself. Although David Beckham actually endorses Pepsi Max, so my analogy doesn't really work in this instance, but I hope you get the point I'm trying to make.

I've got nothing against KFC, or Pepsi Max for that matter, but I think they should stick to advertising their products in an honest way. Here are my suggestions.

KFC Bargain Bucket Meal - for when you're emotional, drunk, or both.

Pepsi Max - for times when there isn't Coke.

To prove that I don't have an agenda, I'm happy to point out that KFC's website is extremely up-front and honest. The calorie content of every meal is clearly stated, and each meal is given a percentage against the Guideline Daily Amount. KFC also point out that they have cut saturated fat by 25% and that they no longer add salt to their chips; in fact they have gone one step further and signed the government's salt pledge. I'm not sure what a 'salt pledge' is, but it would be reasonable to assume that it's a pledge set out by the government, whereby people commit to cutting out salt. Just a thought, but perhaps we should all consider putting together a pledge for the government to sign. How about the 'meaningless gesture pledge'?

While on the KFC site, I also noticed that they are still banging on about that secret blend of herbs and spices, and there is a quotation which says "We'd run blindfolded through bees before revealing our 11 herbs and spices", which is ironic because that is exactly what I would rather do than eat one of their meals. Can it really be that much of a secret? At least with Coke, the 'secret recipe' is actually a closely guarded secret. KFC have not only decided to tell us the two main types of ingredient, they've gone and told us exactly how many we will need. In fact, with the clues we've already been given, anybody with a spare couple of hours and a half-decent spice rack should be able to crack the code.

I'm aware that today's chapter is a bit product-placement-heavy, having mentioned Cadbury, KFC, Coke and Pepsi, and I'd like to take this opportunity to make it clear that other food products are available.

Unless of course it's 2am, alcohol is slurring your speech, and your girlfriend has just dumped you; in that situation, no other product will do.

Wednesday 9th January 2013

It was announced today that fizzy drinks and fruit squashes are being linked to depression, after a study involving more than 250,000 people. I normally glaze over when the results of a 'study' are announced as the studies are often random and have little relevance. "It was announced today that eating cheese can make you go blind, after a study involving 20 patients from Moorfields Eye Hospital. A source from www.wevegotnothingbettertodo.com said that all of the patients had some form of blindness and all of them had eaten cheese at some point in their lives."

The study on fizzy drinks and fruit squashes made me take more notice though, as they had studied over 250,000 people, which I consider to be a fairly big sample. I also took more notice because I drink a lot of fizzy drinks and fruit squashes. The study says that "Downing four cans of sparkling drinks a day raised the risk of mental illness by 30 percent, while the same amount of squash increased it by 38 percent. The danger was greatest for those that opted for diet products".

After I gave up drinking alcohol almost three years ago, I rapidly increased my intake of other fluids, mainly Coke Zero, squash and coffee. I was therefore relieved to read the next sentence, as it confirmed that "People drinking four cups of coffee a day were 10 percent less likely to develop depression."

I really don't want to suffer depression, so I've decided to crunch some numbers to work out the likelihood of me developing depression. I tend to drink an average of one can of Coke Zero a day and roughly the same amount of fruit squash.

4 cans of sparking drinks = 30% more likely, so with one a day it would increase my risk by 7.5%.

Equivalent amount of fruit squash = 38% more likely, so with one a day it would increase my risk by about 9.5%.

So, in terms of my consumption of sparkling drinks and fruit squash, according to the recent study, I am 17% more likely to suffer from a mental illness.

It's time to factor in the coffee.

I drink an average of six cups of coffee a day. I know it's a lot, but this book would not get written without it!

So, 4 cups of coffee = 10% less likely, so it would decrease my risk by 15%.

So there we have it, I am 2% more likely to suffer depression than someone who doesn't drink sparkling drinks, fruit squash or coffee. For a brief moment, I did consider increasing my coffee intake to seven a day, thus eradicating the risk altogether, but ultimately I decided this study is a complete load of rubbish.

Ok, so they studied 250,000 people and, yes, they found that lots of people had depression and mental illness, but with 250,000 people, I bet a fair few of them also had chlamydia! Was that down to what they put in their mouths? Well, actually, yes, it possibly was, but what I'm trying to say is that the study was actively looking at the link between drinks and depression and didn't factor in personal circumstances such as relationships, finances or work stress.

In order to make that chlamydia joke, I needed to double check that you could actually get chlamydia from oral sex, otherwise the joke wouldn't have worked, so I decided to Google "Can you get chlamydia from oral sex?"

It's always good to check your facts, isn't it? Well, in this case, no. Within seconds my iPad screen was inundated with more rotten genitals than a whole series of Embarrassing Bodies could handle. Worse still, the people in the carriage behind must have been having a party, as what can only be described as a smartly-dressed conga danced its way past me, just as the genitals graced my screen.

It's quite depressing to think that half of the train now assumes that I have chlamydia, but then that's nothing another quick coffee can't fix.

Friday 11th January 2013

My wife went out last night on a rare night out with the girls, and I was left to fend for myself. The term 'fend for yourself' is described on thefreedictionary.com as "looking after yourself, supporting yourself, sustaining yourself, taking care of yourself, providing for yourself, making do".

I managed to carry out all of the above, but there is one element to 'fending for yourself' that isn't covered by the dictionary description, and it's one thing I have always struggled with. Entertaining myself.

I can happily look after, support, sustain, take care of and provide for myself, but I have never been able to entertain myself. I am useless in my own company. Assuming you've read up to this point, you've probably noticed that I can be a little bit grumpy at times, and the thought of spending an evening with only the thoughts of a grumpy old man to keep me company is a depressing one, no matter how much coffee I might drink.

So after our daughter was safely tucked up in bed and I had re-enacted my student days by cooking a meal for one, using random items from the cupboard, I decided I needed something to keep me entertained, and this is where a little thing called Sky + comes into its own. As I reminisced over my student days, eating the food that was once so familiar, I pondered where my life would have led, had I had access to the wonders of Sky + back then. I'm pretty sure I'd still be in my pyjamas, eating beans on toast and watching old re-runs of "Have I Got News For You" on Dave.

As I settled down to my meal for one, I made myself comfortable and scrolled though the recorded programmes list. For a very brief moment, I hovered over a film we'd recorded at Christmas, but I could hear my wife's disappointed voice in my head, saying "No, it's fine, I just thought we might have been able to watch it together…"

I decided that to avoid disappointing my wife, I needed to watch something that she wouldn't be interested in, so I was delighted to spot "Spice Girls Story - Viva Forever". I'm not exactly sure why it was recorded, but it was nestled in amongst a host of Christmas programmes, so I can only assume I got a bit carried away over the festive period. I'm not a massive Spice Girls fan, but I was 16 or 17 at the height of their fame, and they certainly didn't escape my adolescent attention.

After an hour or so, my wife called to check and see if our daughter had settled and to see how I was getting on with Mr Grumpy. When I told her I was in fact enjoying the "Spice Girls Story", she could not stop laughing.

"So you waited until I was out to try to recapture your youth and sit and gawp at the Spice Girls," she giggled.

"I didn't, honest; it's just that it was the only thing that I didn't think you would want to watch with me..." I squirmed.

"Sure, darling," she said. "I'll be home around 11-ish, you get back to your Spice Girls!"

I felt dirty. I can understand now why my dad decided to stop watching Felicity Kendall in The Good Life – it's just not worth the awkward line of questioning. I felt like a naughty teenager getting rid of an X-rated magazine as I stood up and pressed the yellow delete button on the remote.

We haven't spoken about it since, but I've a feeling the union jack dress I bought her for Valentine's Day might need taking back.

Monday 14th January 2013

Last week was a long and tiring one for both my wife and me, so we had decided that come Friday, we were going to have a takeaway. We weighed up the pros and cons of going for Chinese or Indian, eventually deciding on Indian as it was freezing outside and it seemed more suited to the weather.

My wife finished putting our daughter to bed as I ventured out to pick up the food, as well as the mandatory pint of milk from the local shop on the way back. When I returned, I was greeted by a scene that wouldn't have looked out of place in a horror movie: all of the lights in the house were out and our daughter was screaming at the top of her voice.

We had simply had a power cut, but that didn't stop me bursting through the door like an action hero, armed with nothing but a bag full of spicy food and a pint of milk. Feeling my way down the hall, I shouted up to my wife and asked if everything was ok.

"Fine," she said, "she's just a bit scared of the dark."

I'd never really thought about it before, but my daughter had never experienced complete darkness, (apart from in the womb, obviously). She has always slept with a night-light, and she has a thermometer in her room that glows various colours, depending on the temperature; so when the power went off it was a moment of true terror for her, and she screamed until my wife was able to reach her. In truth, it was a moment of true terror for me too as I quickly realised that with no power, my wife and I might have to resort to an evening of talking to each other.

I felt my way to the kitchen, placed the food and milk on the side, (I decided there was no point in putting it in the fridge, and I wasn't 100% sure that I'd find it) and commenced the search for candles. I was suddenly immersed in this strange world where somehow I had gone from going to pick up some takeaway food to starring in my own extremely low-budget bush-tucker trial, where instead of searching for stars in order to feed the camp, I was searching for candles.

I felt around in various drawers and cupboards, going from room to room, occasionally tripping, often swearing, and just when I was about to turn to Ant and Dec and shout "I'm an inadequate man, get me out of here", I stumbled across my first candle. Encouraged by my find, I went in search of more, and before long I had four candles of various shapes and sizes in my possession. I felt my way to the living room, headed for the log fire, felt around the mantelpiece for the box of matches, and lit my first candle.

"I got four!" I shouted up to my wife, as she clapped and cheered as any hungry "I'm A Celebrity" camp-mate would. I lit the other candles and placed them safely in various rooms and then commenced the search for torches. Eventually I found a wind-up torch in the cupboard under the stairs and that then led me to my best discovery yet; it was a small battery-powered light that turns on and off when you press the top of it. Of course, the batteries were dead, so I checked the kitchen drawer for spare batteries, of which of course there were none, so I then commenced the tricky job of removing batteries from various toys with a screwdriver that even Tom Thumb would have nightmares about.

Eventually I made it to my daughter's bedroom with a working battery-powered light, and to our delight, our daughter settled beautifully, enabling us to get on with eating our well-earned meal.

We quickly commenced the 'Takeaway Tango', whereby each of us will delicately dance around the other in a well-choreographed routine, in which plates are removed from cupboards, spoons are removed from drawers and the food is slowly removed from the big brown bag. (White if you've opted for Chinese of course). Incidentally, while we're on the subject, why is the rice always at the bottom of the bag? Everyone serves rice first, right? How difficult can it be to put the rice in last, so we can serve the rice first? Eventually, after taking our food through to the dining room, putting it down and going back for the drinks that we had forgotten, we were finally ready to eat.

It was at this point that we both realised we had unwittingly stumbled across a second bush-tucker trial. The candles I had worked so hard to find were in fact scented ones, and had not only filled the room with a grapefruit scent, but had actually managed to make the room taste of grapefruit. So we were subjected to cold food, flavoured with grapefruit, and as we couldn't see what we were eating, we were gagging on bay leaves and cardamom pods every other mouthful.

I used to think people exaggerated when they talked about the 1970s and how difficult it was with all the strikes and the power cuts, but after Friday, I have nothing but sympathy for them.

Tuesday 15th January 2013

Somehow, I've managed to get almost a fifth of the way through my second book without having a whinge about technology. I'm not exactly sure how I've managed it, as I seem to come up against technological breakdowns at every turn. Let's start with this very program that I'm using right now. It's clever enough to spot errors when I'm typing, and corrects them after I've made a mistake, which is great, but then it starts getting cocky and oversteps the mark by predicting what I want to say. It's like the annoying kid from school who liked to finish everyone's sentences. I only have to start typing a word and it starts chipping in with its own suggestions. Even as I went to type the word 'sentences' it popped up with 'sentiment' and 'sentimental'. Here's a phrase it can finish for me: "You can take your predictive text and stick it up your ar......."

The iPad I'm using now is a fairly new purchase, and it often accompanies me to coffee shops and restaurants in order to pass the time if I'm eating or drinking alone. Everything always starts out fine and I'm able to read my emails, catch up with the news and poke my friends to my heart's content; that is, until those dreaded words appear on the screen.

'BT Openzone'.

For those of you who have no idea what I'm talking about, or for those of you reading in the future, accessing the internet via the chip in your brain, BT Openzone is a 'public' Wifi service, which enables anyone within a certain range to access the internet. If you're struggling with the term 'Wifi' it's probably just best to skip to the next chapter, this one isn't for you.

'BT Openzone', like any other public Wifi service for that matter, just renders your device completely useless. After fifteen minutes of messing around filling in forms and typing in pass codes all you're left with is a screen, empty save for the word 'Searching'. I've actually had to stop replying to emails whilst on the move, for fear of passing a coffee shop and entering the Bermuda triangle that is BT Openzone. The most stupid thing of all is that if you do manage to fill in the form, crack the code and with an amazing stroke of luck gain access to the service, it's absolutely terrible. You are far better off using the mobile Internet connection that you were happy to use in the first place, before BT bloody Openzone started taking over.

Another annoying thing about technology, and I'm only annoyed by it because I feel like I was tricked, is targeted adverts. Targeted ads are adverts that are tailored to you, based on your recent search history. I once had someone explain it to me, but as soon as I found out that the cookies involved were in fact computer files and not Chocolate Chip and Hazelnut, I soon lost interest. Last February my wife and I decided that we would go on holiday, and we liked the idea of Center Parcs (Sorry Spellcheck, you can underline it in red all you like, but you got it wrong, it is actually spelled like that!). With my wife being a teacher, we always have to go away in the school holidays, which means we end up having to pay more, but this particular trip seemed just a little bit too expensive. A little later, I'd forgotten about the search and gone onto a news website, and within just a few minutes an advert for Center Parcs appeared in a little box to my right. I couldn't believe the coincidence, and thinking it was fate, I clicked the link, parted with the cash and booked the holiday. Over the next few minutes I realised that everything I had searched for on Google was appearing as an advert, and the penny finally dropped when I had gone onto Halfords to buy a spare headlight bulb for the car and then ten minutes later, the very bulb that I had searched for appeared in an advert.

I'm approaching my destination and I'm frustrated that I've not been able to discuss all of my technological frustrations, although to be truthful, I could complete a trip on the Trans-Siberian Railway and still have plenty to moan about.

Let me finish this off then with the five most frustrating words that you will ever hear when dealing with technology. Five words which will turn you from someone who is placid, timid and caring into someone who is angry, irrational, emotional and happy to commit damage to public property at a moment's notice.

Those five words are......."Unexpected item in bagging area".

Wednesday 16th January 2013

It was announced this morning that Blockbuster is to appoint administrators, following hot on the heels of Jessops and HMV. It's incredibly depressing news all round, as there are thousands of people who stand to lose their jobs. There are also hundreds of thousands of people, including me, with worthless Christmas vouchers. I'd like to point out that I didn't have HMV vouchers, though – I was given vouchers for Hobbycraft.

The general feeling among analysts seems to be that it was inevitable and that although the current economic climate can be blamed in part, blame also has to be attributed to their structural model, some organisations being slower to react than others. I suppose you only have to look at the fact that Blockbuster still display their full name, "Blockbuster Video", on their shop fronts, despite the fact that that format departed our homes in the late nineties. Mind you, try telling that to the people who run charity shops and car-boot sales.

If people want to watch a film these days, they can either press the red button or log onto a myriad of dedicated film sites that will stream them for a fee. If people do want to physically own a DVD, they will invariably go online to purchase it, so it's no wonder that these companies are struggling. It's why you no longer see sex shops anymore. We still have the same amount of weirdos willing to buy the stuff, they just go about satisfying their weird fetishes online, meaning they kill two birds with one stone – firstly they avoid the embarrassment, and secondly they no longer have to change out of their wife's underwear.

It's easy to see why Jessops struggled too, because people hardly print photos any more. Sure, we'll print the odd one off at Christmas so Aunty Joan can see what our daughter looks like in a Christmas hat, but that's not exactly going to pay their overheads is it? I remember the days when we would have to buy six rolls of film before we went on holiday, we'd then snap away to our hearts' content, buy another four rolls while we were there, and then come home and get them all developed. Looking back now, it's staggering to think that not only did we spend money on film, we spent money on pictures we didn't want. We all knew that when the photos came back, two rolls would be of the local cats and dogs licking their balls, but we had to get them developed because there might have been a nice one of the sunset somewhere in there.

Nowadays, we'll either upload them to the computer, never to be seen again, or they'll get loaded onto a digital frame and appear in a constant loop until next year's holiday. In extremely rare situations we might find a really nice photo to go in a frame, and print it off, setting us back 49p. So Jessops went from earning £30 per holiday to 49p (or 39p if we're feeling tight and decide to plump for the 6x4) once or twice a year. And they went under? Staggering...

Tuesday 22nd January 2013

It's fair to say that the last few days have been a bit on the chilly side, and it's because of this that there's a slight gap in this book – no commuting, no writing. If there's one thing this country can't cope with, it's snow, and there only has to be so much as a light dusting for the country to go into complete meltdown.

Every country has a major weakness; with Japan it's earthquakes, with Australia it's wildfires, and with America it's Paris Hilton. It just so happens that Britain can't handle the snow. There only needs to be a light flurry for schools to close, airports to shut down, trains to stop running and roads to get gridlocked.

Of course, because this is Britain, we like to panic, and what do we do when we panic? We buy bread and milk! Some of you might be surprised to learn that the reason we very rarely go to war with other nations is not because of the potential loss of life or the effect it has on our economy, we just can't produce enough bread and milk to cope.

Why they call it panic buying, I'll never know – to me it seems fairly considered. Coming home with ten packs of dog biscuits and twenty tins of dog food, now that would be panic buying, especially if you didn't have a dog.

Another thing that annoys me when it snows is the news. When the snow arrives it becomes the headline story. There are people dying all over the world in horrific acts of violence, but let's just cross to "Christine in Chesham, who has the latest on the snow chaos."

"That's right Huw, I can now report that the snow is starting to settle on the rooftops and it won't be long before it starts to settle on the ground. Back to you in the studio."

There are hundreds of news reporters stationed throughout the country reporting back on people's cars not starting. This isn't news. If there's an avalanche, go ahead and report on it; until then, please only update us on the snow during your weather and travel reports.

Lastly, why has there been a sudden shift when referring to snow? It always used to be reported in inches, now it's centimetres. I know this is the metric age, but when reporting on queues of traffic on the M25, they don't talk about it in kilometres, they describe it in miles, and when people fall tragically to their death, they don't describe it in metres, they talk in feet, so why is snow suddenly settling in centimetres and not inches?

I'll tell you why – because 7 - 10 centimetres sounds so much bigger and more impressive than 3 - 4 inches. Surely it's only a matter of time before us men begin to catch on...

Friday 25th January 2013

I've spent the last couple of days limping like a kid who's just come last at sports day and it's beginning to get me down. It seemed like such an innocuous stumble at the time, but I clearly did more damage than I realised.

As my wife pulled out of the driveway yesterday morning, I could see that the passenger door wasn't shut properly and, eager to stop her driving off, I leapt to action. I slipped on the first pair of shoes I could find (a pair of Crocs, usually reserved for quick journeys to the bin and back) and flew out of the house.

Unfortunately, we have a shingle path, unfortunately it had frozen overnight and unfortunately I was wearing Crocs. The path had frozen with footprints embedded in it, leaving it resembling a scale model of the Alps. What made it worse is that there are two steps down from the house to the garden, so I wasn't just leaping forward with all my weight, I was falling too. I landed awkwardly on my right foot, immediately stumbling to my left as the Croc decided to go a different way, and the momentum had me hop once with my left foot and then smack, with moderate force, into the back of the car, while the other Croc decided it wanted to find its friend. To help you picture the scene, I imagine I looked a little like a triple-jumper would, if someone had untied their laces and parked a car in the sandpit.

My wife, unaware of the situation, but having heard a bang, got out of the car to see me lying on the floor, shouting "I think it's broken". Quick as a flash she surveyed the scene and replied "Don't worry, darling, it would take more than that to break the car!"

I'm pleased to report that the car was fine and the door did get closed properly, but thanks to my efforts to save my wife from having to journey to work with a slight whistling sound, I now have a sprained ankle. In fact, I haven't had much luck with shoes in the last few days. On Wednesday night we realised we were running very low on milk. As it was late and the shops were about to shut, I grabbed the nearest jacket and slipped on the first pair of shoes I found. Luckily for me, this time they weren't the Crocs. I have only ever ventured as far as the petrol station in Crocs, deciding that as I can purchase at the pump, no-one ever need know, other than my wife that is, who was mortified when she found out.

I got to the shops five minutes before they were due to close, and the staff were carrying about their closing duties. As I entered the shop, I was greeted by a lady to my left who was stacking the baskets and a guy to my right who was sweeping the floor. The guy to my right was looking down at the floor, busily sweeping away as my feet emerged from the darkness. Now it's easy to put on one black shoe and one brown shoe in the dark, but it's difficult to forgive someone who puts on one shoe with a heel and one without. I had somehow managed to slip on a black work shoe on my left foot and a brown trainer on my right. There was nothing I could do but shrug and say "It's late, and I'm tired!"

I went the long way around to avoid the other customers in the shop, and it afforded me the opportunity to look back at the crime scene. Needless to say they were pissing themselves laughing, and the most annoying thing about it all is that I had to hang around in the aisles waiting for the laughter to die down before I could pay.

I'll tell you what, though – I've never been so happy to see a self-service till!

Monday 28th January 2013

On Friday I finally succumbed, and I am so disappointed with myself. I only had a few days of January left to hold out. I was so close. I'm ashamed to announce that on Friday, I joined a gym.

Every January I announce that I will get fit and lose some of the Christmas bulge, and I also proclaim that I will do so without using a gym. What a waste of money! Why would I need to join a gym, when I can simply lace up a pair of trainers, open the door and run? (Which is generally far less hazardous than slipping on a pair of Crocs and charging out of the door).

The thing is, gyms are so appealing in January, it's difficult to resist their charms. They know that we've all gone into the New Year thinking 'New Year, new me!' and they play on our emotions. I can hear them in a low, hushed tone, whispering to me as I slowly catch pneumonia, "It's minus five degrees, why are you jogging around the block dodging dog poo, when you could be jogging indoors, in the warm, watching Deal or No Deal?"

Another thing that makes gyms so appealing in January is the price. Suddenly, joining fees have been scrapped, monthly direct debits have been slashed and Tony, the resident personal trainer, is willing to give you two free 'taster sessions'. (I'm anxious to make it known that it wasn't Tony that swung it, although looking at the size of him, he could probably swing me).

So as I am sitting at the desk, talking to Natalie, who is explaining the second most complex cancellation policy known to man, (the most complex obviously being mobile phone contracts) I start to hear the voice of Noel Edmonds, somewhere in my subconscious. "So, Andy, £50 a month, with no joining fee, two free taster sessions with Tony, a welcome gift, and a contract even Houdini would struggle to get out of......deal or no deal?"

Deal!

No doubt I'll continue to open the remaining boxes over the coming months, undoubtedly proving that not only shouldn't I have dealt, but also that I shouldn't have even been playing in the first place. There is a well-known saying in the casino that the house always wins, and when it comes to a gym, I'm inclined to agree.

I'm still on the mend from a sprained ankle, so you could be forgiven for thinking that either I have the pain threshold of a hippy giving birth or I'm an idiot. I'm happy to announce that I'm an idiot. I just couldn't let an apparently good deal pass me by. I knew that in a week or so I would have recovered enough to start some light exercise but by then it would be too late to take advantage of the January deals. Also, I am still able to swim, which will help strengthen my ankle before I'm able to run on it.

Of course, there's also the free gift. Who could turn down the chance to spend £600 a year when there's a keyring that's also an ice-scraper on offer?

Tuesday 29th January 2013

Hot on the heels of last week's decision to join a gym, I decided that part of the 'New Year, new me' process should involve buying some new clothes. Stupid really, when you consider that the whole point of joining a gym is to get fit and lose weight, meaning that if I'm successful, I'll have to go out and buy new clothes again.

It had been so long since I last updated my wardrobe that the shop I would normally buy clothes from was no longer there, so I was left frantically searching my phone for the nearest branch. I made a simple promise in my head about how far I was willing to walk – under a mile and it's game on, more than a mile and it's game over!

It was 0.93 miles.

After walking 1.37 miles, I found the shop I was after, and just two minutes and twelve seconds later I was in a changing room with four pairs of trousers and five shirts hanging patiently, waiting to be tried on. I squeezed into the first pair of trousers. They were ridiculously tight. Maybe they looked ok in the mirror? My mirror in the changing room was covered up with clothes, so I backed out of the changing room and looked towards the mirror at the end of the corridor. It was at this point that I realised I had broken one of the rules. There was a sign on the mirror which said that I should have waited for assistance before entering. Immediately underneath that notice was another one which read 'Maximum five items'.

In my eagerness to get it all over with as quickly as possible, I had managed to break the only two rules that existed. I stood there for a moment, pondering what to do next. Should I confess? Should I waddle back into the shop and admit that I am an impatient, rule-breaking idiot? There were a couple of reasons why I didn't. Firstly, I was wearing a pair of trousers which were so tight they looked like they had been painted on, and secondly, I just didn't have the balls. Ironically, I then proved the latter was only metaphorically true by catching a glimpse of myself in the mirror.

Flustered by the rule break and frustrated by the trouser tightness, I waddled back to the changing room in an effort to remove them as quickly as possible. Through a combination of balancing on one leg and hopping I managed to remove the first leg, but the second was proving more troublesome. I continued to pull, yank, balance and hop, and was now clattering into all four walls in an effort to get free. I felt like the ball in the arcade game Pong.

Eventually, I sensed that the trousers were ready to relinquish their grip, and in a last-ditch effort I pulled with all my strength. The trousers left my body with such force that they smacked into the changing-room door, creating a noise that reverberated around the shop. I couldn't understand what had managed to make such a loud noise, but the culprit soon revealed itself as a small black disc rolling away from the scene of the crime. The trousers had hit the door with such force that the security tag had become detached and was now making a bid for freedom under the changing-room door. It was at exactly this point that the sales assistant arrived to ask if everything was ok.

I opened the changing-room door to be greeted by a confused seventeen year-old boy holding a security tag. As I explained what had gone on, his confusion was replaced by amusement and I could see that he could see the funny side. It was either that or the sight of me in my underpants.

I eventually managed to find a couple of pairs of trousers that fitted and moved on to the shirts. With the disaster of the tight trousers still fresh in my mind, I decided to check that I had selected the correct size. I had. So why, then, did it feel like I was wearing a condom? The shirt was hugging parts of my body that even my wife is unfamiliar with. I removed it to check the size once again and it's then that I spotted the words 'Slim Fit'…

I'm still confused as to whom the 'Slim Fit' is aimed at. Is it muscly guys who want to show off their bodies, or is it skinny guys who don't want to look so skinny? Of course there is the possibility that these shirts are aimed at people like me, who constantly wash clothes on the wrong setting, often rendering all clothes a 'Slim Fit'. Anyway, I gave up on that particular shirt and moved on to the next one. It certainly fitted better, but it seemed to be cut very short in the body and the sleeves were too long. Once again it didn't feel right, so I removed and saw the words 'Tailored Fit' on the label. Hang on a minute – doesn't tailored mean made to measure? Made to measure what – an orangutan?

I moved onto the third shirt and, like Goldilocks, was hopeful I would find success at the third time of asking. I checked the label this time and it stated that it was a 'Regular Fit', which gave me far more confidence than the previous two. It fitted perfectly and I was pleased that I could finally be on my way. I quickly changed back into my old clothes, gathered up my wanted items, and made my way to the till. There was an awkward silence as the seventeen year-old tried to complete the transaction as quickly as possible. The quicker he tried to be, the slower he got and the silence was so excruciating that I had to break it.

"You look the kind of guy that could carry off a 'Slim Fit'!"

I'd like to point out that he was a skinny kid, and I certainly wasn't complementing him on his muscles. I hate small-talk, but if there's one thing I hate more than small-talk, it's awkward silences, so something had to give. This poor boy had not only seen me in my underpants, as far as he was concerned, he was now being chatted up.

I left as quickly as I could and vowed never to go clothes shopping on my own again.

Friday 1st February 2013

As you will hopefully remember, I joined the gym last week and I decided that yesterday was the official start of the 'New Year, new me' process. I rummaged around on the top shelf of the wardrobe, amongst the never-to-be-worn hats and scarves from Christmases past, and found the gym gear I was looking for. I soon neatly packed it away again. You see, unfortunately, this was the gear that I bought towards the end of the 'New Year, new me' process last time, when I was excited about having lost weight and feeling fit and healthy. I eventually found a combination of 'old me' T-shirt and shorts and headed out of the door.

Of course, I was still recovering from a sprained ankle, so on the way to the gym I was adamant that I was only going to have a light swim and then maybe reward myself with twenty minutes in the steam room, but as I got changed, I began to feel guilty. There were guys coming in, twice the size of me, dripping in sweat, collapsing in tears; could I really just pull on the trunks and do a few gentle lengths? I decided that I needed to build up a light sweat in order to enjoy the benefits of the pool downstairs, so I reluctantly trudged up the seventeen steps to the gym floor. For a very brief moment, I thought that the seventeen steps had done enough to start the sweating process, thus earning me my early bath, but I was in fact just being showered with someone else's. Someone had been lifting some heavy weights, above and to the right of me as I climbed the stairs, and the combination of a heavy lift and a puff of the cheeks resulted in a string of top-lip sweat hurtling onto the side of my neck. It was enough for me to want to dive straight in the pool, and if the guy hadn't been so big I might have done more than simply wipe it off with my hand and then onto the back of my shorts.

I had a sprained ankle, so going on a running machine would have been stupid, but the bikes were full and the rowing machines lacked a fundamental piece of equipment – they weren't attached to a telly! Well… what harm could walking on a treadmill really do? Yesterday I managed over two and a half miles and that was in work shoes and laden with shopping.

I selected the machine that was furthest from another human being, partly because I felt stupid walking, but mainly because I didn't want another run-in with someone else's sweat.

Just three minutes into my medium to fast-paced walk, Mo Farah stepped onto the treadmill next to me. Ok, it wasn't Mo Farah, but it might as well have been. There was no warming up, no stretching, no fiddling around with the TV channels only to give up and carry on watching Cash in the Attic, he just whacked it straight up to 15km per hour and ran. It was making me tired just watching him, and to make matters worse, I was sweating more than he was at just 6.5 km per hour.

I shouldn't have been surprised. I'm always being humiliated. I remember being at a charity event in the city once where they were running a penalty shoot-out competition. They had a goal set up in the car park and I got drawn against a guy that I had actually seen throwing up outside not one hour earlier. He could hardly stand and, to swing things further in my favour, he was wearing the shiniest, pointiest pair of work shoes imaginable. Needless to say, he wiped the floor with me. To rub salt into the wounds, we were reunited at the urinals an hour or so later, where he humiliated me once again.

Monday 4th February 2013

My wife and I are terrible at making decisions. In fact it's one of the few things that we regularly argue about. Neither of us wants to be responsible for making a bad decision and we would both happily go with someone else's decision, even if we knew it was a bad one, so that we could smugly sit back and say "It wasn't my idea".

The problem is that when there are two people who can't make a decision, a stalemate ensues. There have been countless times when we've woken up at the weekend and come up with a few ideas over breakfast. We've then spent so long deciding on what to do that ideas are longer viable as there's not enough time left in the day. Eventually, due to the fading light, the decision gets made for us. I know people can be indecisive, but I really do think we have a problem that needs sorting with some sort of professional intervention. I mean, how many people trust the sun to make decisions for them?

After three hours of pondering yesterday, we eventually made a decision. Once again though, it was an extremely exhausting and emotional process. It started with those dreaded five words over breakfast....."What shall we do today?" and was followed by a brain-storming session that any City firm would have been proud of.

"We could do..." "What about...?" "Have you considered...?" "Don't forget that we could also..."

The only things missing from our morning meeting were a flip-chart, a speakerphone and Christine, to take the minutes. Normally, when companies have morning 'breakfast' meetings, the breakfast element is introduced to help the meeting along. It helps people to settle, fills their stomachs and makes them more able to focus, but for us it just makes things worse.

"Darling, would you like jam, marmalade, honey, peanut butter or Marmite?"

It's a good job we both like cold toast.

Eventually, by each of us discarding one option at a time, we got it down to two possibilities.

They were:

Shopping and a trip to the park, or a trip to the seaside.

Obviously, I wanted to go to the seaside, and I'm pretty sure that my wife wanted to do the shopping and park option, but of course, neither of us would take the plunge. A lot of people, once down to two options, would use the trusty paper, scissors and stone method of decision-making, but that would require one of us to be backing the shopping and the other the seaside, and of course neither of us could decide who would be which.

Eventually, we did what we always do in this situation – we let our daughter decide; but, unwilling to burden her with such a responsibility, we also added an element of chance. With the jam representing the shopping and the Marmite representing the seaside, I placed both arms behind my back and asked my daughter to pick a hand. She picked the Marmite hand, so off to the seaside we went.

As soon as we pulled up, we knew she'd made a mistake. When you think of a day at the seaside, you picture deck chairs, ice cream and old people with purple hair, but yesterday there was none of that. Just a few hardy souls walking their dogs. It was utterly bleak. Going to the seaside in winter is like seeing your partner first thing in the morning. Ugly, depressing and troubled by wind.

Having gone to the seaside, there was one thing we were expecting to see, and that was the sea. Unfortunately, due to a low tide and a rapidly approaching sandstorm, it was impossible to make out. Our daughter was visibly upset, and the reassurance "Honestly, it's out there somewhere" did nothing to liven her spirits. Neither did the half-mile walk to the beach-side cafe that was closed. As we made our way back to the car I had mixed emotions. Part of me was pleased that we could finally get out of the freezing wind, but part of me was annoyed that we still had forty minutes left on the parking ticket. I didn't even get to enjoy the satisfaction of handing the ticket to someone else in their hour of need, as there wasn't anyone as stupid as us around.

Ultimately, the day has taught me two things, which I am willing to share with you all. Firstly, the seaside is definitely not the place to go in winter, and secondly, wherever possible, try not to entrust your decisions to breakfast condiments.

Tuesday 5th February 2013

Yesterday I realised for the first time just how competitive I am. I enjoy walking, and I especially like walking fast. Walking fast serves two main purposes. It gets you to your destination more quickly, and it raises the heartbeat that little bit more and therefore, in my eyes, passes as a more acceptable form of exercise. I'm one of those people who weave in and out of pedestrian traffic. If I were in a car, I would be that arsehole in the Mercedes, minus the sunglasses and fake tan.

Having said that, I do it with care. I always make sure there is plenty of room to weave, often having to take bags, terrain and traffic into consideration. I'm effectively the Mercedes man who gives way at a junction – one who weaves in and out, but uses his indicators while doing so.

Yesterday, a man overtook me. It happens from time to time, and I can accept that there are people who walk more quickly than me. What annoyed me, though, was that after overtaking me, he slowed down. Was this deliberate? Was it a challenge? The problem I had was that I was now stuck behind him, having to walk far more slowly than I would normally walk. I had to overtake him. So I did. As soon as I got alongside him, however, his speed picked up, and suddenly I was involved in a race. We must have gone one hundred metres, side by side, at top speed. My calves were burning and it took a huge effort not to break into a jog.

Up ahead the pavement narrowed, allowing only single-file traffic, and I knew that I needed to get ahead. He must have sensed my urge to win, because without warning he peeled off to the right and crossed the road. I didn't dare look across, but I was desperate to see if he was still alongside me. I risked a quick glance, and I could see that he had slowed to a trundle and I was sure I could see a slight limp developing.

When I replayed the incident in my head a little later, I couldn't believe how petty I had been. Why was I so desperate to win a battle with a stranger? It was then that it dawned on me that this wasn't a one-off. On Sunday evening I had been filling the car with petrol when a car pulled in behind me. The driver and I exchanged a brief glance and carried on with our business.

After a minute or so the glances became more frequent, and it became obvious that we were both anxious to finish the filling process and commence the queuing process. Was he filling it to the top? If so, I would almost certainly be ahead of him in the queue, as I started first and he had a bigger car. Annoyingly, he looked like the sort of guy who might just top it up, and he didn't seem like a guy who cared about rounding it up to the nearest pound either. As my pump clicked, I was horrified to see that it was showing £49.93, costing me vital seconds, as I am most definitely one of those people who like to round up.

As it ticked over to £50.01, I secured the petrol cap and made my way to the shop. I could see that he was finished too and my suspicions were confirmed when I glanced at the pump to see £15.07 showing on the screen. Would it be childish to jog at this point? It was cold after all, so I went for it, but so did he. As he had pulled in behind me he was slightly closer, and I was gutted when he made it to the door first. With a smug look on his face, he opened the door and said "After you, mate".

I felt like such an idiot. The thing is, I just can't help it. The more I thought about it, the more I realised I did it. Even when buying a sandwich, I worry about getting a good place in the queue, to the point where I'll grab anything, just to secure my place ahead of the next guy. I'll stand there smugly, thinking "Ha ha, I beat you", only to look down to find I've bought a vegetarian meatball sandwich.

Even when there isn't a stranger around to challenge me, I still feel the need to win. Village fetes are a nightmare as I go from stall to stall, spending a fortune trying to win raffles, tombolas and coconuts. I remember one particular holiday after which I very nearly required counselling due to not being able to win a cuddly toy from one of those arcade machines with the claw.

Time to bring the chapter to a close because even now, as the train pulls into the station, I've got my eyes on the people I need to beat to the door, and they're starting to make a break for it.

Friday 8th February 2013

Why is booking a holiday so difficult? I suppose that in my case it's down to a lack of practice. When I was a child, my parents always made the destination decisions, much to my frustration. I had always dreamt of meeting Mickey and Minnie Mouse in Orlando, Florida, but instead had to put up with meeting Sybil and Cyril Squirrel in Milford-On-Sea, Hampshire.

As a young adult, I went on a couple of 'lads" holidays, the decision generally being entrusted to the person who had enough money to book the deposit; needless to say, I was never called upon. Then there were the few holidays that I took with girlfriends, again, always leaving the decision to them, for three very good reasons.

1) If there was one thing I knew, even back then, it was that women like shopping.

2) If it all went wrong, I couldn't be blamed.

3) I still didn't have the money for the deposit.

Eventually, when it was time for me to 'man up' and book a holiday, it all went horribly wrong. In October 2003 I thought it would be a good idea to book a surprise trip to New York and while there ask my then girlfriend to marry me. I had it all planned. The plan was to surprise her on Christmas Day with tickets to the theatre, hoping that when she looked closely, she would see that the tickets were for Broadway and not the West End. We would then have a lovely trip to New York, culminating with a marriage proposal on New Year's Eve in Times Square, for it was on New Year's Eve that we had met. That was the plan.

I researched the trip for days, looking at various flights, accommodation and excursions, and I just kept going around in circles. This was the chance to have a trip of a lifetime, so in my mind, only the best would do, but I also had to buy a ring as well… Eventually, I just went ahead and booked it. The best flights, the best accommodation and every excursion we could fit in. I decided that this was indeed a once-in-a-lifetime event and that I didn't plan on getting engaged again. It also helped that Barclaycard were offering six months interest free on all new purchases.

A few days later I went to grab something from the fridge, and I couldn't believe what I was seeing. I suddenly started to feel very sick, and for once it had nothing to do with the state of the vegetable drawer. My wife is a teacher, and every year, with the help of the 'School Sucks!' fridge magnet that she bought three months into her first teaching post, she attaches the school term dates to the fridge. These particular school dates confirmed that we were due to fly back from New York on the day she was meant to be back at school. It said the word 'Inset'. I had no idea what that meant, but the words in my diary on that date read 'In New York', not bloody 'Inset'. I frantically called the school and got through to the assistant headmistress, who was very understanding and said that she would get the headmistress to call me back.

They were the worst ten minutes of my life. I haven't been that nervous waiting to speak to the headmistress since I got caught drawing a penis in the snow outside her office window. (Different headmistress, fortunately). Her opening line to me when I got dragged in was "You've got some balls!" Ironically, the one part I hadn't got round to drawing…

Anyway, eventually I got the call. "Unfortunately, Mr Leeks, we have some essential training on that day and I can't afford for anyone to miss it."

I was devastated. She was understanding and very apologetic, but essentially her school's finances were more important than mine. So I spent hours on the phone, trying to get the flights rearranged, speaking to managers and managers of managers and finally the manager who manages the managers' manager. No luck. The flights were non-refundable and non-transferable. I had to book the flights again and, as they were awkward dates, I had to pay through the nose, which left me no money to buy the ring.

So the one time I did book a holiday resulted in me having to book it again and my wife having to buy her own engagement ring. (She did get the money back, by the way, but in the spirit of Barclays it was interest free and over six months; although I think she went a bit far with the monthly statements and regular late fees).

I was therefore pleased last night when I finally managed to book a holiday, paying in full, without having to resort to begging, crying or re-booking. I don't even have to buy a ring. I would have had a celebratory drink, but I'm too scared to go near that bloody fridge…

Monday 11th February 2013

Yesterday I found myself listing my top ten most depressing places on Earth, adamant that the service station I was sat in would feature high on the list. I'm glad to say that it didn't disappoint and came home in third, a whisker behind doctors' waiting rooms and funerals.

I remember the good old days, when we could fly down the motorway safe in the knowledge that we wouldn't have to stop, laughing at the indicating cars as they approached the turn-off. Then it all changed. My daughter learned how to use the toilet, and nappies suddenly became redundant. Friends have often remarked that I have the bladder of a three year-old, and now I'm being punished by having to deal with the consequences of an actual three year-old's bladder. It now means that we need to stop every 37 minutes, (about seven minutes longer than I could go on a night out) so we find ourselves having to frequent service stations when travelling.

When I was a child, a stop at the services was exciting. It was a chance to break up the monotony of a journey, stretch the legs and ultimately hit my brother without the fear of him hitting me back, because I was no longer strapped in next to him. I had absolutely no consideration for the ambience, the cleanliness or the cost, three factors which yesterday were key in placing service stations at number three on my most depressing places list. In fact, it was only the close association of death to positions one and two which stopped service stations ranking higher.

Service stations are quite strange, in that they bring together a lot of people from a variety of backgrounds for a short period of time. It is the perfect place to people-watch, but a frustrating place too. When on holiday, you have a similar scenario where people from different backgrounds are brought together, but you have the luxury of seven to fourteen days to piece the puzzle together. No wedding rings, but three kids between them – I wonder which are hers and which are his… Are they all his? Maybe they're all hers? He doesn't seem that interested in the little girl – the girl is probably hers, so the boys are probably his… It really doesn't matter, but for some reason you feel compelled to work out the inner workings of their family life.

It's exactly the same in restaurants when you try to work out the relationships between the diners and the occasion they might be celebrating. Are they work colleagues? Maybe it's a club of some kind, or is it a family gathering? Is someone leaving work? Maybe they've just played a match, or is it a birthday? None of it matters, but you have less than two hours to crack the case and suddenly this is more important than any birthday or anniversary that you might be celebrating. It's even worse in a service station – you get ten minutes if you're lucky and half an hour if you're really unlucky. It's hugely frustrating as all you ever end up doing is speculating, meaning that almost everyone is either a criminal or involved in some sort of extra-marital affair.

Service stations have to be just about the most unwelcoming place on Earth. Already desperate for a wee, you exit the motorway only to be sent on a cross-country slalom, dangerously swerving left and right as you try to work out if that last right turn was for cars or HGVs. Eventually you find the entrance, only to be met by someone intent on selling you breakdown cover. I'm certain that selling breakdown cover at a service station is already high on the list of difficult jobs, even before you consider the fact that 95% of your target market is in dire need of a wee.

Service stations tend to have a bad reputation when it comes to food, but I'd like to take this opportunity to defend them. I'd like to, but I can't. It's terrible. It's a whole restaurant full of overpriced, overcooked and under-seasoned slop. It's the only place I have ever been where even the food on the promotional posters and the menus looks like it's already been eaten. In a way, I admire their honesty. "Here, look, this is what you'll end up with if you order this." I'm pretty sure that the terrible food is the reason you always see 'Costa' and 'M&S' on the signs on the motorway. "Look, we know we serve shit food, but there's always the option of a cold coffee and an overpriced egg sandwich!"

The only thing that got me through the whole experience was the bittersweet irony of having to order a happy meal.

Tuesday 12th February 2013

I haven't been able to sit in my normal seat for the last two weeks and it's starting to annoy me. I like that seat because it offers plenty of leg-room and sits alone, meaning no-one can read over my shoulder. The only downside is the proximity to the toilet, meaning I'm often left having to hold my breath for the full commute – a small price to pay for being able to write in peace.

Commuters tend to follow set routines, and I'm no different. Leave at the same time, buy the same paper, stand in the same place and sit in the same seat. I have been able to carry out three of the above, but the final and most crucial stage has been impossible due to someone not only sitting in my seat, but falling asleep in it. Every day I've been standing in the same place, hopeful that it's just a phase she's going through, or maybe it's an experiment – maybe, like Goldilocks, she's just trying out various chairs to see which one is the most comfortable. Every day I hope that she'll disappear as quickly as she arrived. Unfortunately, unlike Goldilocks, she has decided to stick around, so this morning I had to make the difficult decision to change where I stand on the platform. By changing where I stand I give myself a better opportunity of getting a similar seat further down the train. The train I catch has twelve carriages, and every fourth carriage has a toilet and consequently a handy little seat that sits on its own and has plenty of leg-room.

In the last two weeks, after discovering that my old seat has been taken by 'Sleeping Ugly', I have had to walk through four carriages to get to the next suitable seat, but by the time I get there, that too has been taken. It has meant that I've had to resort to writing this book in the vestibules. (When I explained to my mum that I was writing the book in the vestibules, she asked what the weather was like! I politely explained that they are the little spaces between the carriages, not a group of islands in the Pacific. Bless her).

Standing in a new place is strange. I was only standing fifty metres from where I used to stand, but I may as well have been at a different station or even in a different country altogether. The rules had changed. Instead of looking straight ahead and ignoring everyone else, people here actually seemed to be communicating. There were little pockets of conversation, and I swear I even caught the tiniest glimpse of a smile. It was a completely different atmosphere to what I was used to towards the back of the train.

It made me wonder why the front of the train was so much happier than the middle or back, where I used to stand. Then it suddenly dawned on me. I was standing amongst the optimists. It's common-sense to assume that in the event of a train crash, the safest place would be towards the rear, so unbeknownst to me, I have spent my commuting life seated amongst the pessimists. No wonder I'm always so miserable… The people up the front, though, they don't give a shit! They're the sort of people who don't bother with insurance, the ones who discard the lid of their coffee, the ones who wouldn't think twice about passing wind the morning after a curry. They're not only optimistic though – they're keen too. Being at the front guarantees a quicker exit, meaning they get to work that little bit sooner. So not only have I been sitting amongst the pessimists, I've been sitting amongst the work-shy too.

I've really enjoyed it down the front, so much so that I'll be here again tomorrow. I might even celebrate my new found optimism with a curry tonight…

Friday 15th February 2013

It's fair to say that most people have a bad habit or two, and I'm no different. In fact, two of my bad habits are having an effect on my ability to write today's chapter. Firstly, I've always bitten my nails. I think it's disgusting, and I wish I didn't do it, but I've never been able to stop. The reason I've never been able to stop is that I genuinely don't know when I'm doing it. It happens completely subconsciously. I could have a perfectly normal nail one minute and the next it could be gone, with me having absolutely no memory of having ripped it from my finger with my teeth. It's a really scary thought that I walk around each day subconsciously subjecting my body to abuse.

I sometimes wish I had a more socially acceptable habit, perhaps one that didn't involve self harm. I remember at school there was a kid in the year below with long hair and glasses who was constantly flicking his hair off his face. The flick of his head, however, meant that his glasses fell down his nose, which meant he then had to push them back up the bridge of his nose. The process of pushing his glasses back up his nose meant that he lowered his head, which meant that his hair fell back over his face. I suppose it was cruel to laugh, but I could spend a fair chunk of my lunch-hour just watching him try and fail to get his hair and glasses in order. Funnier still was watching him two years later, with short hair and contacts, still suffering from the same old habits.

Habitual behaviour is generally deemed to be unhealthy – hence habits are often described as 'bad'. I think it's a shame we rarely seem to develop 'good' habits, like taking the bins out or moving the wet towels off the bed. (My wife probably thinks that's a shame too).

I also think it's a little unfair that people with bad habits get grief, but people with addictions get sympathy. I could argue that my habit is worse than an addiction, because I don't even know when I'm doing it. Of course, it would be insensitive to seriously compare the two; addictions are usually complex and often have a terrible impact on people's lives, whereas habits are just annoying. That said, I see no reason why we can't have Nail-Biters Anonymous. In fact, there might just be such a thing already, and who knows, I may even have attended a meeting subconsciously.

On a serious note, I am really keen to break the habit because not only does it look terrible, but – and here's where it becomes an issue vis-à-vis the book – it's also causing me pain when I type.

The other bad habit I suffer from, and the other reason I am struggling to write this chapter today, is channel-surfing. It's an easy enough habit to deal with when my wife is around as she simply doesn't stand for it, (a cushion is her weapon of choice) but when she's not around I suffer terribly. Time seems to skip forward while I'm channel-surfing, and what feels like ten minutes often ends up being closer to two hours.

Last night I was staggered to discover that two terrestrial channels screen live roulette late at night. I've played the odd game of roulette at a casino, but I've never been particularly interested in it. Last night, though, it was the most fascinating thing I had ever seen. The set looked like it had been put together by my three year-old daughter, and the presenters looked like they had been dragged in off the street, but never mind all of that – would it be the return of the reds on the next spin? The blacks had held a 60/40 advantage in the previous ten spins, so it was looking good for the reds. The people betting at home agreed, explained the presenter, and they also seemed to be favouring the lower numbers too.

Black 35...followed by...Black 31...followed by...Black 26.

Then the presenter did his best Noel Edmonds impression and tried to work out if people had a 'system' and whether they were playing 'tactically' enough.

What a load of absolute rubbish. So much so that I turned off after only an hour and a half.

Monday 25th February 2013

Those of you who keep an eye on my imaginatively titled chapters may have noticed the gap between this and my last chapter. This was due to a well-earned rest (from work, not just the book) and I was determined to return today, refreshed and revitalised, ready to take on whatever stood in my way. My excited optimism lasted approximately four minutes, however, as three people have already literally stood in my way.

My wife and I decided to holiday in England for numerous reasons, not the least of which is because I hate winter tans. Having a tan in winter is totally wrong. It's against the rules. Winter exists to make us miserable and to help us truly appreciate the spring, summer and autumn.

Going on holiday is vital for a commuter. It's obviously essential to combat the stress, but it also reminds us that strangers can not only talk to one another, they can be polite to one another too. When commuting, you seem to do everything you can to avoid eye contact and you develop a strange ability to look through people. If someone does catch your eye, there's always an uncomfortable moment as you both slightly acknowledge it, but rather than do anything about it, just look away. You then make a mental note not to look that way again, just in case that weirdo is staring at you. They of course will be saying exactly the same thing to themselves.

At the start of the holiday I was a little cautious – nervously nodding, maybe even raising the rolled-up paper in my right hand when someone wished me a good morning, but by the end of the week I was actively seeking out and waving at strangers across busy roads. I was wishing people a good morning, a good afternoon and in some cases a lovely day. I knew something inside me had changed when at one point in the holiday I wished a complete stranger a safe journey home. To be fair, I often silently wish everyone a safe journey home when commuting, but that's only because I'm on the same train as them.

We visited a local market on Saturday, and at times it was reminiscent of a busy train. There were queues of people hustling and bustling about, but there was but one big difference – people apologised when they bumped into you. They were uttering phrases I hadn't heard in years, like "After you", "Go ahead", and "You were first".

There was one particularly busy area where the street narrowed and a queue began to form. I found myself nervously awaiting those five awful words being bellowed from somewhere behind me: "Can you move down please!" But of course they never came.

As nice as it was to have a break, I found that I genuinely missed the daily grind and it feels good to be back into the swing of things and writing again. The problem with being on holiday, feeling relaxed and being stress free is that it leaves you absolutely nothing to bloody moan about!

Tuesday 26th February 2013

There's a new addition to my morning routine today. As well as drinking coffee, writing this book, and trying desperately to avoid eye contact with other commuters, I can now add eating biscuits to the list.

A couple of days ago my wife came back from the shops with a big yellow box, which I assumed at the time was a box of cereal.

"These were on offer, so I thought we could try them out," she said.

"What are they?" I asked.

"Belvita breakfast biscuits," she said.

"Breakfast biscuits?" I queried.

"Yes, they're specially designed for breakfast, slowly releasing carbohydrates over four hours, giving you energy for the whole morning," she happily stated, having evidently committed the blurb on the box to memory, and clearly prepared to go toe-to-toe with me on this one.

"But they're biscuits. You don't eat biscuits for breakfast!" I explained, going on to remind her that biscuits are for afternoon tea when her Nan comes round. She knows the routine – we open the rich tea and digestives just before she arrives and then Hobnobs once she's gone.

"But they're perfect for when we're too busy to eat breakfast – we can just eat them on the go," she argued.

"If only there were anything else you could just pick up and eat on the go…" I thought aloud. "Oh yes," I said as I made my way to the fruit bowl, "How about a banana?"

"But does it slowly release carbohydrates over four hours?" she enquired, keen to make me look silly.

"I'm pretty sure that any food slowly releases things over a period of time," I stated. "I doubt there are foods out there which inject your body with an instant shot of fibre, or a sudden hit of fat. The body is designed in such a way that food (and the properties within) get carried around the body and delivered to wherever needed. This is a fairly slow process, so I'm guessing that the four hours it takes the carbs in a Belvita breakfast biscuit to be couriered about the body is the same four hours it would take for a banana. Or any other regular biscuit for that matter." I opined.

So what was her answer to my rather pompous and frankly unsubstantiated statement?

"But they taste like breakfast cereal!"

I patiently explained that if she liked the taste of breakfast cereal, perhaps, instead of buying breakfast biscuits that taste like breakfast cereal, she should just eat the breakfast cereal instead.

Of course, this solution didn't cater for the one major advantage of the breakfast biscuit – the fact that it can be eaten on the go. My daughter seems to be getting through more bananas than the primate house at London Zoo at the moment, so when I discovered that the fruit bowl was empty this morning I was resigned to grabbing that little packet of Belvita breakfast biscuits.

And you know what? They taste great, and my wife was bang on when she said that they taste like breakfast cereal. It doesn't stop me feeling like a naughty schoolchild, however, and I have an uncontrollable urge to conceal as I consume. I've since found out that it's extremely difficult to be covert when eating biscuits. If the crunch of the biscuit itself doesn't alert nearby passengers, the rustle of the packet certainly will. I feel like I'm at the cinema, having to wait for the action sequence before I can open the Minstrels and wine gums, then going in for big handfuls every time a bomb goes off or a helicopter arrives. For once I'm actually looking forward to the inevitable announcement apologising for the delay and advising me to look after my possessions.

The thing is, if breakfast biscuits were such a good idea then surely a biscuit giant like McVitie's would have spotted the gap in the market and come up with the idea first. But they didn't. They simply reacted to others and came up with their own take. So even a biscuit giant hadn't ever considered a biscuit to be a viable breakfast option.

Yes, they are tasty, yes, they are convenient, but no, they are not breakfast.

Wednesday 27th February 2013

As you are hopefully aware, this book is titled 'As They Slept', and it was given its name thanks to the plethora of snoozing passengers on my morning commute. I was frustrated that so many people were wasting precious hours of their lives and I argued that they could be spending that wasted time doing other things. This morning I've changed my mind. This morning I simply want people to be asleep. More specifically, I want the two women with the big hats and big mouths to be asleep.

I absolutely love people-watching, in fact there is nothing in this world that I would rather be doing. Give me a hot coffee and a corner seat and I could happily sit and watch people all day. The key thing about people-watching, however, is the watching. It doesn't necessarily matter if you can't hear what's going on; in fact sometimes it's better, as it allows you to be a little more creative. I'm currently sitting with a hot coffee and a corner seat and quite frankly, people-listening isn't working for me.

Perhaps it would if the subject matter involved something more edifying than the fact that "Tony came back pissed from the pub again," and "it's no wonder the dog shits in the house all the time as he's never there to walk the bastard thing!"

"Did he take him out when he got back?" Came the reply, after lots of head-shaking.

"You're joking! He wasn't able to walk, let alone walk the pissing dog." Big hat 1 retorted.

Big hat 2 then said, "I wouldn't stand for it. When Dean comes home pissed, he has two choices. He either sleeps in the car or he sleeps in the shed, and if he doesn't like it he can piss off to his mum's."

I was desperate to point out that strictly Dean has three choices, but I didn't have time, because there were further aspects of Tony's flawed character that the train needed to be informed of.

"He seems to ignore me all the time at the moment, even on poxy Facebook. I honestly don't even know if he likes me any more," Big hat 1 blathered on.

"Yeah, but he still 'likes' your status updates!"

I couldn't take it anymore. I had to put the headphones on, so now I'm trying to type while listening to Bruno Mars. I'm not sure what's more annoying to be honest…

Why is it that the two hats felt it necessary to subject the rest of the train to their inane chat? They must have realised that everyone else could hear. Or maybe they were actually so insensitive and inconsiderate that they were oblivious to it. The fact that I could hear them in the first place was annoying, but it annoyed me more that they didn't seem to realise how noisy they were being, and it annoyed me even more that the rubbish they were spouting wasn't worth listening to in the first place.

The only thing more annoying is having to listen to Jeremy taking a call from the office and explaining that they are on the same page, so they must touch base soon in order to drill down the numbers and take it to the next level. There has already been lots of research carried out into the physical effects of excessive mobile phone use, and I just hope that they never use Jeremy for their research as they would be forced to conclude that excessive use can turn you into a pompous prick.

Monday 4th March 2013

Noise annoys me, but unnecessary noise really annoys me. Sure, the alarm clock is a pain in the backside, but it's also a necessity in order for me to get to work on time. With the guys digging up the road, sure, the noise is annoying, (and the sight of their bum-cracks first thing in the morning is almost enough for my breakfast to make a second appearance) but those cables and pipes aren't going to upgrade themselves, are they?

Unnecessary noise is noise that can be avoided because its source serves no purpose. For example: cars and bikes revving their engines, people playing loud music in public, and anyone attempting to engage in small talk.

The most annoying unnecessary noise, however, is the noise of a noisy eater. I've got one on my train today. I didn't think it was possible to eat a banana noisily. It hasn't really got anything to make a noise… There's no liquid to slurp, there are no hard bits to crunch and no chewy bits to chew on, so how is this guy managing to sound like a Neanderthal devouring a carcass? What's more worrying is that he still has his really noisy food waiting to be eaten. He's lined it all up on the table in front of him. Banana, followed by yoghurt and granola, and finished off with an apple. Let's hope he dies choking on the granola before he gets to that apple.

I'm joking of course; I wouldn't wish death on anyone, even a guy who has the table manners of a two year-old… Hang on, he just coughed with a mouth full of banana and he didn't cover his mouth! Death-wish reinstated.

I've since realised that this guy is not just a noisy eater, he's just a noisy person, and by that I mean that every thing he does is accompanied by a noise. Everyone knows that you can yawn silently, but this guy has to do it as if he is auditioning for a Night Nurse advert. There are times when we sigh, but in public we choose to suppress it and do it under our breath. Not so our Neanderthal. He has to let the whole train know that he's received a shitty email from work. There are "Hmphhs" followed by "Phhhrrrs" followed by "Tsssssks".

I really feel like introducing him to a new noise – the noise of my fist connecting with his nose, but I'm pretty sure that with the lack of a nose to breath through, his eating would only get noisier. I did decide to subject him to one of my own noises, and it was the noise of a grumpy pacifist. The tut. It's something we Brits have mastered. Never quite brave enough to say anything, but brave enough to make a muted gesture under our breath, often accompanied by a shake of our heads.

He didn't get the hint at all. In fact, rather than put him off, it seemed to spur him on. If anything, he treated my tuts as a kind of percussion to his medley of noises, and just when I thought it couldn't get any worse, the rhythm section kicked in as his phone sprang to life.

What happened next was to annoy me more than anything that had taken place in the previous ten minutes. Just as I was preparing for a bit of light relief from the assorted noises, he whispered, "Sorry, Jane, I can't talk – I'm on the train!"

Tuesday 5th March 2013

I saw an advert last night that confused me. It was for Netflix. The advert itself was fairly self-explanatory – pay them X amount of money and in return they will allow you to watch some films; no confusion there, but then came the warning.

Watch responsibly!

I couldn't work out if this was Netflix's way of being funny. 'We offer such a dazzling array of fantastic films that you may well become addicted, so we advise caution when watching'? Maybe it's their way of asking you to go easy and leave some for the rest? But this is Netflix – there are no actual physical films, they surely exist purely on some hard drive or cloud somewhere. I can only conclude, therefore, that they are being serious and that excessively watching feature films can harm you somehow.

So now, we not only have to drink and gamble responsibly, we have to watch responsibly. I'd never really considered it before, but by boarding a plane, you are being subjected to one 'addiction' after another. You barely get a chance to unbuckle your seat belt before they start plying you with booze; ten minutes later they come around with the scratch cards, and ten minutes after that the film starts. Never mind the pre-flight safety demonstration, we should all be reminded to drink, gamble and watch responsibly before we take off.

Being told to watch responsibly reminds me of my dad warning me that if I watched too much TV, my eyes would go square. Parents tell a lot of lies. I spent my childhood petrified of my eyes turning square, that if the wind changed my face would stay like that, and that if I told a lie my nose would grow bigger. I now know exactly why my dad's got such a big nose.

Of course not all lies are bad, and there is a pleasant side of lying to your children. In our house we are guilty of lying about Father Christmas, the Tooth Fairy, the Easter Bunny, and mummy's chocolate being poisonous. I'm looking forward to the time when, as parents, we will finally be able to stop lying. This will of course be at about the time when, as teenagers, they will spend every waking hour lying to us.

Wednesday 6th March 2013

Everywhere I go, people seem to be coughing and sneezing in my general direction, as it's still that time of year where everyone seems to be suffering from a cold. I hate colds, but more than that, I hate other people with colds. I honestly think that the sound of someone blowing a snotty nose is one of the most disgusting noises known to man, followed closely by the sound of someone sniffing, both of which I'm experiencing in hideous harmony this morning. While on the subject of colds, I want to make it absolutely clear that these are definitely colds that these people are suffering from, not flu.

I've lost count of the amount of times I've heard people say "Sorry I didn't make it in yesterday, I had flu." That most definitely was not influenza, my friend; at worst it was a cold, but you know as well as me that it is far more likely to have just been a hangover, so why didn't you just go for the standard hangover lie and say that it was a 24-hour bug or a migraine, you idiot? Saying "I had flu yesterday" is like jogging up to football practice and saying "Sorry I didn't make it last week, I broke both my legs".

I remember when the swine flu started taking its first few victims and there was panic around the country. Suddenly there were government warnings about how to control the spread of germs and we were advised to "Catch it, bin it, kill it!" The decision makers at the office were quick to order in huge quantities of antibacterial tissues, wipes and hand gels, but apparently it was too late for some of my colleagues. As soon as it started making the news, people around the office were dropping like flies, developing symptoms quicker than they could Google them.

I don't know how many different types of swine flu there were, but it seems that the people at my work had every one going. Never mind hand gel and antibacterial wipes, in order to combat all the symptoms of swine flu, it seems that we should have also ordered haemorrhoid cream and Gaviscon.

While talking about antibacterial hand gel, I must tell you a story about a colleague of mine called Jockey. Jockey is known as Jockey because he's short and could easily pass for a Jockey. It's a good job that not everyone in my office is awarded a nickname because of their build and their potential in a particular sport, otherwise we'd have more than our fair share of Sumos.

I had just made it back to my desk after one of my lunchtime gym sessions when Jockey came up to me to ask a question. It is not unusual for someone, when standing at your desk, to help themselves to some antibacterial hand gel, as they're dotted around the office and free for everyone to use. While I did my best to answer his question, Jockey, standing just behind me, squirted some gel into his hand and really went to work on it. After about 30 or 40 seconds, it was clear that something was wrong as the frantic hand-rubbing was continuing at full pace, so I decided to turn around to look at him. I was greeted by the sight of a pair of hands, covered in a white lather, dripping foam onto the floor.

It took me a few seconds to realise that Jockey had liberally applied to his hands not the hand gel, but my shower gel for use at the gym. What made it funnier for me was that he hadn't said anything. He must have known within four or five seconds that something was terribly wrong, but he must have thought that if he just kept rubbing, he might achieve the same results. There was further embarrassment and ignominy to come as he reached the door and had to ask somebody to open it for him because his hands were that foamy.

I now keep that bottle of shower gel on my desk, partly as a funny reminder, but mainly in the hope that someone one day might just suffer the same fate.

Monday 11th March 2013

As a commuter, there are two things that you learn very early on. Firstly, it is extremely stressful, and secondly, it is extremely expensive. I find that the best way to deal with it is to make the most of the weekends and ensure they are as stress-free as possible.

Normally this is relatively achievable, but last weekend was more stressful and, I dare say, more expensive than any commute I have ever undertaken. Why? Because yesterday was Mother's Day. Don't get me wrong – I love Mother's Day. I love the sentiment, I love the appreciation and I love the warmth and love that's shown between mothers and their children. It's a wonderful day. What I really mean is that I hate the day before Mother's Day. It should have a special name of its own, maybe something like Black Saturday, or Don't You Dare Buy Flowers from the Garage Day.

The whole thing is just so stressful that I honestly believe they should introduce an extra bank holiday in March, just to give back what is effectively a lost weekend. Now I'm married and have a child I don't just have one mother to consider, I have three. I have my mum, my wife's mum and my wife, who is also a mum to our three year-old.

My wife must know how useless I am because all of last week, I could overhear her talking to our daughter in the bath and in the bedroom, saying things like "Daddy will take you to the shops and you can choose", and "It doesn't have to be expensive..." This was most definitely for my benefit, and was reinforced by what I overheard next: "It's the thought that counts, so mummy thought you might like to remind daddy that she likes Cath Kidston."

In truth, I, like most men, have it pretty easy. My wife will go out and buy a card and present for both parents. I don't really feel bad about it and, mum, if you're reading this, it's for your own good. If I assumed responsibility you would only end up with slippers, and what mum wants to receive slippers for Christmas, her birthday and Mother's day?

Mothers and sons have a special bond, and when sons get married it's quite normal for mothers to feel a little sad, as they are effectively giving their child away to be nurtured and taken care of by another woman. What I would say to you mothers out there is this: think of the improvement in presents on Mother's Day! Think of it as a kind of apology from your daughter-in-law. And if you're still getting crap presents, then they clearly don't like you, so you no longer have to feel bad for resenting them!

When I say I don't choose the card and present for my mum, I actually technically still do have some say in the matter, because my wife will come home with two cards and two presents and say to me, "Which ones do you think your mum will like?" I then choose one and my wife says, "Oh, I thought this would suit your mum better," or "I bought this one with your mum in mind!" All of which begs the question: why did she ask me in the first place?

So with two mums taken care of, I only have one mum to buy for, and weirdly, that mum is my wife. When it comes to buying my wife things, I reckon I'm pretty good. The thing is, though, they tend to be special romantic sorts of gifts, not appropriate Mother's Day gifts, so I'm back to square one again. Slippers are out of the question, as she still hasn't worn the ones I bought her for Christmas, so I end up having to drag my daughter around the shops on a rainy Saturday afternoon.

As my daughter is now three, I thought for the first time I would let her choose something special all on her own, without my input. Sure, my wife would probably like something by Cath Kidston, but to know that the present was personally chosen for her by her daughter for the first time – that surely is priceless. After careful consideration, and having completed three circuits of a busy department store, my daughter proudly announced, "Mummy would love this!" My daughter proudly held up a pack of Thomas the Tank Engine paper plates. I had two options. Ask her to put them down, march her over to the Cath Kidston section and get her to choose again, or buy the paper plates.

I bought the paper plates.

I don't regret it for one minute, because the pride on my daughter's face was plain to see. My wife loved them, and we even made a cake and ate off them later in the day.

For those of you thinking that I'm a nasty cheapskate, we did get a little something from the Cath Kidston section too, this time chosen by me, mainly because my daughter hasn't yet mastered the knack of reading price labels.

That said, she's female, so she'll probably never be able to master that one…

Tuesday 12th March 2013

Today marks ten days since the Queen was taken ill with gastroenteritis. We have been subjected to day after day of rolling news updates as to exactly how the queen is getting on. The story had just begun to settle down over the weekend as the Queen returned home, but today it was announced that she has had to cancel a couple of royal engagements, which was the perfect opportunity to resurrect the story.

In the last week we've had updates from royal 'specialists', medical experts and even former workers at the hospital, giving us valuable insights into the inner layout of the hospital, confirming that there was in fact a bed and even a bathroom in the room in which the queen was residing. Fascinating stuff!

Day after day we were subjected to detailed analysis of the illness, often being provided with hi-tech graphics and diagrams of what was, essentially, someone suffering from the shits. At one point, one of the experts mentioned that the queen had been on the throne for sixty years, and I'm pleased to confirm that it was a royal expert and not a medical one.

I suppose we should just be thankful that the Queen has led a relatively health life up until now. It is an unfortunate fact of life that the older you get, the more susceptible you are to illness. Can you imagine what the news would be like if the Queen had the same medical history as the average 86 year-old? The TV news would be a feature-length affair and newspapers would have to produce a special Queen supplement at least two or three times a week.

Seeing the Queen suffering an illness is a timely reminder that she is an elderly woman and won't be our reigning monarch forever. I've heard some stories in the press saying that Prince Charles is keeping a keen eye on the situation, hoping for bad news so that he can take over, and I think it's just wrong. I think it should pass straight to Prince William!

I have only ever lived under this queen's reign and, if I'm honest, I don't like the thought of a man taking over. I really like the fact that we have an old woman in charge of things; I find it comforting. I love spending time with my Nan for the same reason – she's worldly wise, she's warm and loving, and she bakes great cakes.

With the Queen's latest illness, it got me thinking about life after she's gone and who would be a good replacement. Obviously, my ideal choice would be my Nan, but I fear it would need to be someone who is popular with everyone.

Mary Berry wouldn't be a bad choice. She's fairly posh, seems perfectly nice and, like my Nan, definitely makes a good cake. She'd also be able to deliver the perfect Christmas speech: a synopsis of the year followed by how to get that perfect Christmas pudding. However, if we are to break with tradition and vote in a new monarch then I think we should go for youth, so, as nice as Mary is, she isn't the perfect choice.

In fact, I know who would be the perfect choice for our next Queen. Ladies and gentlemen, I give you Adele!

Ok, so she might need a few elocution lessons and she'd have to learn to swear less, but she has already been declared the queen of pop, she is usually immaculately dressed, and she could even do a turn on the Royal Variety Show.

Can someone please send a memo to Adele telling her to brush up on her baking?

Wednesday 13th March 2013

Last week I received an email from Pizza Express headed "Winter is so last year, get that spring feeling with 25% off fresh pizza" or some such.

I'm sure that seemed a fabulous marketing strategy last week, when the mercury crept into double figures for the first time in months, but I'm certain that today they will be feeling pretty bloody stupid. As I sit here, looking at that very email in my inbox, I can confirm that the fields all around me are covered in a blanket of snow and my train is now running forty minutes late due to adverse weather conditions. So is winter 'so last year', Pizza Express? No, it's not, it's very much this year and it's very much right now, you fools.

I'm sure that in the marketing world timing is crucial – get it right and you are onto a winner, get it wrong and you'll have egg on your face, or, in the case of Pizza Express, snow. I'm sure Pizza Express are feeling a little bit silly, but at least they can seek solace in the fact that their ill-timed marketing email did not cause genuine public outcry. About ten years ago Abercrombie and Fitch were caught up in a racism row when they released a new line of T-shirts aimed at trendy young Asian-Americans. The series was almost entirely based around Asian puns, with one of the T-shirts depicting a Chinese laundry and declaring that "Two wongs can make it white". Needless to say, A&F soon withdrew the T-shirts, but not before a PR company speaking on their behalf had declared that "We personally thought that Asians would love this T-Shirt..."

I remember another far less offensive, but equally under-researched, advert which came from McDonald's. In 2005 they released an ad campaign aimed a using street slang. A new advert for their "Dollar Menu" showed a guy staring adoringly at a burger, with the words "I'd hit it" printed next to it. Presumably McDonald's thought that "I'd hit it" was street slang for "I want it" or "I will get it", and not what it actually means, which is "I want to have sex with it".

So while Pizza Express did annoy me with their smug assertion that winter was over, they didn't offend a whole ethnic group and they didn't invite me to have sex with their food, so I suppose I should be thankful.

Thursday 14th March 2013

When you travel on trains, you are expected at some point in the journey to have to produce a valid ticket for travel. Today was no different. A very polite gentleman entered the carriage a few minutes ago and asked, "May I see any tickets that haven't already been seen, please?"

It's a daily ritual that I'm used to, so I stop whatever I'm doing, reach into my back pocket, and produce my Annual Gold Card, which disappointingly, despite the cost, isn't actually made of gold. It's made of card and it isn't even a gold colour, it's a yellow brown. Today, the process of showing my ticket felt decidedly different and I couldn't put my finger on why, until about twenty or thirty seconds later as I watched the train conductor move down the carriage. Not one person gave him any eye contact at all. Every single person simply opened up their train pass with one hand and carried on what they were doing with the other, whether that be typing on the laptop, reading a paper or trying to get three stars on that particularly tricky level of Angry Birds.

I realised that today was different because I, for once, had stopped what I was doing and had given him some eye contact and he had reciprocated with a warm and genuine smile. I know it's not the crime of the century, but I'm annoyed that I've been rude for so long, without even realising it. Now, I'm not trying to make excuses for my inadequacies, but I have to say that I often find writing chapters in such a short space of time difficult, and breaking concentration even for a second can result in me losing my train of thought.

I often think how stupid it is to write a book in this way – constantly worrying about what time it is and often praying for signal failures or train congestion. Can you imagine J K Rowling thinking "I'd best finish off this chapter as we'll be pulling into Cannon Street any minute"?

Now I've taken the time to think about it, I realise I have even been guilty in the past of removing my train pass from my pocket, opening it up and placing it on the table in front of me, in anticipation of the train conductor's arrival. This removes any sort of acknowledgement or even interaction, as it doesn't even require me to move when the conductor arrives.

I first saw this move used successfully a few years ago while travelling from Euston to Watford. A guy was very obviously under the influence of alcohol and so had gone to great lengths to ensure that he could sleep it off on the way home. Firstly, he had attached his train ticket to the work pass that hung around his neck, but secondly, and rather ingeniously, he had scrawled the words "Please wake me up at Leighton Buzzard!" on his ticket. I can confirm that part one of his plan worked perfectly and the train conductor did not have to wake him up to check his ticket, but whether part two was successful I will never know as I alighted before his desired destination.

Back to this morning. As I continued to look down the train, I observed a very well-dressed man, who I would guess was in his mid-to-late-fifties, audibly huff and throw down his paper. He then stood up, produced his pass, showed it to the inspector and said "I don't know why you need to see it, I show it to you every day!"

So not only was Mr Grumpy expecting the inspector to be able to recognise his face amongst the thousands that he encounters each day, most of which are looking down the whole time, he also thought he should be able to memorise the dates on the passes too.

New vacancy: Train Conductor. Good starting salary and pension. Fantastic travel opportunities. Uniform provided. Must have the patience of a saint and an IQ of 140 or above. To apply, please make your way to platform 7 and await further announcements.

Monday 18th March 2013

The weekend papers were once again full of depressing stories about double-dip recessions and parliamentary reform, so it was a relief to read that, even in this uncertain climate, MPs still have time to disgrace themselves by cheating on their partners.

Why is it that newspapers feel the need to report on affairs as if their information has been taken straight out of Viz magazine? People never have sex during an affair – they have a romp, a bonk or a tryst, and when the mistress is interviewed, she hasn't slept with anyone –she's bedded them. In fact, the word affair itself is very rarely mentioned, with the papers favouring phrases like 'Love triangle' and 'Love rat'.

Can you imagine anyone in the real world ever saying that they have been involved in a love triangle, or that their partner was a love rat? "That's right, Shell, turns out we were in a love triangle, and Tony's a love rat!" I think we all know that after the initial shock, the two or three litres of vodka, and the obligatory back-to-back viewing of Bridget Jones' Diary One and Two, the phone call would go something like this: "That's right Shell, the little bastard has been cheating on me, so I took a pair of scissors to his suits and changed my Facebook status to 'it's complicated'."

Romp is a particularly funny word that newspapers like to use and, not content with using it to describe extra-marital sex, they also use it to describe enjoyable movies and books as well as big sporting wins. When reading a newspaper, I personally enjoy reading about the demise of sleazy MPs as well as movie reviews and sport, so there's every chance that I could encounter a romp on pretty much every page that I read.

Another strange thing about newspapers is the insistence on publishing everybody's age. Some would argue that knowing somebody's full name and exact location is more than enough for a story about arable farming, but no, we apparently need to know that Stan Arthurs from Frome in Somerset is in fact 63.

Tuesday 19th March 2013

I couldn't get my normal seat yesterday as there had been numerous cancellations, meaning the train was almost full by the time I got on. I did manage to get a seat at a table, however, and the seat next to me was empty, so I was able to get to work on yesterday's chapter.

I've written before about how important it is for me to get the right seat, and that writing with someone watching over my shoulder is extremely difficult, especially when that person becomes the subject of that day's chapter. I've often thought about writing "PLEASE STOP READING WHAT I AM WRITING AND GET BACK TO YOUR BORING BOOK", and if that doesn't work, following up with "I'M TALKING TO YOU, DICKHEAD".

In fact, I'm sure there are times when everyone feels like people are watching over their shoulder, and this approach could work well in those situations too. Simply take out your phone, hold it in such a way that they can see the screen, open up a new text message and type the words "I'm sitting next to the ugliest person in the world" and pretend to send it. If you want to be a little more mischievous and a little less rude, you could always try typing something like "I'm having an affair with your brother and I'm pregnant with his baby. Oh, and I'm keeping it!"

Today the trouble started at Tonbridge. After stowing his jacket and bag in the overhead compartment, Mr Annoying landed next to me with a huge sigh. He landed with such force that the air rushed out of his seat and flapped at both his tie and his ridiculous quiff. Landing heavily in a train seat often has a further, more disgusting consequence as the released air also brings with it the smell of the previous passenger, but thankfully today I was spared.

Without warning, the armrest started to lower and slowly began imbedding itself into my arm. Instead of pulling back the armrest and asking me if I would mind moving, let alone whether I would actually mind it being lowered in the first place, Mr Annoying pushed down on the armrest with more force, until eventually my arm popped out from under it.

So that was it, yesterday's chapter had to be put on hold for a while, mainly because I had lost the feeling in my right arm, but also because, thanks to the armrest, there was no longer enough room for me to type. I wonder where I would have stood had I just told him that, no, sorry, I didn't want it lowered. I mean stood metaphorically, obviously. If I had been standing, we wouldn't have been in the mess we were in. I know it's childish, but by being there first, doesn't that give me control of the armrest? Kind of like the first person in the lift, the one who gets to be in charge of the buttons?

The middle armrest on a train is a contentious issue. Whom is it for? Some would argue that it's there to share, but it's barely big enough for one arm, let alone two, so I can only assume that it's the property of whoever sat there first. The great thing about train armrests is that if you don't bag the middle one, you can always seek solace in the other one at either end. Theatres and cinemas are trickier, because there are often situations where you don't get to use either, as people on both sides try to fight for what they regard as theirs. I've been guilty in the past of purposely elbowing the person next to me in order to get exclusive use of the armrest, but my wife said if I did it to her again, I wouldn't get any more Maltesers.

The London Underground has hundreds of escalators, and they all operate on a system of standing to the right, meaning that if you just want to ride up or down, you stand to the right, and if you want to walk, you use the left. I think theatres and cinemas should operate an armrest system where you can only use the one on your right; that way, everybody gets to use at least one of them.

A few years ago, I went to see Saturday Night Fever at the London Palladium and sat next to a very stubborn old woman who hogged the armrest for the entire first half. I wouldn't normally have been that bothered, but she had a smug expression on her face that said "Ha ha, look at me, I've got the armrest and you can't have it!" It turned out that she wasn't the only one who could master the art of expression, as I gave her my best "Don't mess with me you bony-armed bitch!" look.

As the curtain lowered to signal the start of the intermission, she started to shuffle in the direction of the toilets, taking her bony little arms with her. I had two options: rush to the toilet myself, risking getting caught up in the queues and losing the perfect opportunity to seize control, or stay at base camp, ignore the chance to empty my bladder and ensure victory. I decided to stay at base camp and therefore guarantee victory. The woman's expression on her return from the toilet was far less smug, and simply said "You little bastard…"

I soon realised that if I was to ensure that I kept the armrest for the entire second half, I would not be able to applaud. Fortunately the cast must have known about my predicament as they went on to provide the most underwhelming performance I have ever witnessed (and from a Watford fan, that really is saying something).

So I sat there stubbornly, desperate for the toilet, with my arms spread and my legs crossed. I was in total agony, but I've got no-one else to blame really, as it was me who booked the tickets…

Wednesday 20th March 2013

From a very young age I've been told that I don't listen, and as I've grown older, people have adapted it to inform me that I am in fact a 'stubborn arsehole', or words to that effect. Well, for the first time in my life, I am prepared to admit that this is true. Throughout my life people have constantly told me to 'be careful', to 'take care', and to 'mind how I go'. They may just be figures of speech, but they always seem such stupid things to say to someone. I feel like saying "Thanks for the timely reminder – I was just about to walk up the road naked and blindfolded into oncoming traffic!"

If I'm completely honest, the reason people feel the need to constantly remind me to take care and to be careful is probably because I do have a bit of a history of not taking care and not being very careful. I dislocated my shoulder while wrestling with my brother on my parents' bed when I was seven, I broke my collarbone while playing British Bulldog in the playground when I was twelve, and I suffered head trauma when a car knocked me off my bike when I was 17. It seems that every five years or so I do something very stupid indeed. In fact, to further support that theory, when I was 22 I decided it would be a good idea to move to Devon to live with a girl I had met on holiday. Having completed a quick bit of mental arithmetic I've just worked out that it was five years later, when I was 27, that I got married... So I suppose, in case my wife's reading, this is the part of the story where everything changed and I broke the cycle! Although, it was five years after that that I started this book, so clearly my stupidity hasn't gone away entirely.

However, I've always been reluctant to buy insurance, only ever taking it out when it's a strict legal requirement. My theory is that, without insurance, I know that I'm playing a dangerous game, meaning I end up being more careful. I happily adopted the same theory with life insurance, until my wife pointed out that should I suffer a tragic early death it wouldn't be me who would lose out financially, it would be her. So I agreed to take it out as long as she paid the premiums, ensuring that it was not me that was to lose out financially, it would be her. I'd like to point out that I'm not a totally miserable git – I do understand the need to take out life insurance, especially when you have a young family, but it doesn't stop me being annoyed by having to do it. Anyway, my wife got her own back, because even though I said that she should pay the premiums, we do in fact have a joint account and all of our finances are shared.

Last night reminded me exactly why I should listen to the people who tell me to be careful, and exactly why I should insure everything from my toaster to my toothbrush. Last night I discovered that I had lost five chapters of this book. When I say lost, I don't mean mislaid, misfiled or misplaced, I mean lost. Gone. Forever. Never to be seen again. Ten hours of my life completely wasted. But on the plus side, ten minutes of yours saved.

When I started this book, I set out to prove that sleeping on trains is a waste of time, but then so is writing five chapters of a book and then losing them. In truth, I might as well have slept. So today I've decided that living life dangerously just isn't for me. I'm taking out my own insurance policy on the book. I'm emailing a copy to myself every five minutes, taking a screen print every ten, and when I get home I'll back it all up on the home computer.

I've just got to make sure I don't leave my iPad on the train because, you've guessed it, it's not insured!

Thursday 21st March 2013

I don't normally like to write about stories that have appeared in the news as I often worry about how relevant they might be should someone read this book in ten years' time. But every so often there's a story that's so big it is impossible to ignore, so today I have decided to break tradition and dedicate this chapter to the story everyone is talking about.

Poppy the Hamster.

Ok, maybe not everyone is talking about it, but it did make the feature page of the BBC news website. For those who may have missed the story, here is the headline: "Hamster found wandering in blizzard".

To get you fully up to speed with this earth-shattering story, here is a brief synopsis:

Hamster found in street.

It was snowing.

Someone named it Poppy.

Er....... that's it!

Duncan Robertson of the Scottish SPCA said "Poppy is around a year old and is in good condition. It is very lucky that she was found by someone who helped her as there was a severe blizzard on Monday evening and it was bitterly cold. Poppy was found in Leith which is a built-up area with lots of flats nearby. Hamsters are fast creatures and can wriggle through small spaces so there is a chance she has escaped from home."

Ok, Duncan, I agree that hamsters are fast and they can wriggle through gaps, but I'm pretty sure they haven't yet mastered the ability to fly. I think it's far more likely that with the current horsemeat scandal restaurants are just trying out alternatives. The SPCA did say that she was in good condition, but they neglected to tell us whether she was covered in olive oil and garlic.

Duncan went on to say that he was keeping an open mind and could not rule out the possibility of the hamster having been abandoned by her owner. So a sweet story about a missing hamster suddenly turns a little more sinister. As important as animal welfare is, I don't think that the BBC news website is the place to be hammering home messages about the rise of rodent abandonment. That said, I'm seriously worried that this might be the start of something terrible because I might already have stumbled across a case of animal abandonment myself this morning. I can see the headlines now: "Cat seen wandering the streets of Headcorn".

Duncan finished off by saying "We're keen to hear from anyone who recognises Poppy, and in the meantime we'll ensure she receives the care she needs." If I'm right with the local restaurant theory, that means Duncan will be ensuring she is well seasoned and basted every half an hour or so.

Friday 22nd March 2013

A few of us went out to lunch yesterday to say goodbye to a colleague. It's very rare that I go out with people from work any more, not because I don't want to, just because it's often a choice between seeing my daughter before she goes to bed, and going out for a drink after work. My daughter nearly always wins that particular battle. Admittedly, it might require a tactical text from my wife saying that my daughter is "Really looking forward to seeing her Daddy", or if my wife is particularly concerned that I might be coming home late, it isn't unusual to receive a call from my daughter herself, who even at the age of three seems to have mastered the art of blackmail.

Going out at lunch is the perfect compromise, as I get to socialise with colleagues, guilt-free, while also getting to see my little one before bed. Win win. Or so I thought. It turns out that eating lunch with colleagues is rubbish. Firstly, whether you mean to or not, the conversation always comes back to work. After all, it's the only common ground you all share, and it's also the middle of the working day. Instead of raising a glass and wishing our colleague every success in her ventures abroad, we spent the whole time talking about whether she was fully up to date with her filing and whether her replacement was enjoying her training.

We chose to go to a Mexican restaurant, and while it was great to experience the full Mexican treatment, there is no getting away from the fact that no business talk should ever take place while wearing a sombrero and fake moustache. Maybe in Mexico City, but definitely not in the City of London.

Another reason I didn't enjoy eating out with my colleagues is that we decided to get a sharing platter for starters. To be honest, I find it uncomfortable sharing food with loved ones, let alone near-strangers. The whole thing is so stressful – there's the stress of taking something that someone else wants, the stress of someone else taking what you want, and then that's all overshadowed by the stress of someone double-dipping a nacho. When you finally think that the stress of sharing is over, the bill arrives.

As much as it was nice to be sociable with colleagues and to say goodbye to a good friend, I'm going back to buying sandwiches from Pret, so there's no fear of anyone stealing my sandwich and absolutely no doubt as to who has to pay.

Monday 25th March 2013

I think I could count on one hand the number of times I've been out socially in the last six months. I'm not complaining – my wife and I knew what we were getting ourselves into when we decided to have children, so it's no surprise that our social calendar is as empty as the bread aisle after a snow storm.

Imagine my surprise then, when not only did I go out for a leaving lunch last week, I also went out for dinner with an old friend the following day. Two days, two meals out. It had been in the diary for weeks, but unlike every other time, it didn't get cancelled at the last minute due to either his or my child's ridiculously weak immune system. We both put ourselves first for once, leaving the wives and children at home to fend for themselves. If it meant us both rolling home in the early hours then so be it, we were going out and there was nothing anyone could do about it!

We decided in the end it was probably best to meet early so we could get back at a reasonable time, and we were both of the opinion that it was probably best to drive, just in case we were needed back home at short notice. After carefully selecting the restaurant based on the phone signal strength, we sat down to enjoy a tasty curry, each with our phones out in front of us, set to 'loud' and 'vibrate'.

As expected, the restaurant was relatively empty due to our insistence on meeting early; in fact there was only one other occupied table in the whole restaurant. It's natural upon entering a restaurant to scan the floor, looking for the best available dining spot, factoring in the distance from the front door, the distance from the toilet and the distance from any other diners. All of these distances are crucial – too close to the door and you get a draft, too far away and you are starved of fresh air. Too close to the toilet and you run the risk of smelling it, too far away and it's a pain to reach it. Too close to other people and they start to listen to your conversation, too far away and you become unable to hear theirs.

I'm sure everyone makes these mental decisions, although I suspect not in so much detail, and I'm sure that everyone has followed their waiter or waitress, silently saying to themselves:

"Walk that way, over there, no, not there, the other way. Ok, well, at least don't sit me next to....."

"Is this ok, sir?"

Inside we're thinking "No, it's not, look at them! Why would I want to spend an evening sat next to someone covered in tattoos, with a dodgy ponytail and a cigarette stuck behind both ears? And don't even get me started on her husband!"

But we actually say "Yes, fine, thanks."

You've probably guessed by now that, after taking our coats, the waiter sat us right next to the only other occupied table in the restaurant. If we had been any closer we would probably have felt obliged to split the bill.

I hadn't really considered it before, but by going out on a Friday night, it wouldn't necessarily be assumed that my friend and I were business contacts, and thanks to the waiter seating us at a candle lit table for two, it didn't look like we were just friends either... So naturally, once seated and comfortable, I came up with the one line that would leave the other couple in no doubt as to our relationship. I checked to see whether either of our wedding rings was visible, and whether either of our phones was displaying any clues such as a photo of a wife or child, and when I was absolutely sure that they weren't, I simply stated "You look a lot nicer than you did in your profile picture!"

As my friend's face dropped to the floor, I realised that there was every chance that my social calendar will once again be empty for a long while to come.

Tuesday 26th March 2013

I've always had a weird knack for being able to find my way. I didn't learn to drive until well into my late twenties, so I was often given the job of navigator and entrusted with the directions. I was particularly good at memorising routes, confident that once I had found a place once, I would be able to find it again with very little assistance. Being a passenger allowed me to take in all the details like landmarks, buildings and place names. There were times, in built-up areas, when I remembered the route based purely on the pubs that we passed, a technique that often came in handy six or seven hours, and indeed six or seven pints, later.

Nowadays, with a sat nav, it's very rare that I get a chance to test myself, although every so often I do like to 'forget' to use the sat nav, much to my wife's annoyance.

"If it's there, then you might as well use it!" she will often say.

"But I know that in order to get to Cambridge I need to take the M20, followed by the M25 and then onto the M11. If I get stuck after that it'll be signposted." I will reply.

"What, 'this way to Colin's house'?"

The thing is, my wife hasn't been able to truly experience my inner compass due to her reliance on, and insistence on always using, the sat nav. I think the reason that she is so reluctant for me to rely on instincts is that she doesn't trust her own, a point backed up by what happened to her yesterday. She was driving along the main road, happily taking in all of the beauty that the countryside had to offer, when she was met with the sight of a police car blocking the road ahead of her. The policeman had conveniently blocked the traffic at a crossroads, offering cars the opportunity to either go left or right.

"Ok, so you turned right?" I asked.

"No, I turned left" she said.

We live in a fairly rural area and you only need to make a slight deviation from the main road in order to completely leave civilisation, by which I mean mobile phone coverage, behind. Undeterred, my wife battled on for another twenty minutes until she was completely lost and finally gave in and opted for the sat nav. If I'm honest, I'm surprised she left it that long, but she explained that initially it seemed quite a simple task, in that because she had turned left she just needed to find a right turn further down the road and she would be back on track.

"That would have worked had you gone right," I smugly explained. "You follow the road down the hill, past the post-box, past the row of bungalows and then there's a turning on the left that brings you back onto the main road about half a mile further down."

"How do you even know that?" she asked. "Have you ever even gone right at that crossroads?"

"I have once," I said. "There are a couple of nice pubs down there!"

Unfortunately, it seems that not only is there a dearth of mobile phone masts in the countryside, there is also a distinct lack of satellite coverage, much to my wife's frustration, as the sat nav wouldn't work.

"What did you do then?" I asked.

"I just sat there, waiting," she replied.

"For what? For someone to build a mobile phone mast so you could phone for help? For a friendly passing satellite?"

"I don't know. I didn't know what to do. I didn't want to get any more lost than I already was," she said.

This truly amazed me.

"So you were lost, but you were afraid you might get really lost?!" I asked.

"Yes," she replied, "Exactly!"

I tried to explain that being lost was final. There aren't multiple stages of being lost. You're either lost or you're not. No one says "I'm very nearly lost, give me a minute and I'll be lost".

No, getting lost tends to go something like this: I know where I am, I think I know where I am, I thought I knew where I was, where the hell am I? No, dear, I'm not going to ask for directions.

I tried to explain that as she was already lost, she had nothing to lose by continuing to drive, but she immediately replied with "What about petrol?"

I could sense that she was becoming frustrated with my smug 'I know better' demeanour, so I decided to put an end to the conversation and simply ask how she got home.

"I got out and looked in the boot and found a map," she said.

"Excellent, so you used the map to find your way home?"

"No, while rummaging in the boot for a map, I received a text and realised I had a small amount of reception, so I called my mum!"

Wednesday 27th March 2013

I've always been terrible at seeing things through to the end. I've lost count of the books that I started to read and never bothered to finish, and there have been many films and TV series that I have never seen the end of. The awful thing is that it has nothing to do with the quality of the book, film or TV show, and has everything to do with me and my weird ability to lose interest at the critical point. It's a wonder I've ever been able to have children!

I'll often watch a whole TV series, like Masterchef or X Factor, and then not bother to watch the final. I remember buying the box set of 24 when everyone was raving about it, but as far as I am concerned, it may as well have been called 17.5. I've seen films right up until the crucial twist and then simply switched off because I've lost interest. I have to trust that people are telling the truth when they tell me that [spoiler alert] Bruce Willis was in fact a ghost all along, or when I hear that [here comes another one] Darth Vader is in fact Luke's father and Princess Leia is his sister. I genuinely had no idea as I had only seen both films up until about their respective half way points.

In a way it's more fun, as I can simply make up my own ending, meaning everything finishes up exactly how I want. Never again will I be disappointed by the ending of something. The reason I mentioned earlier that I have to trust people when they say that [spoiler again] Darth Vader was Luke's father and Princess Leia was his sister, is because in my mind, Darth Vader was in fact his sister and it was Princess Leia that was his father. It made for a far more powerful, if confusing, ending.

I'm so used to making up my own endings that it can lead to genuine confusion, months and sometimes years later. I'll be watching a programme and the presenter will say "coming up later we will be speaking to…" and it will either be last year's X Factor, Britain's Got Talent or Masterchef winner, and it won't be the person I'm expecting. I obviously don't just make something up in my own mind for a bit of fun, I seem to actually believe it too.

Having boldly stated that I am terrible at seeing things through, it is with genuine surprise that I find myself at the end of Part 2 of this book. (I originally wrote and released the book in four parts via Amazon Kindle) Of course I shouldn't be surprised because I get to make up my own ending and I also get to make sure that this finishes exactly the way I want it to!

Wednesday 27th March 2013

This part of the book is going to start out much like the last one. I've explained in the past that coming back from a Christmas break feels much the same as coming back from a holiday abroad: you constantly worry about how much money you've spent, how much weight you've put on and how much work you have to go back to. The only real difference between an Easter break and a Christmas break is that the extra weight is thanks to gluttony of the sweet kind, rather than the savoury.

My daughter is now of the age where she not only knows who the Easter bunny is, she's actively hunting him down. Every child loves an Easter hunt, but I think she's taking it a little too far with the camouflage and binoculars. This year, thanks to a combination of her covert operations and a particularly generous Easter bunny, she's received a record haul, and at the last count this morning she still had about eight eggs left.

We have always been careful with how much chocolate our daughter eats, and until recently she hardly ate any at all. In fact, it was only when we discovered the power that chocolate could have as a bargaining tool that we started to increase her allowance. A small piece of chocolate is all it takes for a room to get tidied, for vegetables to get eaten and, after a much more recent discovery, for cold drinks to be fetched from the fridge.

I very quickly realised that my daughter had accumulated far too many eggs and, in an effort to stop her following her mother's footsteps into a lifelong addiction to all things Cadburys, I decided that I should help her out. My wife was clearly annoyed this weekend when I started to eat the surplus eggs, but I think it was less to do with the fact that I was eating them, and more to do with the fact that she wasn't!

One of my self-appointed household tasks is to do the weekly food shopping, and I have no problem doing it because I'm also the self-appointed chef. Actually, scrap that, the word 'chef' is probably a little ambitious - let's stick with cook. I am the self-appointed cook. So, as I get to control exactly what food comes into our household, I naturally get to keep close control of the chocolate reserves. At times, when my wife is suffering terribly from chocolate withdrawal, I feel more like a drug councillor in charge of the methadone than a caring and loving husband.

Although I'm the main cook, my wife does prepare our daughter's meals, as I get back far too late in the evening. My wife recently decided it was a good idea to clear out one of our kitchen cupboards and make it into a special cupboard, just for our daughter's things.

'It means we can keep it all in the same place and we'll know exactly where it all is,' she said.

'It's so much easier to grab snacks and to make packed lunches,' she continued, hammering her point home.

I thought it sounded like a sensible suggestion, and she went ahead and re-arranged the cupboards in a way that only women can. What I didn't realise at the time is that it was nothing more that a ruse to disguise her real intentions. A few weeks ago, while putting away some of our daughter's snacks, I discovered a secret stash of chocolate.

'How can you be sure it's your wife's secret stash?' I hear you ask.

'It could be chocolate bought for your daughter,' you might conclude.

Well, unless my daughter had suddenly developed a taste for her mother's three favourite chocolate bars, I was more than happy to conclude that this secret stash did in fact belong to my wife.

I wondered for a while just how I should deal with the situation. Should I just come straight out with it? Should I drop hints and then let her admit to it? I decided that the simplest solution was just to go ahead and eat it. My theory was that she would be too scared to mention it, as that would first involve having to admit to it, and I was confident that she wasn't at that stage of her recovery just yet. Obviously this approach doesn't work in every situation, and I would strongly advise police officers to steer clear of this method and stick to the tried and trusted bagging up of evidence ready for the trial.

So tonight, after finishing off the last of my daughter's eggs, I will be happy in the knowledge that not only will I have helped to reduce the chances of my daughter growing up to be a chocoholic like her mother, I will have also helped my wife further along the road to recovery.

What a considerate husband and father I am. And I bet neither of them even bothers to thank me.

Wednesday 3rd April 2013

Bank holidays are generally a good thing. I say generally because to self-employed people they probably seem a bit pointless. As an employed person, however, I couldn't be happier when they come around as it means that I get paid to stay at home.

That said, there are times when bank holidays can be a complete pain in the arse. Trying to travel anywhere on a bank holiday is a nightmare and I can think of nothing worse than spending my paid day off sitting in a car, stationary, behind a bloody caravan in the middle lane of the M25. Actually, I can think of something worse. It's sitting in a car, stationary, behind a school coach in the middle lane of the M25.

There are only so many spotty arses I can tolerate, and after four or five hours of being told on multiple occasions by a multitude of children that you're a wanker through the medium of mime, I defy anyone not to seriously consider the benefits of bringing back the cane.

Another problem with a bank holiday is the confusion it creates when you go back to work. I spent the whole of yesterday thinking it was Monday, and I've already made the mistake of thinking today is Tuesday. To be honest, it's not all bad because come Friday I'll still be thinking it's Thursday, and what a lovely moment of realisation that will be. It's like the feeling you get when you wake up at the weekend thinking it's Monday and then it dawns on you. I'll have to be careful though, because if I don't synchronise my internal calendar by Friday, I could well end up travelling into work on Saturday.

This week though, my brain has been dealt a double-whammy. Not only have I had to deal with the confusion of the Easter bank holidays, I've had to deal with the clocks going forward too. My internal calendar was already screwed up, and now my internal clock has taken a hit as well.

How is it that a complex and sophisticated organ such as the brain can be so easily tricked? Why is it that the brain is able to retain some detailed information, but equally able to forget the most basic of things? Why is that I haven't yet completely mastered the use of pronouns, but can easily remember the music from the Um Bongo advert from beginning to end?

While on the subject of Um Bongo, after extensive internet research, I can conclusively reveal that they most definitely do not drink it in the Congo. I'm starting to wonder what other bogus claims they may have come up with during their foray into advertising in the early nineties. Come to think of it, it's unlikely they would have hired animals to pick the fruit in the first place, and it seems especially strange that they got a parrot to handle the packaging side of things. Evidently trading standards were far more lenient back then.

Incidentally, back in 1999, Um Bongo brought out a sister product called Um Ognob, but ultimately it wasn't a success and it was discontinued in 2003. I can't seem to find a specific reason why, but I reckon it has a lot to do with the fact that they couldn't find a country to rhyme with it. Surely they could have easily called it Um Bangola? Or Um Bhana?

If you ever need proof that the brain never works at full capacity, all you need to know is that it took me until now to work out that Ognob is Bongo spelled backwards.

Way down deep in the middle of the Congo,

A hippo took an apricot, a guava and a mango.

He stuck it with the others, and he danced a dainty tango.

The rhino said, 'I know, we'll call it Um Bongo!'

Um Bongo, Um Bongo, they drink it in the Congo.

The python picked the passion fruit, the marmoset the mandarin.

The parrot painted packets that the whole caboodle landed in.

So when it comes to sun and fun and goodness in the jungle,

They all prefer the sunny funny one they call Um Bongo!

Friday 5th April 2013

Every so often there's a gap in this book and this is down to me either taking a holiday, working from home or, very rarely, being ill. Yesterday I was ill. Well, if I'm honest, I wasn't strictly speaking ill, but I wasn't in a fit state to work.

To tell the story fully, I need to go back a little bit further.

On Thursday, March 7th 2013 my wife had a wee on a stick. We weren't on a Bear Grylls survival course, and she hadn't been caught short on a woodland ramble; the stick in question had a thin blue line and the word 'Pregnant' was clearly displayed.

We were so pleased as we'd been 'trying' for over eighteen months. People often say that these kinds of things can be affected by stress, and with my wife being a teacher there was every chance that her occupation had contributed to our lack of success. In mid-February, my wife decided that she wanted to give up teaching and spend more time with our daughter. It was a hard decision and one that wasn't taken lightly, but for the sake of her health and wellbeing, it was ultimately the right choice to make. I was amazed to see how much my wife's stress levels were alleviated immediately, and as if to prove Newton's third law correct, I immediately started to stress out an equal amount more, wondering how the hell we were going to pay for everything.

Three weeks later, while staring at that blue line, my financial concerns were but a distant memory as I hugged my wife tightly while we wiped away our tears. 'We're having a baby!' we said together, not quite believing that it could be true. We spent the night and the next morning doing what everyone else in our situation does: checking if the blue line is still there, wondering if we'd dreamed it, and ultimately wasting another £7.50 by taking another test.

We announced the news to close family and friends within a week or so of finding out, even though I'm sure there will be a collective sharp intake of breath from the 'You shouldn't tell anyone until 12 weeks' brigade. The thing is, should the very worst happen, these are the people whose support we would inevitably fall upon and they're also the people who will be there for us through the whole process, so it's nice to be able to let them in on the secret and to give some good news back.

It's been a little bit strange announcing the news in this way. As much as I'm okay with letting the family know from a very early strange it feels wrong to be announcing the news so publicly and so early on. I needn't have worried though as I quickly realised that the book will be released after the crucial 12-week scan.

I started this chapter by announcing that I was unfit to work yesterday, and now that you are fully up to speed, I can finally tell you exactly what happened. At around 8pm on Wednesday, my wife returned from the bathroom with a worried look on her face.

'I think something's wrong,' she said.

Within minutes my mother-in-law had arrived to take over childcare duties and we'd arrived at the hospital in under an hour. The next few hours were tough as we patiently waited for someone to tell us whether everything was okay. My wife was clearly in pain, both physically and mentally, and I tried to comfort her as best I could. When the effect of my kisses, hugs and dry wit had begun to wear off, I played my trump card: a bar of Dairy Milk from the vending machine.

While tea and coffee will invariably come out of a hospital vending machine tasting of cat urine, a chocolate bar from a hospital vending machine tastes like a chocolate bar. In fact, it tastes better out of a hospital vending machine than it does out of the cupboard or fridge at home. This is because when you indulge in chocolate at home you'll invariably have other home comforts that come into play, such as comfortable seating, soft lighting and a lovely little romcom on the telly, all of which distract you from the chocolate. In a hospital waiting room, it's all about the chocolate bar.

We were eventually invited in to see the consultant, and after a lot of pushing, prodding and poking, he finally agreed to take a look at my wife. Sorry, that wasn't the best time for a joke. He agreed that it was best to have an ultrasound to check everything was in order and he said we would be first on the list to be seen. It was now 3am and we were relieved that we'd finally find out whether everything was okay.

'You will be the first to be seen when they open at 8am,' he said.

The doctor was keen for us to go home and come back in the morning, but it's a 45-minute drive to the hospital, which would mean an hour-and-a-half round trip. We figured that we wouldn't get any sleep at home anyway and we'd rather be in a safe place should the very worst happen.

I decided to let my wife get some rest, and I thought I would try to get some sleep in the car. It was impossible. If anyone is ever on the lookout for a new torture technique, you could do far worse than making someone sleep in a car. But if you do make use of it, you didn't get the idea from me.

I returned to my wife's bedside with a fresh cup of cat urine at 7am and we spent the next hour telling ourselves how lucky we were to already have one beautiful child. By the time we entered the sonographer's room, we were both prepared for the bad news that we were sure would follow, but to our astonishment the news was good. Our baby was happy and healthy.

We arrived back home twelve hours after we'd left, exhausted, emotional and relieved. Our dream, which had threatened to become a nightmare, could still become a reality…

Monday 8th April 2013

After our little scare last week, and on Doctor's advice, we decided to take it easy this weekend. 'You should rest up and not do anything too strenuous,' he had said. Unfortunately this advice was for my wife and didn't extend to us both, so I was still expected to find time to cut the grass and wash the car at some point.

The thing is, with a three-and-a-half-year-old it's actually very difficult to rest at all. In fact, staying indoors with a three-and-a-half-year-old can, at times, be far more strenuous than going out. My daughter is particularly imaginative and one of her favourite games is role play. This means that, thanks to her vivid imagination, any part of the house can at any time become anything that she desires. One minute she'll be a princess in a castle, and the next minute an astronaut on a spaceship. This is all well and good, you might think – my daughter, happily able to entertain herself while my wife puts her feet up and I grudgingly wash the car.

Not so.

Immediately my daughter will start barking directions at us, telling us where we should be and what we should say. She'll shout instructions like a seasoned director on the set of a Hollywood blockbuster, and we'll sometimes even be required to redo our lines. 'No, not like that – like this,' she'll say. 'Don't do that – do this'. Constant pressure to get it just right.

Once again, you might think this is a standard part of parenting, and to indulge our daughter in these fantasy Hollywood productions is as good as taking it easy. Surely there's nothing too strenuous about any of this?

Again, not so.

I'm sure there are many differences between shooting a movie in Hollywood and shooting one in our living room, but the one major difference that I've noticed is that the actors seem to be doing all of their own stunts. There are dragons that need slaying, horses that need riding, spaceships that need flying and cars that need crashing, all of which required my wife and I to be leaping around, all the while being told 'No, not like that – like this!'

It was no good – we had to come up with another plan. So on the first bloody sunny day for what seemed like a year, we decided to go to the cinema. We've never taken our daughter to the cinema before, partly because we felt she might get bored and lose interest, but mainly because we were worried she might start shouting out 'No, not like that – like this!'

Having never been to the cinema, our daughter didn't really know what to expect. We told her it was like a big television that lots of people watch together, but she didn't quite get it. 'Can I watch Peppa Pig there?' she asked. 'No, we're going to watch a film,' we explained. 'Okay,' she said, finally getting it. 'Can I watch Toy Story there instead?'

Tuesday 9th April 2013

I've noticed that some advances in technology have had a dramatic effect on the life of a commuter. It wasn't so long ago that the only way a commuter could work on the train was with a piece of paper and a pen.

We're used to a rather noisy environment nowadays, often having to put up with phone conversations and text alerts, but before the technological revolution, train journeys would have had a very different backing track, consisting purely of paper-shuffling and scribbling. I'm pretty sure that people didn't really get much done back then. Sure, people could prepare for a meeting or two, and no doubt put the odd date in the diary, but they certainly weren't sealing huge deals while trying not to spill their cappuccino on the 17:48 from Euston.

Of course, nowadays, people are. In fact people aren't just signing huge deals while on the move – people are holding conferences, board meetings and even hiring and firing their bloody staff. I know this because I see it and hear it. While I'm rambling on about chocolate eggs and Um Bongo, big business decisions are being made and carried out all around me.

Or so I thought.

This morning I had to listen to the full inner workings of a small recruitment firm located somewhere near London Bridge. A rosy-faced chap in his mid-to-late fifties seemed to be having a conference call with two other senior people at the firm. He was certainly pulling no punches. He was accusing certain people of being lazy, other people of ignoring his instructions, and one poor bastard got blamed for being off sick. Throughout the conversation he furiously swiped and tapped at his iPad, throwing up his arms and gesticulating wildly. It was only as he finished his call and got up to start getting his coat on that I was able to see what was on his screen.

It was Angry Birds. (But I can't confirm whether it was the Star Wars edition or not)

So while new technology allows us to do far more work on the move, it also gives us ample opportunity to destroy little green cartoon pigs with the help of a selection of 'Angry Birds'.

In fact, I would go as far as to say that the iPad could well be responsible for the economic slowdown. Just a few years ago, I would have seen hundreds of commuters furiously beavering away on a company laptop, happily firing the entire middle-management team, whereas now these very same people are content with firing little Angry Birds.

What I find more disturbing, however, is not the fact that the work isn't getting done anymore – it's the fact that sixty-year-old men are playing computer games in the first place! I think it only fair that commuters should stick to the games they grew up with, even if it does mean that we have to find extra luggage space for hundreds of hoops and sticks. (Younger readers, ask your parents).

Wednesday 10ᵗʰ April 2013

I've heard a lot of people talk about what they would do if they won the lottery. The first things people tend to want to do are clear their debt, go on holiday and buy the perfect house. Once these fundamental bits of admin are sorted, the list tends to be extended to giving money to friends or relatives, and then finally onto the treats. The little things that you've never been able to have and probably never will have, but nonetheless would really love to have. Whether it's a Harley Davidson, a home sauna or a lifetime subscription to Woman's Own, everyone has their 'Wouldn't it be great to have…'

My dear old Gramps could fill a whole afternoon listing the things he would have done with a lottery win and it was with genuine regret that he passed away, bereft of the win that would have bought him the thirty-foot yacht he was so desperate to skipper. He would list in great detail exactly who would get what, and go on to explain exactly how he would spend his portion. 'I'd buy a big house on the south coast, with enough space for everyone to stay, and I'd moor the yacht at Lymington harbour,' he used to say.

Gramps grew up in the East End and joined the Royal Air Force as soon as he turned 18. After his initial six weeks' training in Bedfordshire, he was posted to Felixstowe to serve with the Air Sea Rescue service. His crew was responsible for rescuing downed pilots over the North Sea and the English Channel during the Second World War. He was immensely proud of this, and I know that his dreams of owning a yacht and living by the sea have everything to do with those years serving queen and country.

It was great listening to Gramps spend money he didn't have, but it must have been hard for my Nan to listen to the bold claims of huge houses and private yachts while at the same time being told that there was nothing wrong with the knackered old sofa and that it had a good few years left in it yet.

So once the debt's cleared, the new house has been purchased and the holiday is but a distant memory, what would be next on your list of purchases? A new car? A nice motorbike? A home cinema? Maybe a whole load of clothes to fill up that nice new walk-in wardrobe in the new place? Me, personally, I'd get hiring some staff. As much as I enjoy cooking, it frustrates me that in order to cook you need food, and in order to get food you need to go food shopping, and in order to go food shopping you need to have ideas about what you want to cook. Wouldn't it be great to have a chef who would not only cook the food, but research the recipes, source the ingredients and, who knows, maybe even wash up afterwards? I also like exercise, but after a hard day at work, it's extremely difficult to get motivated to do it, so a personal trainer would be a nice 'Wouldn't it be great to have…' too. And if I'm honest, I'm not all that crazy about driving, so while I'm hiring staff, I wouldn't mind a driver too.

Of course all of this is pointless because I'm not going to win the lottery, and if I did I would give up my job immediately anyway, giving me ample time to exercise, plan recipes, drive to the shops and go shopping.

Thursday 11th April 2013

I seem to get lots of spam. And when I say spam I mean the email variety, not the tinned stuff. Among the plethora of unsolicited emails this week I have been offered diet pills, a masters degree and my personal favourite – a bigger penis, GUARANTEED! All of these services can apparently be obtained with absolutely no questions asked, which, as we all know, is a complete lie as the first question is almost always 'What are your bank details?'

How is it that spam still exists? Leaving aside the technical issues of filters and the like, surely no-one falls for this nonsense? For a start the emails tend to make absolutely no bloody sense. They usually go something like this:

'My Dear Friend,

May I be sorry four contacting you in such a short Space of time, for I am adviseing of a fantastic opportunity that should never be missed.'

I can only assume that there are people out there who actually do fall for this rubbish; otherwise these spammers wouldn't be doing it. It's a scatter-gun approach which works by targeting hundreds of thousands of people in the hope that a few take the bait. A friend of mine, who shall remain nameless, had a very similar approach while frequenting Watford's Kudos nightclub in the late nineties. He would approach a group of girls and the following short script would play out.

'Hello, I wonder if you could help me with something…'

'Sure, what is it?' would come the reply.

'I'm trying to lose my virginity!'

Nine times out of ten he would be told to crawl back under the rock from which he had come. But unbelievably, every so often, some poor girl of questionable judgement would either pity him, or maybe assume he was joking, and strike up a conversation. A chat would lead to a drink, a drink to a smooch, and the rest is history. Let's just say that thanks to his unique 'spamming' technique, he lost his virginity a fair few times in the late nineties.

So this morning, after clearing my daily spam, I was delighted to see an email which was effectively the complete opposite. This email was not asking me to part with cash in return for a product that doesn't exist; it was confirming that £9.99 had been deposited in my bank account and that I'd also been given five free products. I know what you're thinking. Surely, that can't be right? But it was! Here's how…

Last weekend I found myself at home looking after our daughter while my wife went shopping in London with her mother. I was offered the opportunity of going, but after a long three seconds, I decided it was best to stay at home as there were some urgent bills that needed paying and some crucial filing that needed catching up on. I was expecting my wife back around 5pm, and the plan was for me to then pop out to watch the Watford game at the local pub. I don't often get a chance to see my home team, and Watford were doing quite well this season. They were playing Cardiff, who at the time of writing were top of the league, and the game was on Sky, which we don't have. At about 4pm, my wife called to say that they were running a bit late and wouldn't be home until after 6:30pm, meaning I wouldn't be able to go out and catch the game.

Coincidentally, not three minutes after receiving that call, an advert appeared on the TV that answered all of my prayers. 'Haven't got Sky Sports, but want to watch the big match? Welcome to Now TV…' I did as the advert instructed, immediately! I downloaded the app on my iPad and purchased the Sports Day Pass for £9.99. Not only was I able to watch my beloved Watford, I didn't even have to sit still and watch it on the TV – I could watch it on the move. That particular feature was actually invaluable, as it turned out my wife had asked me to do a few chores, which of course, thirty minutes before she was due back, I still hadn't got round to. I figured that £9.99 was a lot to watch a game of football, but I was extremely happy with the service and I would probably have spent that much at the pub. All of this brings us to today's email…

Here's what it said:

'Due to an unforeseen technical issue we know some of our customers couldn't access our service. As sports fans we totally understand the frustration you must have experienced if you came to watch the big game. Having identified the cause of last night's problem, we are now working hard to make sure it doesn't happen again.'

The 'big game' was the Manchester derby, which had been on just after the Watford game, but I hadn't been watching it. Then came the next, staggering paragraph.

'For anyone who has ever purchased a Sky Sports Day pass since launch, we have refunded all of your £9.99 passes. It will be in your bank within 3 to 5 days. By way of an apology, we will also be sending everyone affected 5 free Sky Sports Day passes so you can try the service again. Apologies again from everyone here at Now TV.'

I still, even now, can't quite believe what Now TV did. They had a small error which would have affected a limited number of customers, but instead of blaming it on others and leaving it down to their customers to complain, (like every other company I seem to encounter) they held their hands up about the error and refunded EVERYONE who had ever used the service. They then went one stage further and gave EVERYONE five free passes, worth £49.95. Not one, to essentially replace the one which hadn't worked, but five.

So, as annoying as spam email is, I say it's the price we have to pay for receiving those very few pleasant emails.

Tuesday 16th April 2013

I feel I need to provide you with a warning before you read this chapter. If this chapter were a film, it would probably come complete with the warning 'Contains content that some viewers may find disturbing'.

Yesterday, while chatting to a colleague in the middle of our busy office, I stifled a laugh. There were lots of people on the phone near me, so I thought it best to keep the laugh internal. I can't remember exactly what I was laughing at, but I can confirm that it was one of those fake laughs which serve only to break the silence and keep the small talk ticking along. There was some brief business to conduct with a colleague I barely knew and the information we both needed was taking its time to appear on his computer screen. I was more than happy to ride out the awkward silence, but without warning my colleague stepped in and delivered a piece of classic small talk. I can't remember exactly what it was, but it was intended to break the ice and create a little giggle. It was probably poking fun at the time it was taking to return the information on the screen. It could have been the classic 'Shall I try turning it off and back on again?' or maybe it was 'It might have been quicker to send it by Royal Mail.' Whatever it was, it was immediately discarded from my long-term memory because of what happened next.

Without warning a nine-inch stream of nasal mucus flew out of my right nostril and, using my chin as a mooring point, began swinging wildly back and forth. I had no idea where it had come from. There was absolutely no warning. I didn't have a cold, I wasn't suffering from hay fever and I hadn't even needed to blow my nose at all that day. What made it even more annoying was that the 'joke' wasn't even funny – I was just doing us a both a favour in an awkward moment. Well that awkward moment had just got a whole lot more awkward.

There is not much you can say to someone whom you barely know when a nine-inch piece of snot is not only dangling from your face, but swinging back and forth mere inches from theirs. As it had arrived completely unannounced, I was totally unprepared and the nearest box of tissues was at least three desks away. At best I was hoping my colleague would laugh, and maybe at worst he would get up and walk away, but he simply stared in total horror at the situation that had unfolded in front of him. After what felt like a good four or five minutes, he simply backed away and said 'I'll email you the details when they come through…'

I've said it before and I'll say it again. I bloody hate small talk.

Wednesday 17th April 2013

My wife recently took it upon herself to do some decorating. Don't get me wrong – had the decorating involved scraping the mouldy wallpaper from the bathroom walls, or applying a generous lick of magnolia to the skirting boards, then I would have been a very happy man, but no, the decorating started and finished with our marital bed. A few weeks ago I noticed a small, round pillow with a frilly edge had snuck onto our bed.

'What's this?' I enquired.

'A pillow,' my wife explained.

'What's it doing on our bed? It's not big enough for our daughter, let alone us!' I argued.

'It's for decoration,' she went on. 'It looks pretty.'

The pillow was then removed from the bed and placed on the floor. The following morning, the bed was made and the pillow was back on the bed again.

'So that's it? That's what it does? That's its job?' I asked.

'Yes. Pretty, isn't it?' she said as she hopped towards the bathroom.

'Just let me get this right,' I said, chasing her towards the landing. 'That little pillow sits on our bed all day, looking pretty, while we both go to work?'

'That's right,' she said.

'What's the point?' I asked. 'Who gets to see it? You spend more time moving it than you do looking at it and appreciating it!'

'That's not the point,' she said.

'So what's next? A poncho for the vacuum? A doily for the kettle? Earrings for the taps?'

'You're just being stupid now.'

'If you wanted something to pretty up the bed before you get in, just give me a nudge and I'll hop in first! I'd happily be your little decorative pillow!'

I could see my wife was getting angry and, as if to prove my point, she said 'Fine, that's a deal! Don't forget the pillow stays on the floor overnight!'

Over the next few weeks the pillows multiplied, and we now have a total of four decorative pillows as well as a silky piece of fabric draped across the foot of the bed. Unlike the pillows, this useless piece of fabric remains on the bed at night, although only ever for a maximum of an hour, as that's all it takes for it to slide off one way or another.

I would estimate that it now takes my wife around twenty minutes to make our bed, which is at least fifteen minutes longer than it used to take her and a full twenty minutes longer than I will ever take

Monday 22ⁿᵈ April 2013

Against my better judgement I've decided to go on another diet. Christmas and Easter have finally taken their toll, and it's time for me to start watching the weight again. I tend to go on a new diet approximately every six months, and it's usually in April and October. I like the thought of starting to lose weight in October in anticipation for Christmas. My theory is that if I lose a few pounds before Christmas, I can then sit back and eat whatever I want over the festive period, safe in the knowledge that I'll only return to what I was back in October. Also, as an added bonus, because I won't have officially put any weight on (compared to the October weight) I don't have to go crazy and lose any in the New Year. April is another good weight-loss month as there are always a few post-Easter pounds, especially this year (see chapter dated Tuesday April 2nd 2013)…

In the past I've tried Weight Watchers, Slimming World, the Atkins Diet, the Grapefruit Diet, the Cabbage Soup Diet and, most embarrassingly of all, a diet called 'Six Weeks to OMG'. This last one involved, amongst other things, taking cold showers and blowing up balloons (I kid you not). If I'm being honest, I have no idea why I ever bother to go on a diet. The only time I've ever successfully lost weight and kept it off is when I didn't diet at all. A few months after my daughter was born I stopped drinking, started exercising more, cut down on my portion sizes and stopped eating as much junk. I didn't see it as a diet – I wasn't counting calories and I didn't stop myself from eating anything at all, I simply started being a bit more sensible. After a while I naturally started to eat less as my stomach reduced in size, and I started to crave healthier foods. I don't know what's gone wrong this time around, but I just can't get back into that healthy mindset. Christmas and Easter certainly didn't help, and the long hours I work make it difficult to plan, prepare and eat the healthier foods. I'm sure the large bar of chocolate in front of the telly every night isn't helping things either.

So I've decided to try a new diet with the intention of using it to help kick-start the weight-loss process. It's called the Dukan Diet and starts with an attack phase which only allows you to eat foods that are high in protein. It lasts five to ten days on average and is designed to lose the first few pounds very quickly. On average people lose between seven and twelve pounds during this phase. This then leads into a cruise phase in which other foods are introduced. There are four phases in total, but I'm hoping I never have to find out what phases three and four are as I'm hoping to use my own common sense from there on in. If I were searching for an analogy here, I would say that I'm a glider plane. Gliders need the help of either a winch or a plane called an Aerotow in order for them to achieve flight, and I truly believe that in order for me to lose weight I need a winch or an Aerotow. Of course, it isn't the perfect analogy because a glider will eventually fall to earth and be reliant on others once again, whereas I'll be hoping to go it alone permanently once I've reached my desired altitude.

I'm aware that it could be considered a tad strange to read about a 'bloke' having issues with weight and his tactics on how best to deal with it. I imagine it's an issue more often attributed to women, but I think that's only the case because women tend to talk about it more. I'm certain there are as many men as women who are unhappy about how they look and are keen to do something about it. You only need to look at the growth in the male cosmetics industry in recent years to see how times are changing. Thirty years ago, your average guy would own three products which would loosely fit into the category of 'Male Grooming', and they would simply be soap, shampoo and aftershave. The market was so small that I can say with some confidence that 90% of men would have used Imperial Leather soap, Head and Shoulders shampoo and either Old Spice or Brut aftershave (applied liberally). That was it. In fact, had I been a grown man at that time, I would only have needed two of those products, as my hair and I have long since parted ways.

Nowadays, men regularly use lip balms, moisturisers, gels, eye creams, fake tan and even foundation. Gone are the days where men who looked after themselves would be labelled 'Metrosexual' with a sneer. In fact, it's far more likely for a guy to be singled out when they look 'a bit rough'. It used to be every man's right to look dishevelled and downtrodden, but those days are fast disappearing. So while I agree, it is a bit strange that I've been so open and honest about my weight-loss plans, I reckon it won't be long before men ditch the football talk at the local pub and start meeting in juice bars to discuss the merits of the Atkins and the Dukan.

Tuesday 23rd April 2013

Every so often I see people walking the busy streets of London, dodging in and out of the crowds, with a book held out in front of them. Part of me wants to knock the book out of their hands and shout 'Your journey isn't over yet! Concentrate on the world around you, bozo', but the other part of me just has to accept the skill that's on show. Somehow they manage to negotiate extremely congested train aisles, stepping over feet, bags and passengers in the process. Then with their free hands they're able to remove tickets, put them through barriers and return them to their rightful place, all without so much as looking up from the book once. I've nicknamed these book-reading street-walkers 'Zombies', mainly because they look like zombies, but also because 'book-reading street-walkers' is a little on the clunky side.

Of course, the advent of various e-reader devices has made this activity somewhat easier to carry out, and thanks to the popularity of said devices, the number of zombies is on the increase. It's the purists whom I respect most though – those able to walk the streets with a good old-fashioned book in their hands, somehow managing to negotiate pedestrians, traffic and page-turning, all without so much as a glance up from the text. I remember my Gramps talking about football in much the same way, saying that it was so much better in the 'Good old days'. I'm not sure what was so 'Good' about pitches resembling ploughed fields and a ball that knocked you out cold every time it came into contact with your head though.

This morning I encountered a zombie of a different kind – one which surpasses the e-reader zombie – a thoroughly modern zombie. Ladies and gentlemen, I give you the 'iPad zombie'. I would have been extremely impressed had he been composing an email or even playing Angry Birds, but alas, he was just watching something on the BBC iPlayer. I weaved my way through the crowd, desperate to get close enough to see exactly what he was watching. What could be so engrossing that it needed to be watched in the zombie state? Some sort of enthralling thriller? Maybe a murder mystery?

No, it was University Challenge! The draw of needing to know which fictional village lies just off the B3980, six miles south of Borchester, was obviously too much.

It was Ambridge, home of 'The Archers', by the way.

Wednesday 24th April 2013

It was a hellish commute home yesterday. There were multiple points failures across the network, resulting in a huge number of cancellations and delays. After waiting for about 25 minutes I gave up on the direct train and started making plans to at least get part-way home. I've learned that I can pretty much get any train to London Bridge from Cannon Street and once there, there's a much greater chance of catching a train towards where I live. The problem with this, however, is that everyone else has the same idea and although there's a better chance of getting a connection, there are ten times as many people trying to do the same thing.

Here's where tactics and a little inside knowledge come into play. I'm going to share with you a little secret. When London Bridge is experiencing overcrowding due to cancellations and delays it can often take over an hour to board a train, and when you finally do, you can guarantee that you'll be standing all the way. Instead of waiting around and trying to squeeze on a train, I've worked out that if I take a train the other way, back towards central London, then out again, I have a greater choice of trains and a guaranteed seat. Even better still, some of those trains don't even stop at London Bridge on the way back, and there's nothing more satisfying than being on a train that's whizzing past the very people I was standing behind only ten minutes earlier.

When I finally put the key in the door, I was surprised to find that the door wouldn't open fully. My wife and daughter were out, so I knew there couldn't be anyone behind the door, so why wouldn't it budge any further? I briefly thought that it might be a burglar, but what kind of burglar hides behind the door you're coming in through? I gave the door a bigger shove and it finally gave way to reveal a plethora of crap on the doormat. Of course I'm talking about junk mail, not faeces; in fact our doormat has been faeces-free ever since I plumped for the trick rather than the treat last Halloween. I remember my wife being totally disgusted and questioning just how that could be considered a trick.

'You try doing it!' I said.

There were five pieces of correspondence. I was going to call them letters, but that would have been inaccurate – these were definitely not letters. They were a combination of leaflets, pamphlets, catalogues and plastic-wrapped magazines, and were advertising double glazing, laser eye surgery, debt management, pizza and God. Incidentally, had I decided to go ahead and buy double glazing from that particular firm, I would almost certainly have required the laser eye surgery, then debt management, then pizza as a pick-me-up, and eventually God.

Why do companies insist on sending so much rubbish through the post? I'm sure it only exists to keep Royal Mail in business. I'm always tempted to ask the postman to hang on just a second and then get him to pop the junk in the recycling on the way out. My dad always used to insist on returning the prepaid envelopes empty, arguing that they will get sick of paying the postage and will stop. 'But they won't know it's you, dad…' I countered. 'Exactly!' he said, 'That's why I've started filling them with untold amounts of crap! If they can do it to me, why can't I do it to them?'

It's not just junk mail that he gets a kick out of – he loves receiving telesales calls as well. He has two ways of dealing with them. If he likes them, he'll keep them on the phone for as long as possible, chatting about anything and everything, before eventually saying that he has no money, but it was lovely just to have someone to chat to. If he takes an immediate dislike to them, he will simply say 'Let me just get the homeowner for you', and then pop the phone on the side and carry on with what he was doing. Every few minutes he'll pick it up and say 'Won't be long', much to his own amusement. His personal record is 48 minutes.

So after arriving home to an empty house after a hellish commute I did what anyone would do in the same situation. I ordered a pizza.

Junk Mail 1 – Andy Leeks 0.

Monday 29th April 2013

How is it possible to have so much love for your own child, but so much hatred for somebody else's? The weather wasn't the best this weekend, so we decided to take our daughter to an indoor activity centre. It's a wonderful name for what is essentially a dilapidated warehouse set in the scenic surroundings of an industrial estate. I'm sure most of you have heard of the Wacky Warehouse; well, this weekend we seem to have somehow stumbled across their poorer cousin, the Chavvy Warehouse.

After a very one-sided transaction in which we traded five pounds and a pair of shoes for a paper wristband, we made our way to a table, empty save for the crisp packets and a plethora of brown stains. The room was filled with the echoing sounds of excited children and it reminded me of the atmosphere when you go swimming, only with the smell of chlorine replaced by the subtle aroma of socks and Wotsits.

Smells have always conjured up powerful emotions for me – the smell of freshly cut grass takes me straight back to being seven years old, kicking a ball around the park, the smell of roast beef takes me back to lazy Sundays around my Nan's house, and the smell of freshly baked bread always reminds me of being told to shut up while being pushed down the bakery aisle at the supermarket in a trolley.

Anyway, it was with genuine fear that we agreed to release our daughter into the wild, and in order to get through the next hour or so we decided we were going to need some coffee. Some very strong coffee. Once purchased, I became an unwitting participant in the game 'dodge the hyperactive child', ultimately failing and adding to the stains on the table. Any thought of sitting back and relaxing soon disappeared as we watched child after child bump, push and even tread on our daughter.

Every parent's nightmare is to hear that their child is being bullied, and here I was effectively watching it play out in front of me. I looked around, fully expecting to see swathes of parents stepping forward to reprimand their children, but I was met with nothing but a wall of Bella and Woman's Own. At that exact moment, all I wanted to do was round up all of the children who had bumped, pushed and trod on my daughter and give them a piece of my mind. In fact, I was prepared to go one stage further and give them a taste of their own medicine by bumping, pushing and treading on them back, just to see how they liked it.

It was around four or five seconds into my crazy thoughts of retribution when I realised that what I was considering effectively amounted to child abuse. Even Robin Hood never resorted to targeting children. I felt truly ashamed, and I'm pleased that the moment passed and I avoided the temptation of tripping up little Tyler or Courtney.

Strangely, it wasn't the prospect of a lengthy prison sentence which allowed me to move my thoughts elsewhere; it was simply the realisation that nothing is ever settled by resorting to violence. Oh, and the fact that Tyler's dad was the size of a house.

Tuesday 30ᵗʰ April 2013

In order to get to Cannon Street station, I have to negotiate half a mile of London's busy streets, and as I'm too tight to buy an extension to my Gold card, it's a journey I have to carry out using my own two feet.

I hate that half-mile walk!

It's not that I hate walking. Walking I like. It's the crowds, the traffic and often the weather that I hate. If someone said that I had to do a 500-mile walk, but they could guarantee that there wouldn't be a single person with a bag on wheels, that the walk would be completely free of cars ready to kill me at a moment's notice, and that the weather would be pleasant at all times, I would sign up tomorrow. The half-mile walk should take no more than fifteen minutes, but it often takes up to half an hour thanks to idiotic pedestrians, kamikaze taxi drivers and the lamentable English weather.

Yesterday evening, however, everything fell into place. Spring had finally sprung and it had the pleasant side-effect of clearing London of its idiots and kamikaze drivers. It felt amazing to have the warmth of the sun on my back for what must have been the first time this year. One of the first things I do as I complete my walk and reach the steps at Cannon Street station is to check whether there are any delays, and I was delighted to see that displayed on the departure board in front of me was a full set of 'On Time's.

I walked up the platform surveying the seats, and as if to prove that absolutely everything at that moment was right with the world, my preferred seat was empty. I sat down, happy and content, and decided to reach for my iPod. On the very rare occasions I get to listen to my iPod I tend to listen to podcasts or audiobooks, but yesterday was definitely a music day. I selected the music app and at exactly the same time as I hit the shuffle button, the train lurched forward. It happened with such uncanny timing that for a very brief moment, I was sure I was in control of the train.

Of course I knew this was completely stupid, but stranger things have happened, so in order to test my theory I tried to perform an emergency stop. I pressed down hard on the stop button and braced, but of course nothing happened – the train just carried on accelerating. Bugger.

As ridiculous as it was, I was genuinely disappointed when it didn't work. I remember as a child being convinced that I had the power to turn off people's lights in their houses, simply by staring at them. I would look out of my bedroom window and stare at the lit windows in the houses opposite, partly because I was thirteen and starting to develop hormones, but also because I genuinely thought I had the power to turn them off. After about twenty minutes, a light in the distance would go off and I would immediately take the credit. The thought that someone might have been getting ready for bed and had simply turned off the light in order to get their head down for the night genuinely never crossed my mind.

I also remember spending my childhood asking people to think of a card, boldly claiming that it was the seven of hearts, getting it wrong and then moving onto the next person. Eventually, someone would think of the seven of hearts and I became a mindreading genius.

I tried pressing the stop button one last time. It still didn't work. Double bugger!

I consoled myself by pressing fast forward as the train sped up, trying to convince myself that it was all down to me, but I knew in my heart of hearts that I'd failed…

As my dreams of being the next James Bond subsided, the music softly rolled into my head and I was immediately imbued with a beautiful, peaceful state of mind. The train rounded the corner at the exact point at which Bill Withers was exclaiming just how lovely a day it was, and I was greeted with one of the most spectacular views in London – Tower Bridge at sunset. It stood there, proud and magnificent, as the River Thames shimmered calmly in its wake. Newer London landmarks, although striking, can often seem arrogant and domineering whereas Tower Bridge has always remained elegant and dependable.

It's amazing how emotive music can be in certain situations. There are times when I'll be listening to a certain song and I'll immediately be transported to another place entirely. It could be Venice, Paris, New York or even Margate; certain songs have the power to transport me anywhere without warning. It's not just places either – sometimes I'll be transported back in time to various family gatherings, birthdays and, more soberingly, funerals.

I haven't been able to listen to 'Sailing' by Rod Stewart or 'Live Forever' by Oasis ever since they were played at funerals I attended. There are certain songs that are able to transport me to a completely different reality. I'm not sure if anyone else has experienced this, but every so often the perfect song will come on at the perfect time. Suddenly, the music becomes the soundtrack to my life and I feel like a movie star during one of those incredibly cheesy Hollywood end-of-movie montages, where the guy gets the girl. It's a very rare moment in my life when I suddenly feel cool, confident and desirable, and can forget for a brief moment that I'm a bald, overweight nobody. It doesn't take long before I catch a glimpse of my reflection in a nearby shop window and the startling reality sinks back in.

Without warning, Bill Withers was interrupted by a screech of brakes, followed by a loud clunk as everything on the train came to an immediate halt. I quickly checked to see if I had inadvertently pressed the stop button and before I was able to register my disappointment, the toilet door started to slowly open. The loud clunk was the sound of the toilet seat crashing down, and it was immediately evident that this had caused the toilet's occupant some difficulty.

Now, as a man, going for a wee on a train is extremely difficult. It's one of the few public toilet situations where women get a better deal than men. Weeing into a train toilet is already a tricky process for a man, as the toilet is effectively a moving target, but you also need to factor in the handicap. In normal circumstances, a wee is a two-hand job, but on a train, one hand is immediately removed from the situation and put on 'balance duties'. This man had obviously struggled – there was clear evidence that he had not only failed to hit the target, but had experienced a couple of messy misfires too. He nonchalantly made his way down the carriage as if nothing had happened, all the while completely unaware that his wee was following him.

Disgusted and faintly annoyed that Bill was still harping on about what a lovely day it was, I pressed the skip button.

Artist: The Clash

Song: Should I Stay or Should I Go

As the wee snaked its way slowly up the carriage, mere inches from my feet, I made my decision. Time to go!

Wednesday 8th May 2013

I always feel slightly sorry for twins, but slightly envious at the same time. Childhood twins will never get to experience the joys of having their own birthday cake, but I suppose this is offset by the fact that at least they'll always have someone to play pass the parcel with. I'd love to be a twin. In fact for about two years I actually had one. Don't worry – this isn't the start of a tragic tale in which I go on to explain the struggle of dealing with the loss of a sibling at such a young age, it's simply the tale of an attention seeking eleven-year-old.

For some reason, when I moved to big school (I've been informed that it's now referred to as Year 7) I had an unfortunate urge to show off in what was simply a desperate bid to try to fit in. (This is something which hasn't really changed in the twenty-odd years since). Unfortunately I wasn't good looking, I wasn't cool and I wasn't willing to gain street-cred by getting into trouble, so I was basically an ugly, geeky nerd. It seemed like the only time anyone ever called my name during that first year was for the register. I don't know why, but during one of those early weeks in the first term, I decided to let it be known that I was in fact a twin myself. I had seen the attention other twins got and I wanted some of the action. Obviously, the major flaw in my plan was that I didn't actually have a twin, and the lack of an actual twin to back up my story was fairly inconvenient right from the very start. So the story went that my twin and I didn't get on so my parents had decided we should go to different schools.

It was fun for a few weeks. People would come up to me and say that they'd seen my twin while out at the weekend, when it was in fact me, and there was even a time when I was approached out of school and pretended to be my twin. Often though, when pressed on the finer details, I would panic and come up with stupid answers, like the very first question I was asked, which was 'What's his name?'

'Andre,' I said.

Now, at that time, on the very rare occasions that people did talk to me, they called me by my full name, Andrew, so what I had in fact done is provide them with my own name minus one letter.

'Andre?' came the reply. 'Like Andrew, without the W?'

'So it seems,' I said, panicking.

In the following weeks I was forced to come up with more and more ridiculous lies, until I finally came unstuck. In one of the more full-on question and answer sessions, I had managed to fabricate that my twin brother Andre went to Parmiters School and had been playing so well for their football team that he'd been offered a trial with Watford. 'What position does he play?' asked one of my newfound friends. 'Right wing,' I stated, going for the opposite wing to the one I tended to play on. A week later, the fixtures went up on the PE board and my worst fears came true – we were playing Parmiters away. So now I'm not only playing football against a prodigy of a twin brother who doesn't exist, I'm going head-to-head with him as he supposedly plays on the right wing, and I play on the left.

I tried to explain that my brother couldn't play because he had an important training session with Watford, but it all came out in the wash as one of our team was friends with one of their team out of school. It's amazing how quickly it was forgotten really, and I'm glad to say that people seemed to treat me as quirky rather than dangerously weird.

I've always found it odd when twins are dressed the same. Obviously as babies it's fairly inevitable that they're going to be dressed in similar clothes, but as they get older I think it's important for them to have their own identities. There's nothing worse than seeing thirty-year-old twins wearing matching dresses, especially if one of them is a bloke. In fact, the reason for today's twin-heavy chapter is that on this very train this morning, I saw a pair of identical twins in their mid- to late twenties wearing identical clothes. I thought for a moment how wonderful it would be if they were in fact pulling off an elaborate scam on an employer by only doing half a job each, but I soon realised how stupid an idea that was. Why would they? They would only have one income between the two of them, and why on earth would they both be travelling in together? Surely one would stay home each day and they would take it in turns.

After staring at them for longer than I should have, I realised that there were in fact minor differences, namely in the detailing on their shoes and handbags. I wondered why they'd gone to so much effort to look like each other, only to slip up on the accessories. Maybe they do it to show that they still have their own identity, but

I think it's far more likely that, as women, they simply love handbags and shoes and this way they get to double their options.

Thursday 9th May 2013

As you know, I'm a commuter. I've commuted to work for a little over ten years. The truth is that I hate commuting, and I've hated commuting for a little under ten years. I remember the excitement of the first few weeks, and I can honestly say that I enjoyed commuting back then. I had a magic gold-coloured card, which got me on and off any train I cared to board and in and out of any station I cared to visit, seemingly without costing me anything. It was on the 25th day of my first month with my employer, however, that I was to find out that the season ticket application form I had carefully filled in on day one was in fact a legally binding contract allowing my employer to deduct the cost of my weight in gold from my salary each month as payment for my journeys.

The first thing I did was to check whether the season ticket was in fact made of real gold. It wasn't. Believe me, had it been, it would have been placed straight into one of those Cash for Gold envelopes. I'd fallen for the biggest swindle since my Dad told me that the ice cream van only plays the music when it's run out of ice cream.

I was originally attracted to London because of the allure of the big city, the big lights and the chance to make something of myself. It was only a few weeks later that I realised that what I'd actually done is add fifteen hours to my working week and developed not only mild asthma, but also a completely irrational hatred of tourists. I decided to look on the bright side. Yes, I'd inevitably die younger; yes, I had to see a councillor about my anger issues, and yes, every so often I'd have to stand because someone was old or fertile, but at least I had my little gold card – my key to the city, the key that didn't just open doors, but barriers!

My joy quickly turned to despair, however, as I found it incredibly easy to lose my little gold friend. The next few years would see me lose my little key to the city on no fewer than twelve occasions and as it's incredibly expensive and time consuming to get it replaced, I decided, for a little while at least, to try travelling a different way. Some time in early 2010 I decided to trade in my precious gold card and became the owner proud owner of an Oyster Card. A chunk of precious metal exchanged for a slimy mollusc!

I wonder why they decided to call it an Oyster Card. I'm assuming some apparently clever guy with a white shirt, loosened tie and thick-rimmed glasses was workshopping the theme 'The World's your Oyster!' But this is the London Underground, and although Hackney can often seem like another world, it is in fact secreted in East London. The furthest anyone can get on the tube is Chesham, so I'm not sure Mr Ad-Man was on the right track. No pun intended.

Having Googled Oysters, I can tell you that they are filter feeders which draw water in over their gills through the beating of cilia. Suspended plankton and food particles are trapped in the mucus of the gills and from there transported to the mouth, where they are eaten, digested and expelled as faeces. So if we were looking for an analogy here, you could say that commuters are simply the plankton, trapped in the Underground's mucus, eventually being expelled as faeces! Well done Mr Ad-Man, I couldn't have put it better myself.

I'd like to add that going for an Oyster card was another one of my 'good ideas gone bad'. Another false economy. I'd worked out that I could save £1,500 a year by travelling from a different station and using an Oyster card. However, in order to get to the other station I needed transport, so I needed to get myself a motorbike. I went on to spend £100 on a CBT course (Compulsory Basic Training: a basic course that you're required to take if you want to ride a motorbike under a certain classification) and £1,000 on a second-hand motorbike. I thought that it would take quite a few months to make a saving, but once I passed that point, it would be plain sailing from there on in and I'd be saving £125 every month. Unfortunately, I didn't factor in the £1,800 I ended up spending on the bike in the first six months. In that short time the exhaust fell off, the brakes failed, the electrics failed, the key snapped in the ignition and I had three flat tyres. During those six months I was on first-name terms with the AA, and I found out that not all of them are very nice men. I can also say with absolute certainty that there were weeks when I pushed that bloody bike further than I rode it.

Just as I had made up my mind to give it up and go back to my trusty Gold Card, the bike had one last surprise in store for me: it decided to slide from under me as I was going at low speed around a busy roundabout. There was no oil spill, the brakes hadn't failed and I wasn't speeding – it seemed the bike just didn't want me riding it, and it flicked me off like a wild stallion, fed up with the idiot trying to ride it.

The only positive I could take from the experience is that it happened on the way to the petrol station, so at least I saved nearly a tenner on petrol.

Monday 13th May 2013

This morning I overheard the following conversation:

Stranger 1:   'So how was your weekend?'

Stranger 2:   'Not so good actually.'

Stranger 1:   'Why?'

Stranger 2:   'I've broken up with my girlfriend and things are just awful.'

Stranger 1:   'I'm really sorry to hear that. Did it happen this weekend?'

Stranger 2:   'No, it kicked off a couple of weeks ago, but we're still living together and she's being such a …'

Unfortunately, that's all I managed to overhear. I've no idea what she was being. Was she being such a good sport? Was she being such a pain in the arse? It's highly likely that she was being such a bitch, but I will never ever know. I'll never know because I was in a lift with them, and at the crucial point in the conversation the lift arrived at my floor.

In fact, if I'm being entirely truthful, the conversation actually went like this:

Stranger 1:   'So how was your weekend?'

Stranger 2:   'Not so good actually.'

Me: 'Excuse me – can I have floor number three, please?'

Stranger 1:   'Why?'

Me: 'Because that's where I work…'

Stranger1:   'Sorry, I was talking to him. Why – what happened?'

Stranger 2:   'I've broken up with my girlfriend and things are just awful.'

Stranger 1:   'I'm really sorry to hear that. Did it happen this weekend?'

Stranger 2:   'No, it kicked off a couple of weeks ago, but we're still living together and she's being such a …'

Lift: 'Ding'……floor number three.

I was extremely tempted to let the doors shut and carry on up to the fifth floor to hear the conclusion, but how would I ever explain that one? I couldn't tell them I'd made a mistake – they'd already questioned it once. I thought about running up to the fifth to catch the tail-end, but there was too much risk of being spotted, so, searching for closure, I was left to make up the ending myself. Well, it turns out that she really was a total bitch. Not content with cutting up his best suit and sleeping with his best friend, she deleted the unwatched Match of the Day on the Sky Plus. What a bitch!

When I got back to my desk, I started to get a little bit paranoid. It was almost too perfect. Within three seconds of being stuck in a lift with two strangers, I'm privy to the intimate details of a difficult breakup. Had I been the victim of a prank? Had they set me up? I bet they do it every day to make people uncomfortable, just for kicks! Today it's a difficult breakup; tomorrow it'll be erectile dysfunction.

Tuesday 14ᵗʰ May 2013

Whilst staring bleary eyed into the bathroom mirror this morning, I was shocked to discover my very first grey hairs. It wasn't so much the fact that I had a couple of grey hairs that shocked me, it was more the location. The hair on the top of my head has long since gone, with the hair on every other inch of my body stubbornly holding on. I've never worried about going grey and so I've never bothered to check, but this morning the rogue grey hairs were difficult to miss, even as I squinted in the bright morning light. The hairs in question are secreted in my right eyebrow and after giving them a tug, switching the light on and off and soaking them with water, I can confirm that they are definitely grey hairs and neither a rogue piece of fluff nor a trick of the light. I can confirm that my eyebrows are going grey.

I'd always assumed that my eyebrows would stay dark. Eyebrows always seem to be the last to go. Look at poor old Alistair Darling (if you don't know him, he's worth Googling). With my lack of head hair, I was resigned to my facial hair and even my chest hair changing colour at some point, but not my eyebrows. I can't even begin to imagine just how stupid I'll look with dark facial hair and grey eyebrows. The reverse Darling! People always say that going grey can make you feel distinguished and even dignified, but I'm certain those people are referring to the hair on people's heads and not the hair above their eyes. Right now going grey above the eyes is not so much a reason to feel distinguished and dignified, more a reason to feel anguished and terrified.

I think the real reason I'm starting to fret is that I have particularly bushy eyebrows. I remember an old school friend, Ellie, saying I reminded her of Noel Gallagher and at the time I was extremely flattered because I was the lead in the school musical. I had assumed, wrongly it turned out, that she was referring to my voice, when she was in fact referring to my eyebrows. It's with a certain amount of embarrassment that I find myself contemplating plucking my eyebrows, having spent ten years explaining to my wife that men who pluck their eyebrows should be ashamed of themselves.

If I do decide to pluck though, where will it end? Two grey hairs have sprouted overnight. If it was to continue at that pace then I'd have no eyebrows by Christmas, and as weird as I might look with grey eyebrows, I'd certainly look a lot weirder with none. On the plus side, if they do go fully grey by Christmas, at least they'll make my Santa outfit look a tad more realistic.

Wednesday 15th May 2013

Who'd have thought it? You wait ages for a chapter on lifts and two come along at once. As per usual, two of the three lifts at work are 'Currently undergoing maintenance'. The phrase 'currently undergoing maintenance' is hugely misleading. I've undertaken my own research and I can exclusively reveal that there has never been any 'current' maintenance work being carried out; there's only ever future maintenance work to be carried out. There was a time where the sign would read 'Lift out of order, engineer en route', and after three days a hand-written response would be affixed to it, asking 'What, on a boat from New Zealand?' I suppose that the new approach, while being a complete lie, is at least a little more encouraging.

With only one lift working, not only do I have to wait an age for it to arrive, but when it finally does, I have to share it with at least four other equally lazy people. I'm prepared to describe us as lazy because the building we work in only has six floors. When the day eventually arrives when all three lifts are 'Currently undergoing maintenance' (and it's definitely a case of when and not if) I'm pretty sure that 75% of the people who work in our building would rather wait for the maintenance to be completed than actually have a crack at the stairs. Within hours the reception area would look like a community centre during a natural disaster. In my defence, I do have a simple rule which I've always stuck to. If will always go up in the lift, but come down via the stairs. Apart from the exercise, it's good practice in case there's ever a fire.

This morning I waited about five minutes for the lift to arrive, and by the time it did, there were five other people keen to take the lift up with me. I was the first in the queue, so I made my way to the back of the lift and began to remove my rucksack from my back. In another futile effort to get fit and healthy, I'd crammed my bag full of gym gear and fruit, but before I had a chance to fully remove it, I was squeezed into a position which meant that removal was not an option. The lift is mirrored on all sides, meaning that everyone can see everyone at every angle, so there's no chance of pulling a funny face, even when the person to one's left has extremely questionable personal hygiene. With so many mirrors, the lift often reminds me of the hall of mirrors at the fairground, only in this version I seem to be fat in every single one…

Suddenly, without warning, a strange noise reverberated around the lift. I know what you're thinking. In a way, I would rather that had happened. A fart would have been a welcome relief compared to what actually did happen. The noise continued for a few seconds, until eventually everyone turned their attention to me. They weren't so much accusing looks, they were more quizzical. Eventually, I too had to turn my own attention to me, and luckily I had the mirrors with which to do it. The noise was a weird kind of high pitched rumbling. It sounded a little like a coffee percolator. All of a sudden, smoke started emanating from my rucksack, and it was at exactly that point when the doors opened to the second floor and my five lift buddies ran for cover. I held up my hands as if to prove that I wasn't a threat and, as I did so, the noise and the smoke immediately stopped. Suddenly the smell hit me and I started to gag, so I too emerged from the lift, to what can only be described as an extremely hostile audience.

'It's okay.' I said. 'It's not a bomb.' I'm pleased to say that is the first and almost certainly the last time I will ever utter those words.

I was confident that it wasn't a bomb because I had suddenly recognised the smell. It wasn't the smell of burning; it was the fresh and pleasant smell of my antiperspirant. What looked like smoke was actually the chalky vapour escaping from the can as it was being squashed up against the back of the lift.

While it's true that I gave five people the biggest fright of their life, I also like to think that some good did come of it. You see, there's no way anyone could have stood more than a few seconds in that lift for the next few hours, so there should have been more people getting some exercise by taking the stairs. Happy to help.

Thursday 16th May 2013

Okay, I'm just going to come out with it. Last night I ended up getting locked in a train toilet with a stranger. As I've never harboured an interest in becoming a politician, it's not something I ever expected to end up admitting to. In truth, there's a fairly simple explanation, but then again there have been countless people who have uttered those words and still ended up with a hefty sentence.

It all started on the 19:19 from London Bridge to Dover Priory. The train pulled in and was as busy as ever. At times like this I head for my usual carriage – the one with the toilet – as it affords more room when the train is standing room only. I managed to squeeze through the crowds and perched at the end of the carriage between the toilet and the sliding doors to the next carriage. When standing is the only option, it's as good a place as any, toilet smell aside. I got on with my usual routine of checking, re-writing and editing my morning's work, albeit at half the pace as I had to do it standing up, when suddenly I heard someone shouting. I've been a witness to many shouting incidents on trains, but they usually take place on the last train home and involve an exceptionally large quantity of alcohol, so I was a little confused.

'Snacks, crisps, drinks or coffees, anyone?'

I looked down the carriage to see a woman in her late fifties edging her way slowly down the aisle. I desperately wanted to point out that technically crisps are snacks and coffee is a drink. I wondered how many times she'd uttered those six words when four would have done. Companies are always looking to make cuts, and I'd just spotted an opportunity to cut 33% right there. I didn't actually say anything because I was too pre-occupied with worrying about what was going to happen when she reached me. I was stuck between the toilet and the sliding doors and there was nowhere for me to go in order to get out of her way. Suddenly, the toilet door started to open.

The toilet door in question was an automatic sliding door operated by a series of buttons, and the toilet itself was a spacious elliptical space catering for disabled passengers and baby-changing. A gentleman slightly further up the carriage stepped into the toilet and, with nowhere else to go, I did the same. You can see exactly where this is going, and exactly how innocent we both were, but at the time it did nothing to assuage the sheer embarrassment of seeing those sliding doors slowly closing as the rest of the carriage looked on. Neither of us could look each other in the eye as we accepted the inevitable, and it was left to my toilet companion to hit the door release button as if his life depended on it. But unfortunately, as the doors slowly opened, the lady with the trolley was still blocking our exit. Annoyingly someone had decided to purchase a coffee and, with a packed train ahead of her, this lady wasn't exactly rushing to complete the transaction. Seconds later, the doors were on the move again and I was once again trapped in the toilet with the stranger.

I'm pleased to say that when the door opened for the second time the coast was clear and we were each able to get on with our lives, albeit heavily scarred by the incident. I like to think that I'm a fairly normal guy, living a fairly normal life, but how often does a normal person have to explain to total strangers that he is neither a terrorist nor a pervert, all in the space of 24 hours?

Monday 20th May 2013

While I was rinsing my daughter's hair in the bath last night, she asked me a question.

'Daddy, why is it so dark?'

This simple question reduced me to fits of laughter, and it took a long while for me to respond with 'Try opening your eyes.'

'Wow, magic!' she exclaimed.

As I continued to laugh, my daughter laughed, and after what seemed like five minutes she suddenly stopped and said with a completely straight face 'Daddy, what's so funny?'

They say that children say the funniest things, and my daughter is no different. My wife is currently fifteen weeks pregnant and our daughter has just begun to grasp the fact that mummy has a baby in her tummy. We told her that mummy's tummy is getting bigger because there's a baby growing inside. Her response?

'Is daddy having a baby too?'

Well that stung.

I remember a time when we were returning from a walk to our local shops and our daughter was getting tired, so I picked her up and popped her on my shoulders. Now, what happened next may sound like something out of a Laurel and Hardy movie, but it genuinely happened. A little further down the path there was a low-hanging tree branch and without thinking I shouted 'Duck!' Of course, rather than bending out of the way, all she did was shout 'Where?'

It's not just children who say and do funny things though. I myself have been guilty of a few clangers in the past.

The single most stupid thing I have ever been guilty of is trying to outrun the speed of light. In our old house we would often just have a small lamp on in the evening, and it was situated at the far end of the living room. In order to turn it off I would have to turn on the main light to ensure I could find my way back across the living room. But one night I forgot to turn on the main light. I realised as I got to the switch for the lamp and, without thinking, switched the lamp off and ran.

For some unfathomable reason, I had decided that it was entirely possible for me to get to the other side of the room before the light disappeared. Of course, around four steps in, I realised I was in complete darkness and running at full tilt towards exceptionally hard objects such as walls and doors, so I just froze on the spot.

I actually burst out laughing there and then, in the dark and completely on my own, as I realised just how ridiculous the situation was. I slowly felt my way out of the room, quietly tiptoed up the stairs and slipped into bed thinking I'd got away with it, until my wife asked 'What's so funny?'

Wednesday 22nd May 2013

After keeping quiet for a very long time, I've finally decided to speak out. Every day I watch as they hog the spare seats, bump into people and constantly trip people over. To make matters worse, they don't even pay a bloody fare. I am of course talking about the most frustrating recent addition to the morning and evening commute: the bag on wheels.

As commuters, we managed to get along just fine with our briefcases, rucksacks and shoulder bags, until around five years ago when everything changed. Suddenly, instead of being reserved for an annual trip abroad, bags on wheels started to accompany people on their daily commute. The addition of wheels to large suitcases was an extremely sensible idea – it's often hard to find a luggage trolley and with the average airport terminal being roughly the size of Belgium, they can be a welcome relief. What I cannot work out, however, is why wheels need to be added to business bags and briefcases. Why are people suddenly unable to carry the combined weight of a laptop, notepad and pot of low-fat hummus? Why is it that big shots in the city are perfectly capable of carrying out million-pound takeovers but are completely unable to carry their own bags?

I have always maintained that they are dangerous, and this morning my point was proved. After dodging, swerving and stepping over the usual five or six bags on wheels, I finally made it out of the station and onto the main road. There was a little bit of traffic, owing to some roadworks which were taking place and a temporary traffic light system which was in operation. As I crossed the road, I saw a woman coming towards me, followed by a very strange looking dog. The dog in question was black, around five feet tall and was being dragged on a yellow lead. A few seconds later I realised that it wasn't a dog at all – it was in fact a temporary traffic light which was being dragged into the road by a bag on wheels and its owner. She didn't notice until the traffic light was half way across the road, and I was very close to saying to her 'I reckon that with that kind of strength, you'd be able to manage picking up your bag and carrying it.'

Amazingly, she didn't do what any sane person would have done in the same situation, which is to replace the traffic light as quickly as possible and get the hell out of there, oh no. She decided to have it out with the traffic light, right there and then in the middle of the road. Sensing the argument was a little one-sided, a workman stepped forward to help the traffic light out, but she simply switched her volley of abuse onto him.

The woman gesticulated wildly and trudged off with a final flurry of abuse as the workman wheeled the traffic light back into position. While I watched the workman carefully place the traffic light back where it belonged, I couldn't help feeling that what I'd just witnessed was the perfect visual metaphor for almost every one of my failed relationships. Somehow I manage to embarrass the lady in question, she flies off the handle, my friend tries to come to the rescue, she storms off, and my friend is left to pick up the pieces. Not that I'm projecting.

While careless bag-on-wheels owners are annoying, they are not the worst kind of owner. The worst is the experienced bag-on-wheels owner. The person who has made wheeling bags into an art form. Somehow, and I have no idea how, they are able to produce the handle with a flick of the wrist and be on their way with a simple but flamboyant pirouette. 'Yes,' you think, as they approach the barriers, 'but try negotiating that with your fancy bag-wheeling moves.' And then somehow they bring the bag up beside them and with a twist of the wrist bring the bag round in front of them and push it through the barriers, all in one fluid movement, only to return it to its original position with another devastatingly effectively manoeuvre.

As annoying as it is to watch an experienced bag-on-wheels owner negotiating the station concourse, I'll always know that my plain, old, boring carrying-my-bag-by-the-handle method will always be far superior to theirs. It's for the same reason that I was never afraid of the Daleks.

Stairs!

Wednesday 29th May 2013

Sometimes I think to myself 'Wouldn't it just be easier to live life as a woman?' Don't get me wrong, I know that women have it pretty tough; there's the pain of childbirth, the frustration of always having to queue for a toilet, and the constant disappointment of never having enough shoes, but I would happily suffer all of that if it meant I no longer had to suffer the indignity and embarrassment of the male embrace.

When women meet there's always a simple, effortless embrace. It's often a kiss on the cheek followed by a hug and, depending on the distance travelled or the time since the last meeting, it may well be preceded by a shriek and succeeded by some jumping around. There's never a moment when things can get awkward.

With guys, however, the embrace is an altogether different prospect. It's never simple or effortless. First there's that initial stage when a man spots his male friend from a distance, but, being men, they mustn't actually say anything. So they simply raise at the very most a hand, but usually just an eyebrow, or give a nod. Women on the other hand are free to do what they want, and it seems that it's entirely acceptable for them to shout 'Oh my god!' at the top of their voices.

After the initial stage of doing everything they can to ignore each other for three hundred yards, then comes the difficult choice. It's a crossroads, but instead of left, right or straight ahead, the options are handshake, hug or high five. Actually, strictly there are four options, the fourth one being to do absolutely nothing, which is essentially the same as pulling the handbrake and turning off the engine.

It often depends on the type of person you're meeting – whether it be a member of your family, a long term friend, a work colleague or the most difficult to gauge, the FOF. The FOF is the 'Friend of a Friend' and, as a guy, what you do in that first meeting can determine whether or not you end up being upgraded to a fully fledged 'F'.

No matter how many times we meet male friends, we men will never feel truly comfortable with the embrace. We're left with a lifetime of stuttering handshakes, high fives and hugs, often winding up shaking hands poised for a high five, slapping hands that are poised for a shake, or most embarrassingly of all, hugging those who have opted for the handshake.

What makes a mockery of it all, however, is that it only takes two or three beers for the awkwardness to disappear and then suddenly it's as if we're making up for lost time. It will often start with a backslap, perhaps followed by a friendly headlock or head rub, but it then quickly turns into full-blown bear-hugs. If there's a sport involved as well as the alcohol, and it happens that your team has just taken the lead, it's even acceptable to extend this open display of affection to complete strangers.

As strange as women can be sometimes, I don't think there would ever be a situation where they would find themselves bear-hugging a stranger when only two hours previously they were unable to look their best friend in the eye.

Friday 31ˢᵗ May 2013

It's Friday and, rather than thanking Crunchie, I'm going to go home this evening and pay my very own tribute to Ben and Jerry, Haagen-Dazs and possibly even Krispy Kreme. I've been feeling terrible all week, battling the telltale symptoms: the slightly scratchy feeling in my throat, the slightly runny nose and the occasional cough. Yes, I'm afraid I'm currently suffering from the dreaded 'Man Flu'.

It was announced yesterday that it has been the coldest spring for fifty years and, typically, I managed to get through that period without so much as a tickly nose, but as soon as the sun made its long-awaited appearance this week, I immediately succumbed to the dreaded MF. My daughter has been climbing the walls for weeks, desperate to get outside and do something, yet here we are on a beautiful sunny Friday evening, with good weather being predicted for the whole weekend, and all I want to do is crawl into my warm bed and eat ice cream. I remember Alanis Morrisette famously warbled on about 10,000 spoons when all she needed was a knife, and meeting the man of her dreams and then meeting his beautiful wife. Strangely, however, she called the song 'Ironic', when it should have been called 'Sod's Law' or perhaps 'Shitty Luck'. In fact the only thing that was ironic about the song was the fact that it was called 'Ironic'.

We all suffer from 'sod's law' at some time in our lives, but I honestly think that I suffer more than most. I suppose that's just 'sod's law' in itself. There was a time when I won a family trip to Euro Disney on the radio and we couldn't go in the end because our daughter didn't have a passport and we couldn't get it sorted out in time. That said, call me a terrible husband and father, I did end up going on that trip with a couple of friends, leaving my wife and child at home. Sure, the family couldn't come with me, which was certainly 'sod's law', but not going at all would have been plain stupid. In fact, isn't it ironic that three balding, thirty-something men decided to go on a 'family' trip to Euro Disney with not one child between them?

Just recently I booked tickets to see a comedian who was filming his latest DVD release. The tickets were good value as it was being recorded on a weekday evening, so I decided to get four tickets. Unfortunately only one person I invited could make it, so I ended up with two extra tickets which I didn't need but had already paid for. To add insult to injury, I got an email on the way to the theatre, telling me that I had won an extra two tickets in a prize draw. I couldn't help but feel that they were struggling to fill the theatre due to the unsociable timing, and as they were recording the DVD they were desperate to fill it. So somehow I'd managed to pay for four tickets, been given six, but only required two.

Well, as Alanis also said, life has a funny, funny way of helping you out, so let's hope that my good friends Ben and Jerry can shift this awful Man Flu so I can enjoy the sun tomorrow.

Monday 17ᵗʰ June 2013

As you can see from the date of today's entry, there's been a significant gap since the last one. A lot has happened in the last couple of weeks, and I'll try my best to describe exactly what's gone on in the next few chapters. My ultimate goal with the creation of this book series was to write an informative and amusing commentary on the life of an average commuter. Some people have expressed disappointment that these books are not solely crammed with amusing train-based anecdotes, and if I'm being entirely truthful, it disappoints me too. The problem is, however, that a lot of the time my journeys pass without anything at all to report on. There's nothing amusing or anecdotal at all; in fact, they could easily be described as mundane or even boring. There's only one thing more boring than experiencing a journey like that, and that's reading about it.

I assure you that whenever something amusing or intriguing presents itself on one of my many commutes, it finds itself written into the book; and when I experience one of my many mundane trips, you'll be presented with various miscellaneous musings that either my life or my imagination conjures up. But for now, you'll have to put up with this…

It was Monday 3rd of June, and I was getting fed up with the world. I'm a fairly optimistic person and it's rare for me to feel down. It takes a hell of a lot for me to feel stressed, and my wife often jokes that I suffer from some sort of weird condition that means I only ever see the positives. I doubt there is an official condition, but if they're looking for someone to come up with a name, I'd like to recommend the word Misteroptimistic. Obviously it would be Missoptimistic for female sufferers, and child sufferers would most probably suffer from Minoroptimistic. I could try to come up with a word for elderly sufferers, but what would be the point? There would never be any recorded cases. What person over 75 ever sees the positive in anything? I'm not having a go; in fact I'm certain that I myself will have a dramatic change of attitude when I find myself having to divide 90% of my waking hours between doctors' waiting rooms, post offices and chemists. They say that the optimist sees the glass as half full and pessimist sees it as half empty. I, on the other hand, would be looking for a tap and a bigger glass. But it's fair to say that on the 3rd of June, the water had evaporated and I was left holding an empty glass. I can't put my finger on it exactly, but everything just seemed so pointless. I'd never really felt that way before. Nothing was able to raise my mood – not the sound of my daughter's voice, the smell of fresh coffee and, perhaps the least surprising of all, not the sight of my wife first thing in the morning.

I made my way in to work as normal and tried my best to get lost in my work, so as to shift my awful mood. It worked for about ten minutes before I found myself once again feeling like the world was against me. I'm lucky to have never suffered depression, but I have been around people who have. It's one of those terrible illnesses which a lot of people never truly regard as an actual illness. People often think that someone who suffers from depression just needs a pat on the back, or worse a damned good talking to, but it's far more complex than that. I definitely wasn't suffering from depression, but it's fair to say that I had even more sympathy for sufferers then. However, by the end of my lunch hour on the 3rd of June I was absolutely convinced that I wasn't suffering from depression, my mood had been completely lifted, and instead of feeling down I was feeling hugely excited.

This newfound excitement was down to the last-minute family holiday I'd just booked to Cyprus. We'd be off in less than 48 hours. I'd realised that I probably just needed a holiday, and it had been five years since my wife and I last had a proper holiday abroad. Five years might not seem that long to some, but you have to consider that my wife is currently pregnant and it will almost certainly be another five years before we have another chance. So I figured we'd better seize the opportunity to have a relaxing break, and as my wife isn't currently working and the company I work for are understanding and flexible, we were able to get an incredibly good last-minute deal.

Tuesday 18th June 2013

I've always been impulsive. It's one of my major weaknesses, alongside Sudoku, Watford Football Club and chocolate Hob Nobs. I remember about ten years ago, before I could drive and just after I met my wife, I passed a shop in London which specialised in electric bikes. Up until that point, I hadn't even expressed an interest in an ordinary human-powered bike, but suddenly an electric bike was the solution to a problem which didn't even exist. My wife lived about a mile from me at the time, and she would often come and pick me up from my mum and dad's house and we would go back to the house she shared with her friend. I remember being quite embarrassed that I didn't drive and feeling guilty that she constantly had to drive over to pick me up.

Suddenly, an electric bike was the perfect solution! Why this was preferable over simply walking or buying a normal bike at a tenth of the cost, I have no idea. The salesman must have thought all of his Christmases had come at once as I suddenly produced a credit card before he was even halfway through explaining the features. I also purchased a helmet, a lock and a squidgy seat cover, all at extortionate London prices, and rode out of the shop £1,100 poorer than I had walked in. A mile or so later I was left cursing the fact that I hadn't let him finish his sales patter, as I was sure that at some point he would have had to mention the extraordinarily poor battery life and subsequent outrageously long charge time. Less than a month later I was to fall off of that very same bike, and it remains in my mum and dad's garage to this day, complete with helmet, lock and squidgy seat cover.

There are other examples of my impulsive behaviour, such as me buying a car whilst on a weekend trip to Leeds when I was nineteen. That might not sound too ridiculous a story until you realise that as I didn't have a driving license, (and wouldn't have for another ten years) my brother had to get a lift to Leeds a week later in order to drive it back down, a round trip of just under 400 miles. I never did drive that car. Then there was the time I made a £1,000 bid in a charity auction on Heart Radio. It was to spend the afternoon shopping with Emma Bunton, but to be fair I just heard the words 'afternoon with Emma Bunton' and the rest was white noise, so I immediately made the bid. Luckily I was outbid in the last few minutes and so my wife never had to hear about it. Until now, that is.

And of course I will never be able to forget the day when, instead of booking a romantic weekend in Bath in order to propose to my wife, I booked a week in New York, only to find out that I'd got the dates wrong and had to buy additional flights to fly home earlier. Anyone reading this chapter must think I'm made of money, but alas this is not the case. I'm ashamed to say that nearly all of my many impulses have been facilitated by a small rectangular piece of plastic, and if I ever felt like I was actually parting with real money, maybe I would have stopped a long time ago. There's something about the 'buy now, pay later' mentality which removes all of the guilt from the decision. Somehow my brain is able to disengage all of the synapses responsible for rational thought and guilt, and instead connect up the sort of synapses which are used while drunk or in the grip of lust.

The one lesson I have learned from considerable experience is that people should be wary of the words 'buy now, pay later' because at some point in the future, no matter how attractive the deal may have looked, those words will be replaced with 'bought then, paying now!' As frustrating as it is not doing something because you don't have the money, it's even more annoying to be paying for something you have no memory of buying…

Wednesday 19th June 2013

Back to the holiday. It was booked on the Monday and we had only 48 hours to get everything in order before we flew out. My wife's a former teacher and has spent her working life using charts and lists and planning to her heart's content, and she clearly relished being thrust back into teacher mode. She kept saying things like 'Now, we'll need to get….' And 'Oh, we mustn't forget to buy….' And 'We absolutely cannot manage without….' All fairly straightforward, normal openings to sentences which invariably ended with a cream or medication of some sort, but what I haven't made clear thus far is that whenever she said 'we' she actually meant 'you', and in this context 'you' is of course me.

Initially, I was fairly keen. We live in a small village so it's often easier for me to pick things up on my way back from London. I was more than happy popping into Boots on the way home from work to pick up some sun cream and Calpol, but now I found myself holding a list which included specialist shampoo, conditioner, moisturiser and even bloody hair-removal cream. There were also requests for sunglasses, holdalls, beach towels, games and even a travel pillow. Talking of travel pillows, why is that as soon as the word 'travel' is attached to anything, it immediately trebles in price? Travel pillows were retailing at about £12.99, and can you believe I paid £7.99 for a travel plug? The only thing more frustrating than that was the fact that you don't need travel plugs in Cyprus as they use the same electricity system as we do!

So as the list grew, I had to put my foot down and explain that I could only bring back essential items like travel money, sun cream and tea bags. (Yes, they're essential – have you tried drinking the tea abroad?).

'There's only so much I can carry!' I explained to my wife.

'If you buy a holdall, you can carry the rest of the stuff home in that!'

She had me there. It is a holdall, after all, not a holdsome or a holdabit.

'We can get it when we get out there,' I said, unaware that this was to become my catchphrase for the next 48 hours.

It seemed that there was nothing I wasn't prepared to 'get when we get out there'.

I assured her that even though she was five months pregnant, she'd be able to find the perfect swimsuit 'when we get out there', she'd be able to get her nails done 'when we get out there', and the best place to find something nice to wear for the warm summer evenings would most definitely be 'out there'.

I'm almost certain that had she asked for a divorce, I would have recommended that we do it 'out there'.

Thursday 20th June 2013

As she'd never flown before, I was excited about my daughter's reaction to her first flight. There was excitement initially, but that soon gave way to boredom as she exhausted all of the magazines, books, games and various buttons that were within arm's reach. Even kicking the seat in front of her only kept her entertained for a few minutes, and that's an activity which normally entertains a child for the entire flight, at least on every flight I've ever been on.

It had been an early start and, towards the middle of the afternoon, my daughter started showing the telltale signs of needing a nap. My wife and I were both keen to get some rest ourselves, so we reached into our bag for something which could act as a blanket, and to my wife's frustration, we had nothing.

'I'll ask the stewardess,' I said.

'Certainly, sir, that will be £5,' the stewardess said.

I was sure the stewardess had mistaken my request for something else. What sounds like blanket and costs around £5? The only phrases I could come up with were 'spank it' or 'yank it', and in either case I felt sure she would have been charging more than a fiver for those kinds of services.

'I'm sorry, sir, we have to charge for them now. But you get to keep it, and it comes with a travel pillow.'

The good old travel pillow. Suddenly £5 seemed a bargain, as just the day before I had refused to buy one at £12.99. My optimism was a little premature, however, as the 'travel pillow' actually turned out to be a cheap, neck-shaped, blow-up pillow, seemingly designed with only bouncers and rugby players in mind. Putting this pillow around my daughter's neck had the same visual effect as hanging a horseshoe on a nail.

To our delight our daughter slept beautifully for three hours, enabling me to worry about crashing without any other distractions. I'll be honest – I'm terrified of flying. In fact, that's a lie – I'm actually terrified of crashing. I can trace it all back to the first time I flew without an adult. That makes it sound like I was packed off on a plane as a child and left to my own devices, but what I actually mean is the first time I flew unsupervised. I was about nineteen, and a friend and I flew out to Gran Canaria on the only other last-minute holiday I've ever booked. The flight out to Gran Canaria was fantastic, mainly due to the fact that neither of us could remember it, giddy as we were on cheap champagne, but the flight back was awful. It was a night flight, we were tired and we had turbulence from the moment we took off to the moment we landed. In those terrifying few hours we convinced each other that we were going to die, and I haven't been able to shake that feeling ever since.

A few years later my wife and I flew out to Bratislava for a short break. She was extremely sympathetic and was fantastic at keeping me calm during take-off. Amazingly, while chatting to the guy next to us, it transpired that he was a pilot and was flying to Bratislava for a job interview. He also played a huge part in keeping me calm as he explained how safe the aircraft was, how it was able to land with just one engine and that even with no engines functioning there was every chance of a safe landing. All was going well until the final descent, when at around 500 feet the plane started to bank sharply to the left, with the landing strip looming into view out of my left-hand window.

Now I'm not an expert, but I felt sure that the landing strip should be visible from the pilot's window rather than mine. I was still fairly calm up until the point when the pilot (the one next to me and not the one currently doing his best to crash the plane) suddenly uttered the less than comforting words 'Well, there's nothing in the handbook for this type of landing'. To our amazement (and I dare say the pilot's too) we landed safely and went on to have a lovely few days. That is, until it was time to fly home again.

The flight home was probably worse than the flight out, but it had nothing to do with a kamikaze pilot and everything to do with the fact that a stag party had invaded our plane. You would think that they would have been keen to sleep off their excess or busy themselves with worrying about crashing, like me and my paranoid friend a few years earlier, but no, it seemed that this stag do was still in full swing. The problem was that because they were clearly still drunk, they'd all arrived at the check-in desk separately and so none of them were sitting together. The whole group was spread evenly throughout the plane, and throughout the flight people were shouting and swearing from one end of the plane to the other. The guy in the seat in front of us spent the whole flight knelt on his seat facing backwards, shouting and swearing at his friends, and because plane seats are approximately seven inches apart, I had to put up with this guy's disgusting beery breath in my face for almost two hours. Their behaviour meant that the stewardesses stopped coming round with refreshments, so I was genuinely relieved when they started throwing peanuts at each other, because at least it meant I got something to eat.

Friday 21st June 2013

We arrived in Cyprus in one piece, but having been sat in the middle of the plane, we were the last to get off. I was initially pleased with our seats being right in the middle of the plane as it's apparently the best place to sit in the event of a crash, being the strongest part of the aeroplane and therefore less likely to rip apart. Then I realised that might be the case, but the middle of the plane is also where the wings are attached, and the wings are where they house the thousands of gallons of highly flammable fuel. So while the middle of the plane might just stay in one piece in the event of a crash, it will almost certainly be one very big burning piece.

As we were the last off the plane, we were the last to collect our bags and the last to join the queue for the hire car. In preparation, before we left I booked and paid a deposit on a hire car through Europcar. There were other companies to choose from which were slightly cheaper, but I went for Europcar because I knew the name and knew they were a reputable company. After fifteen minutes the queue hadn't moved and there were still thirteen people waiting to be served in front of us. It was getting late, so I decided to enquire with the local Cypriot car hire company, where there were three people behind the desk twiddling their thumbs. They couldn't have been more helpful, and in less than ten minutes we were being shown to our shiny hire car. I say shiny, but I actually had no idea if it was shiny. I didn't even have a clue what make it was or what colour it was because it was pitch black outside and there were no street lights. I wasn't even 100% sure I was standing next to a car.

A few minutes later an employee scurried out of the darkness and presented us with a child's car seat.

'You have to fit it yourself – we're not insured,' he said. And with that he was gone, back to the bright lights of the airport, ready to snaffle up another couple of disgruntled Europcar customers.

I would probably rank the next 25 minutes in the top ten of the most stressful times of my life. I had somehow found myself trying to fit a child's car seat in a car I had yet to identify, in complete darkness, all with a three-and-a-half-year-old child excitedly shouting 'Come on, daddy, I want to go for a drive in our new car!'

Anyone who has experience of fitting a child's car seat using the seat belt method will be able to sympathise with me here. Even in the perfect conditions of a warm, sunny day, with a seat belt that has no desire to lock up with every tug, and with no children anywhere to be seen, you could be looking at around fifteen minutes and a minimum of four category B swear words. Half an hour later we were all set and ready to go.

I turned the key and… nothing.

'Come on, daddy, I want to go for a drive in our new car!'

I turned it again and… nothing.

'Come on, daddy, I really want to go for a drive in our new car!'

'Third time lucky,' I thought, as I turned the key once again.

Nothing.

I checked the petrol gauge and all looked okay. I say all looked okay, but all I was going on was the fact the arrow was pointing to 'F'. I assumed it stood for 'full', but frankly that 'F' could very well have stood for something else entirely. In fact, after three failed attempts to start the car, I felt like we were totally and utterly 'F'ed.

I then decided I needed to look at the engine. I have no idea why, as all I would be able to do with absolute certainty is to confirm that it had one; beyond that I'm well and truly lost. When I buy a car, I always adopt the 'look and kick' test. I simply circle the car, scratching my chin, look at the engine and then kick the tyres. I've bought four cars using the 'look and kick' test and it's worked every time. I do get some funny looks from other customers, but mercifully no kicks thus far.

So after fifteen minutes of searching for the bonnet release button using the light from my iPhone screen, I popped the bonnet, saw that there was an engine and then closed it again. What now? 45 minutes had passed and we were still stationary.

'Daddy, why doesn't the car work?'

I turned the key and it started! For some reason the car would only start with the clutch pedal depressed. Well that made two of us; thanks, clutch pedal! It wasn't just the clutch pedal which annoyed me – it was also the fact that the car kept telling me when to change gear. A big green light appeared on the dash board with the word 'Shift'. Ironic really, when that was one thing the car was completely incapable of doing. Not only did I have my wife doing her very best back-seat driver act in the passenger seat, the actual car was giving me grief too.

The drive should have taken forty minutes, according to the paperwork, but of course it took us about an hour and ten minutes, mainly due to the fact that we were relying on illegible instructions, being read out once again by the light of an iPhone. I knew we'd been driving a while, because our now exhausted daughter said 'Daddy, can we stop driving in our new car now?'

Eventually we got to the villa, unpacked the car and put our daughter to bed. We'd done it! We'd arrived in one piece. And now things could only get better, right? Right…?

Monday 24th June 2013

Less than an hour after I thought those fateful thoughts, two bad things happened. Firstly, I fell down the stairs. I now realise that marble staircases should not be descended in socks, and certainly not when you're carrying a glass of water. I took a tumble on a step about six or seven from the bottom, and landed firstly on my bum and then on my right arm. The glass had been knocked clear of my hand and smashed on the tiled floor.

My wife looked down the stairs, no doubt expecting to see smashed glass and a pool of water, but I don't think she expected to see me rolling around in the middle of it all. I was fine. I had a beautiful step-shaped bruise on my bum for a week and with the pain in my arm I certainly wouldn't be playing cricket for a couple of weeks, but as I haven't played cricket since I was fifteen, that wasn't too much of an issue.

The second, more serious, issue for us was our daughter's temperature. We hadn't brought a thermometer with us, which surprised me initially as I felt sure the only thing left back at our house was the kitchen sink, but we could feel she was extremely hot. The next morning she wasn't interested in food and had no desire to play in the pool or go to the beach. She kept asking us to close the windows and doors and insisted on sitting and watching DVDs. After an afternoon nap, things took a turn for the worse – she was shivering, her lips had gone blue and if anything her temperature had got worse. We decided we had to go to hospital and, on the advice of our rep, we took her to a private clinic which turned out to be about 25 km away.

The 25-minute journey obviously became fifty minutes as I forgot about the clutch and then proceeded to get lost, but my mood was lifted when I found that we didn't have to pay to park and we could be seen straight away. In England we're used to a very softly-softly approach, but in Cyprus there seems to be no such thing. Whereas a doctor in England will ask if it's okay to do this or do that, the doctors in Cyprus just plough on and do it. When we tried to question ours about this, he simply said 'Do you want her to get better or not?' To which we replied 'Yes, of course,' so he carried on.

After the checks were complete, he once again went against everything we're used to in England by kissing our daughter on the hand. I'm pretty sure that if he practised in the UK he'd have to go on a list for that kind of thing, as ridiculous as that is. We were totally fine with it, albeit a little surprised, until every passing nurse, porter and cleaner did exactly the same thing, with the odd one deciding to pinch her cheek or kiss her on the forehead instead.

The doctor said he would ideally like to admit her to do some tests, but we were reluctant because it was our first day in a foreign country and it could be something as simple as a viral infection which she would recover from without any medical intervention. We simply didn't want to put her through any unnecessary suffering. That is, any more than she'd had to go through already what with all the kissing and cheek-grabbing. Ten minutes and £100 later we were back in the car, with a recommendation to let her have plenty of rest and plenty of fluids. The doctor had given us his card and said that we could call him any time, day or night. For the next two days our daughter remained poorly, stuck indoors either sleeping or watching DVDs, all the while complaining that she was cold.

Eventually we had to test the doctor's 'call me anytime' promise by calling him in the early hours of Saturday morning, when our daughter once again took a turn for the worse. She woke up screaming, saying she was in pain and that she wanted to go to the hospital. What three-and-a-half-year-old child wakes up demanding to go to the hospital? Clearly this was serious. The doctor was fantastic and was able to convince us that the best thing was to stay with her and get prepared to bring her in to hospital later that morning. He made it clear that she would receive better care then as more staff would be in, and we as parents would be better rested. I couldn't help feeling that he had a nice bottle of red to get back to as well though.

Tuesday 25th June 2013

We arrived at a more sociable hour of the morning and were immediately seen by the doctor, who I was pleased to note had absolutely no signs of having been on the wine late into the night. He immediately set about arranging blood tests and chest x-rays, and while I was pleased they were being thorough, I couldn't help but feel that they were doing it to maximise the insurance claim. I was made to eat those words approximately twenty minutes later when the doctor called me into his room to show me the x-ray.

'Do you see this here, Mr Leeks?' he asked, pointing with a wooden ruler he had taken from his desk.

'If you mean can I see a shady rectangular blob, then yes, I can see it perfectly,' I said.

'I'm sorry to say....'

Now when a doctor is pointing to an x-ray and delivers the words 'I'm sorry to say....' you really do begin to sit up and take notice. The world stops for a brief second and you can hear your heartbeat not only beating through your chest, but pounding through your body, into your head and out through your ears. I'm no doctor, a fact I had proved just seconds before, but I would say I was definitely suffering stress and anxiety at that exact point in time.

'...that your daughter has pneumonia.'

'Pneumonia?' I queried, confused. 'But she's running a temperature of forty degrees...'

'It's bacterial pneumonia and it's in the early stages. As long as we can treat it very quickly and very aggressively, she'll be fine. Please, Mr Leeks, don't worry – she's in safe hands,' he said.

I honestly couldn't comprehend how my daughter had been diagnosed with pneumonia in Cyprus. It was 36 degrees outside. As it turned out it was likely that she actually contracted it in England and brought it out with her and the re-circulated air in the aeroplane helped to bring it out.

'You will need to stay here for a minimum of four days in order for the antibiotics to take effect,' he said matter-of-factly.

Four days? Four days took us to Wednesday, the day we were meant to fly back.

'What if it takes longer?' I asked.

'Then she'll have to stay here longer,' he said, truly mastering the matter-of-fact style he had begun to adopt.

'But what about our flight home?' I asked, panicking.

'Oh, I'm sure they'll hold the flight,' he said with a wry smile, moving swiftly from matter-of-fact to sarcastic.

'My job is to make your daughter better, and that will take as long as it takes. I'll do my best to get her fit and well for you to fly home on time, and if it takes longer we'll have to discuss it then,' he said, back to his old style.

The doctor then left the room and I'm not ashamed to say that the three of us cried together.

There was a lot going on in those tears. There were tears of relief. Relief that we were in the right place and that our daughter would now begin to get better. There were tears of frustration. Frustration that we were stuck inside a hospital when we should all have been enjoying our holiday together. There were tears of sorrow. Sorrow that our daughter had been through such an ordeal, that she had plenty more to endure, and that she couldn't do any of the things she had been so excited to do as we flew out. There were tears of loneliness. Even though we were all together, we felt desperately isolated. We were in an unfamiliar country, without any friends or family to lean on for support, and we were constantly having to make important decisions on our own. The first of these was the antibiotics. The doctor said that the antibiotics could be taken three ways: orally, intramuscularly or intravenously. Intramuscularly essentially means a jab in the bum and intravenously means that after fitting a cannula, the antibiotics are delivered together with a saline solution through a drip. We opted for the latter.

The doctor tried and failed to fit the cannula correctly, and the antibiotics were slowly being released into our daughter's arm instead of being delivered around the body via the veins. The results were an arm twice the size it should have been and an extremely distressed daughter. It seems we had got our first decision wrong.

Wednesday 26th June 2013

Eventually the doctor was able to administer the antibiotics via our daughter's bottom and, while her temperature was still dangerously high, she was at least comfortable and was able to tell us that she felt a little better. In fact, her exact words were 'I feel better now, daddy, can we go back to our holiday house and play in the swimming pool?' Tears flowed silently down my cheeks as I tried my best to explain that we couldn't, and I held my daughter tight as she wept with the pain, frustration and confusion of it all. We spent the rest of the day and early evening taking it in turns to read and doze until it was time for me to go back to the villa to get our overnight things. I looked around and could see only one extra bed in our room and when the nurse confirmed that only one if us could stay with our daughter overnight the tears flowed once again.

We waited for our daughter to fall asleep and I crept out of the room, got back into our hire car and set out on the 25km drive back to our villa. I was tired and emotional, and both of these things together with the fact that it was now dark contributed to me taking a wrong turn. I must have taken a right instead of a left at some point, because instead of the sea to my left, I now had land. I tried taking turn after turn to get back to where I'd gone wrong, but I ended up getting more and more lost. Suddenly, I found myself on a mountain road with no way of turning around. At that point I'd been lost for nearly an hour and I was beginning to worry. The weird thing is that I wasn't worried about myself – I was worrying about my wife worrying about me. We had no way of communicating so I couldn't just give her a quick call and tell her I'd decided to do a bit of night-time mountain sightseeing but I'd be back as soon as I could. As far as she was concerned I'd probably been kidnapped by pirates (little did she know that I was in fact nowhere near the sea). For the previous three days we had effectively forgotten that my wife was pregnant. We simply gave it no consideration at all as our daughter's illness had consumed us both. It was only me being lost which brought it all back to me, because I realised that she would worry about me, which was no good for our unborn baby, which in turn worried me.

Eventually, I made it to the top of the mountain and was able to pull off the main road. I asked a local shopkeeper for directions, bought some Peppa Pig stickers and a bottle of water, and finally found my way back to our villa. It was a strange feeling, because once the bag was packed and I was on the way back to the hospital, I knew that I would be returning in an hour or so, only this time to sleep, on my own and once again with no way of contacting my ill daughter or pregnant wife. My daughter had no idea that I wasn't allowed to stay, so I promised my wife I'd return early enough in the morning for my daughter to be unaware that I'd been away . If she was to wake up in the middle of the night and ask where I was, then my wife was to simply tell her that I'd popped out to get something. I just didn't want my daughter to suffer any more than she was already, and if it meant telling a little white lie then so be it.

The drive back to the villa was uneventful, save for the handful of idiots who were intent on getting run over. I was trying once again to read the road signs through tired and tear-soaked eyes and really could have done without the death-by-car suicide attempts of several drunken revellers in Paphos town. I couldn't actually tell whether they were British or not from the front, but from the back I was left in no doubt. From the front, a drunken idiot could be from any country, but from behind with the help of the rear-view mirror, these guys were definitely British. There were three of them, one without a shirt and with his shorts pulled down at the back to reveal his arse, and two who had shown incredible reserve in keeping their arses in their trousers, but had spoiled things somewhat with their T-shirts which said 'Single and Horny'. If I'm honest, I didn't realise what was written on the back of their shirts until approximately 5 km further down the road when I finally worked out what the 'ynroh dna elgnis' in my rear-view mirror meant; in fact, until that point I'd pretty much assumed that the guys were Cypriot.

I got back to the villa at just after 1am, and the whole area was blanketed in darkness and deathly quiet. I say deathly quiet, but it's not actually possible for anywhere in a hot climate to be deathly quiet, thanks to the plethora of nocturnal critters. People in busier areas of the island have to put up with the noise of teenagers in karaoke bars and on quad bikes, but spare a thought for those stuck on the hillside having to deal with a cacophony of insects.

I got into bed and drifted off into a light sleep, mindful of the fact that I didn't have an alarm. I didn't want to let myself get in too deep a sleep as I was desperate to get back to the hospital before my daughter woke up. I needn't have worried. I was wide awake an hour or so later and spent the next few hours flicking through the various foreign shopping channels on the TV, counting down the minutes until it was time to make my way back to the hospital. Happy holidays.

Thursday 27ᵗʰ June 2013

On the way back to the hospital, in order to keep alert and stay focused on the road, I decided to try to work out the miles per gallon of the car I was in. I have never taken any interest in the fuel consumption of any vehicle in my life, but I thought it might give me something to do. You'll realise how ridiculous a task this was when I tell you that I still had no idea what car I was driving. I was still identifying it in the hospital car park by colour alone, and when that became too tough a task I resorted to pressing the button on the key fob, hoping I would catch a glimpse of the flashing orange lights. As if that weren't enough, the petrol prices were in Euro's, a currency I had yet to get a firm handle on, and the vehicle I was in didn't even display distances in miles. I finally came to the conclusion that the car definitely required SOME petrol for almost every journey. (I figured there might be the odd extremely short downhill journey). Scientific, eh?

Once I was done with my self-imposed Mensa challenge, I began to get annoyed. I worked out that no matter the fuel consumption, I could have saved 50 km worth of fuel by just sleeping in the car in the first place.

I successfully made it back to the hospital before my daughter awoke, and I even managed to surprise my wife with a cup of tea I'd bought in the downstairs restaurant. Actually, let me write that last bit of that sentence again. I even managed to surprise my wife with a cup of warm liquid I'd bought from a moody lady holding a mop.

I'm glad to say that the story gets happier from here on as my daughter woke with a fever which was now under control and a condition which was being well treated. Slowly over the next few days she got better and better. After one of my many trips back to the villa, I managed to return with the DVD player and hook it up to the TV in her room. I've not seen a child so happy to see a talking pig since David Bennett announced proudly in the school cloakroom that he had a crush on Miss Piggy.

Every day our daughter showed signs of improvement, which gave us the courage to get over the disappointment of the holiday we knew she'd missed out on. We also found out that the hospital had WiFi, so we were able to use the iPad which I'm writing on now to have video chats with our family. In the past we'd tried and failed to use Skype in order to speak to my folks back in Watford. Somehow we've never been able to see more than a blurry mess, yet suddenly in Cyprus if felt like we were in the same room. I'll give credit to the doctor too, as he walked in during one of our Skype sessions and started joining in with the waving and blowing of kisses.

We were finally discharged the day before our flight home, and although our daughter wasn't well enough to visit the beach or swim in the pool, we did manage to have a short walk in the evening sun and even popped out to grab a little something to eat.

On the flight home, just after taking another dose of antibiotics, my daughter melted my heart when she said 'Daddy, I really enjoyed my holiday.'

That's good, I thought. She's due her tonsils out next year – that'll save me a few hundred quid on a holiday.

Friday 28th June 2013

I always like to use the final chapter of each part of the book to tie up a few loose ends and this one is no different, so here goes.

My wife's pregnancy is advancing very nicely and, 24 weeks in, all is happy and healthy. In case you were wondering, no, I still haven't won the lottery and my Gramps' dream of having a boat moored at Lymington harbour remains exactly that. The decorative pillows on the bed remain, and I've still yet to make the bed. The Dukan diet lasted just under a week (a personal record) and I'm pleased to report that my daughter is recovering well and will be back to full health very soon. Oh and I still have no idea of the make or model of that bloody hire car.

I would like to end Part 3 by once again saying a big thank you. Since the first book was released I've been touched by the number of people who have got in touch, not only to give feedback on the book, but also to share their own stories and anecdotes. It has been fantastic to hear from you and I urge you to continue to get in touch.

Monday 1st July 2013

I've seen a rapid increase in the number of establishments using the word 'Express' in their business or product names recently. For the most part it makes perfect sense, and I can see exactly why the proprietors would want to convey the message of speed.

The word express conjures up images of people dashing around looking as if someone has pressed the fast-forward button. It conjures up images of people standing aside and waving you through, but unfortunately, thanks to fatherhood, it also conjures up images of my wife using an elaborate machine to extract milk from her breast.

'Cafe Nero Express' is a perfect example of where the word express works well. 'Cafe Nero Express' perfectly explains what you're going to get as a paying customer. You're going to get coffee and, so long as they have their business model right, you're going to get it quickly. Pizza Express works much in the same way, and once again I wholeheartedly agree with their willingness to provide the 'Express' in their title and their service. As I see it, people need food and drink in order to survive, and whenever there's a chance that someone might die, I think it's reasonable to demand an express service.

There are a couple of examples, however, where the word express doesn't exactly fit with the product or service. Take the Gatwick Express, for example. It's a fantastic concept: a high-speed train service which will get you to Gatwick in a flash. Except the flash is usually followed by smoke and flames, all as a result of another signal-box failure.

All of this brings me to a company that was brought to my attention yesterday, as one of its branded vans sped around the City of London. The company?

Picture Frames Express!

I've nothing against Picture Frames Express, per se. I'm sure they offer an extremely good range of picture frames and are able to deliver them quickly, but who has ever thought to themselves "I need a picture frame, and I need it now"?

Surely a picture frame is a purchase only ever carried out while casually browsing? I can't imagine someone ever running into a shop and demanding to know where the frames are. "They're over there, sir, right by the door, next to the toilet paper and the morning-after pills!"

Tuesday 2nd July 2013

I was minding my own business, wandering aimlessly around the frozen food aisle on Saturday afternoon when I heard a distant crackle followed by a tinny voice which asked "Would Leroy Brown please make your way to the customer helpdesk? That's Leroy Brown to the customer helpdesk."

What a coincidence, I thought, taking a break from deciding between the Ben and Jerry's in my left hand and the Haagen Dazs in my right. Only ten minutes previously, in the car on the way over to the supermarket, I'd been listening to a song by Jimmy Croce, entitled 'Bad, Bad Leroy Brown'.

Just as I was about to ask my wife if she thought he was being summoned for being bad, the frostbite kicked in and I was forced into deciding on the Ben and Jerry's, primarily because the trolley was to my left and the freezer was to my right.

Only a couple of minutes later, when we'd moved onto the vegetables, the same tinny voice piped up with "Would Richard Whitely please make your way to the checkouts? That's Richard Whitely to the checkouts." Were they having a laugh? Leroy Brown, followed by Richard Whitely? Not only two famous names, but two colour-based names. I immediately started to think of who could possibly be next. "Jason Orange to the store room?" "Cilla Black to aisle four?"

In truth, had Jason or Cilla been next on the staff announcements, I would have had to double-check to see if it was really them; I can't imagine either of them are in the position to be turning down work.

So what was going on? Was it a massive coincidence? Had the supermarket in question managed to somehow legitimately employ a Leroy Brown and a Richard Whitely? Were they using colour-based code names, as part of some silly company directive, or were they having a laugh and playing a game in an attempt to make the day pass that little bit quicker? Unfortunately, I will never know. I waited with bated breath to find out if Professor Green or Pink were next to be summoned, but there were no more announcements.

What I can say, however, is that it's not just supermarkets that seem to be having a laugh at our expense when it comes to names – our trusted NHS is at it too. As my wife read out a letter from the hospital, I had to laugh when she confirmed whom her appointment would be with.

"Dear Mrs Leeks. An appointment has been made for you to see one of our two specialist midwives; you will either be seeing Midwife D. Flood or Midwife G. Gale."

Thursday 4th July 2013

We had the dreaded fire drill at work yesterday. Every six months we have to go through the same rigmarole. "Please stop what you are doing and leave quietly via the fire exit," the fire marshall will shout. There are times throughout the year when you can think of nothing better than a fire drill – when Colin is delivering his quarterly review and you long for the invitation to leave quietly via the fire exit. Why is it then that the fire drill always seems to occur when you're in the middle of the most critical tasks?

I always find myself frantically saving documents and sending out emails, which in a real fire would probably result in me being burned alive. Of course there's only so much you can do before Fire Marshall Simon storms in with his little yellow jacket and demands that you leave immediately.

Fire marshalls are a strange breed. I've always thought that you have to be a certain kind of person to be a fire marshall. You need to be someone who is not only happy to take on extra responsibility, but to do it with no extra pay and the very real possibility of burning to death.

Let's not forget the perks, however. While there may be no extra pay on offer, who could possibly refuse the offer of unlimited access to clipboards, pens and of course that little yellow jacket?

There's always a certain smug look on the face of the office fire marshall. A look that says "Hey buddy, I know something you don't!" Strangely, even though that 'something' is actually only the inside track on the latest fire drill dates, you still feel like you're missing out.

Fire drill day is a big day in the life of the office fire marshall. I like to imagine that they have the date marked on their calendar months in advance (in code of course, so as not to give away the big secret). I've sometimes wondered if they ever wake up to their morning alarm in character. I can imagine them jumping out of bed and reaching for the clipboard whilst shouting "Please leave everything behind and make your way quietly to the fire exit," as their partners and children look on bemused.

The reasons for carrying out a fire drill are obvious. Apart from being a legal requirement, they ensure that the systems in place are in working order, and they help to educate potential victims on the correct course of action. The only problem with this system is that the fire marshalls themselves never get truly tested, as they always have the inside knowledge. The yellow jacket is always freshly ironed, the clipboard has an up-to-date attendance list, and the biro is always fresh from the box.

I personally think they should add an extra fire drill every year, aimed purely at testing our fire marshalls. Let's see how well-ironed that jacket is when they haven't had the date marked in the calendar for three months. Let's see if that clipboard has an up to date attendance list if the alarm starts ringing when they're in the middle of finalising the accounts. Only then would we be able to truly trust our fire marshalls.

Monday 8th July 2013

One thing you learn pretty early on as a commuter is that you are nobody's friend, and it's every man, woman and child for themselves. I say child because school children commute too and, if I'm honest, they seem just as grumpy as the rest of us. Every day I share my carriage with around ten school children, and all they do is moan. They moan about their parents mostly, closely followed by their school work, and then it's everything from relationships to battleships, all the while having to deal with hormones which are slowly turning them into sweaty, spotty, stroppy monsters. Throw in a morning commute and there's no wonder that they are the top trumps when it comes to the grumps.

It's generally accepted that commuters don't speak to each other; in fact it's generally preferred. A paper, tablet or laptop acts as the perfect defence mechanism for most, meaning that we can easily ignore everyone around us. Then of course you've got the inspiration for this book: the commuter who likes to sleep. The closer we get to our destination, however, the busier the train gets, and a busier train means stroppier commuters. There will be some commuters who every day, without fail, will place all of their belongings on the seat next to them, knowing full well that at some point someone will want to sit in that seat. They will then act like a petulant child when someone asks them perfectly politely to move their things.

When taking a seat next to someone, the standard response you tend to get is muted frustration, and the very best you can hope for is a nod or a smile. This generally means that the person doesn't want you to sit next to them, but they accept that there's nothing they can do about it. Every so often, however, you will be greeted with what can only be described as visible frustration, verging on anger, only a small leap from actual rage. This is a look which says "There are other seats on this carriage, why the hell have you chosen to sit next to me, you inconsiderate arsehole?!"

As tempting as it is to stare back with a look which says "Look, baldy, you know as well as me that this train is going to fill up at the next stop and there's every chance you could have ended up sitting next to someone far smellier and fatter than me, so put your frown away and get on with sending out that boring email about next month's strategy meeting." Admittedly, that's a lot to convey in a look. And anyway, as a commuter you don't give them that look – you simply smile, sit down and spend the next twenty minutes trying to read his email about next month's strategy meeting. At some point of course you will get caught, and the best course of action is to pretend to be looking out of the window – awkward when you're going through the Sevenoaks tunnel.

Yesterday on my way home I was greeted by an entirely different commuter. A commuter who welcomed me with a warm and open smile, a smile which said "Sure, sit down, it's nice to have your company." It's fair to say that I was sceptical and somewhat confused by his happy demeanour, and it took me a few seconds to realise exactly what was going on. I had sat opposite a newbie. The person I was looking at was in his late teens, had curly blond facial hair which looked like the fluff that sticks to your socks, and he was wearing a name badge which identified him as a 'Trainee'.

Bless him, he didn't know the rules. So, in an attempt to educate him, I did what would be expected of a seasoned commuter like me – I scowled back at him. He was of course undeterred – buoyed by the exuberance of youth and stupidity, finally rid of the grumpy adolescent hormones (save for the ones responsible for his acne).

He carried on with the game on his phone as I tried my best to work out what he was playing by looking at the reflection in the window. I was just coming to the conclusion that it was some kind of fighting game when the game suddenly came to life and I was kicked hard in the shin.

"I'm so sorry," he said.

Of course I just ignored him – not because I was being rude, but because I was genuinely shocked that he had apologised. As a commuter, I've been the victim of GBH on a number of occasions, and on really busy trains even minor sexual assault, and not once has anyone ever apologised.

He's going to have to learn the hard way!

Wednesday 10th July 2013

It's been what I would describe as "Bloody hot!" over the past couple of weeks, and being British, I've done nothing but moan about it. When it's cold, it's always too cold; when it's wet, it's always too wet, and when it's hot, it's obviously always way too bloody hot. In fact I'm only ever happy with the weather when it's dry and warm but with a little breeze. I'd say we get about ten to fifteen days a year when the weather fits snugly into my 'ideal weather' niche, so I therefore spend roughly 350 days a year moaning about the weather.

I feel bad moaning because I'm sure there are people all across the globe who would give up everything in order to have the diverse climate we enjoy. There are countries which suffer frequent droughts, some which suffer from regular floods, and others which are under the constant threat of tropical storms, yet here I am moaning about the fact that it's a little bit humid for my liking and that it won't be long before the flying ants are out.

It is of course because our weather is so changeable that it's such a talking point. Talking about the weather used to be a cliché – something people would joke about when they were searching for some common ground. Talking about the weather only ever used to be reserved for small talk, but in the last few years it has become a legitimate conversation topic. People regularly open conversations with "Hasn't it been hot today?" and they're not being ironic – they are genuinely looking to converse about the weather. To my amazement, rather than a standard three-word brush-off such as "Hasn't it just?" or a courteous four-word "Tell me about it", or even the positively verbose five-word "Too hot for my liking", people are instead engaging with others and conversing in great depth.

"I know; I've had to start opening the windows at night, much to Tony's annoyance. He nearly choked on a moth on Monday."

People start using expressions they've only heard other people use, thinking it's okay for them to start describing it as being "So close!" It amazes me that when it's cold, people constantly say they want to get away from it all, yet when the Sun arrives, suddenly it's too bloody close.

I do find it funny that as soon as we start experiencing extreme weather, everyone becomes a meteorologist. You've only got to mention the weather and someone will inevitably say something like "Looks like there's a cold front coming in from the east."

They have no idea what they're talking about, but because someone called Sian or Kevin came on the telly directly after the news to tell them, they think they're suddenly an expert.

If you think about it, the weather forecast shouldn't really be offered as part of the news package. The news, while depressing at times, does its best to inform you of the day's events, in which people mainly die, cry or lie. An essential part of the news is that we, as viewers, believe it to be the truth (not always the case with the written press, I might add). But the weather forecast is not based on truth at all – it's based on people in smart suits giving us their best guesses. It could quite easily be sandwiched between Coronation Street and 'Oh god, not another police documentary', but it isn't, because it would suddenly lose all of its credibility.

Of course, the other reason that the news executives like to cling on to the weather forecast is that it's the only thing stopping people from switching over once the headlines are finished with. Next time you have the chance, halfway through the report on fiscal policy, I urge you to reach for your remote – I guarantee you'll hear a faint but audible cry of "Don't turn it over yet, the weather will be on in a minute."

Thursday 11th July 2013

With the rising cost of travel in recent years, I've noticed a significant increase in the number of cyclists on London's roads. In the last few months in particular, I've noticed that more and more 'normal' people are taking to two wheels. When I say 'normal' people, I mean the ones you could never imagine being comfortable on a bicycle. Take Duncan, who has recently had a bit of a health scare and who somehow thinks that cycling to work is the answer to his troubles, rather than cutting down on the twenty fags and two packets of custard creams he gets through each day.

I feel sorry for the seasoned cyclists, the Marks and the Richards of this world, who until recently only had to put up with the dangers of dodging buses and pedestrians, but now have to deal with dodging the likes of Duncan, weaving from side to side as he desperately tries to get to the top of the hill before collapsing.

In the days when it was just Mark and Richard, bikes all looked the same. They had thin tyres, curly handles (you'll notice I'm using all of the technical terms here) and they were either white or black. These days, thanks in part to the London Cycle Hire scheme, bikes come in all shapes and sizes. While fold-up bikes are undoubtedly convenient, they do have a habit of looking a little bit silly when ridden, especially when Duncan's on-board. I've also seen a huge increase in what I call 'bikes from the shed' – ones where people have literally woken up one morning, fed up with the queues and the extortionate travel costs, and thought to themselves "I know what I'll do, I'll ride to work on that bike from the shed." The BFTS have all the tell-tale signs: they have a rusty chain, only one working brake, and a saddle intent on adjusting itself.

This afternoon I've seen the strangest bike of all, and I'll try my best to describe it. While the fold-up bike often leaves the cyclist looking decidedly upright, this bike has the opposite effect. The cyclist was effectively lying down with the back wheel underneath his shoulder blades, the handlebar just above his nipples, and his legs were outstretched horizontally. As he pedalled, his knees came up to be in line with his head, and the whole bike must have been only eighteen inches off the ground at most.

I can't understand what he's achieving by riding such a ridiculous bike. Not only does it look incredibly uncomfortable, it looks like hard work too. Not content with that, the thing looks like a complete bloody death trap. While I imagine it's difficult to spot ordinary cyclists if one is driving a large vehicle, this contraption must be bloody near invisible. If these bikes were really to take off we'd have to scrap Sat Navs and start issuing drivers with bloody radar systems.

Why would someone want to ride to work on something which is so much worse that the alternative? What good can come of it? I often spend a week or so breaking in a pair of new shoes; I put in the hard work because I know all will be well in the end. That bike, though, is never going to be any good in the end, except maybe to the scrap metal dealer who scrapes it off the road.

Maybe he's a guy who just likes a challenge. Perhaps he's someone who's happy to take risks. Well, if that's the case, I urge him to ditch the bike and try getting on a bus or a tube sometime between 7.30 and 8.30am.

Friday 12th July 2013

Buying train tickets these days is pretty complicated. It used to be very simple. You used to form an orderly queue (if you're not from the British Isles, replace 'form an orderly queue' with 'push in') and wait to speak to the polite man in the uniform. You would pay your money and he would give you your tickets. A simple transaction; you stated your destination, he gave you the price, and you handed over the money. You walked away calm, happy in the knowledge that the tickets you'd purchased would A) get you to the correct destination and B) were purchased at the correct price.

You can still purchase tickets the old way, (although you now have to replace 'polite man in the uniform' with 'often grumpy person in a jumper') but with the age of the internet came the age of the commercial booking site. Put simply, this is the middle man. It's effectively the same as the ticket tout you see at every gig, only you don't have to put up with the tobacco-stained fingers and cockney dialogue. They have connections and buy their tickets at one price and sell them at another. The problem with commercial booking sites is that you never know whether they are truly saving you money or costing you more. There are various tactics you now have to employ to ensure you get a good deal. I say 'ensure' but the truth is, you are not 'ensuring' anything. You never truly know whether you're getting your ticket at the best price, and that's the frustrating thing about commercial booking sites. Once the 'Confirm Purchase' button has been pressed you're left with a feeling of doubt. "Did I get a good deal? Could I have got it cheaper?"

The problem is that it's all very confusing. I've been told that when possible I should book early, but of course it also might be beneficial to buy last-minute. A return is usually cheaper, but there are times when two singles may be best. There are also times when splitting my ticket might be beneficial; this means buying a single to a destination en route and then buying a separate single from there. Apparently this is frowned upon and some train operators have rules which say you can't, sometimes even handing out fines.

I've been told that another way to try to save money is to only pay peak fare for the part of the journey which falls during peak times. Thus if I'm going on a long journey I can pay for a single for the part of the journey which is 'peak' and then buy a separate single for further down the line. I have also had personal experience of booking my ticket through a completely different operator and getting 25% off. The part of the London to Kent route that I travel on is operated by South Eastern, but I had noticed that Southern were offering 25% off, so I searched for the same tickets via a different operator and got them cheaper!

Crazy, isn't it?

Oh, and a little tip – try whenever possible to avoid calling National Rail Enquiries from your mobile. The cost can be extortionate, and all of the information can be found via your smart phone and the various apps available.

So now, when purchasing train tickets, I urge you to buy them in advance at the last minute, make sure it's a split return single from a different operator and always go online to call them.

There – that's nice and clear, isn't it?

Tuesday 16th July 2013

After ten years of commuting, I thought I'd seen it all. It seems there's nothing people are not prepared to do on a train in front of a crowd of people. I've seen people have breakdowns, breakups and fights; I've seen people eat breakfast, lunch and dinner; I've seen people reading newspapers, books and even porn.

All of this pales into insignificance compared to what I've seen this morning. This morning I've had to endure a woman basically completing her own personal MOT in front of me. In fact it wasn't just an MOT – it was an MOT complete with a full-service wash and polish.

As soon as I got on I knew I was in trouble. The table opposite was covered in mirrors, brushes, files, pots, creams and lotions. Firstly, she started sanding down the rusty paintwork, or in other words filing her nails. She went at them as if her life depended on it, back and forth, in and out. The morning sun was shining through the train and I could see clouds of nail particles swirling into the air and just as I was thinking how disgusting it was, she blew on her nails.

Suddenly billions of this woman's dead nail particles were hurtling towards my face and the only thing I could think of doing to halt them was to cough without covering my mouth. She looked at me in disgust. There she was trying to suffocate me with her body dust, and suddenly I was the disgusting one.

Next she started wiping down the bodywork with a wet wipe, then began to touch up the paintwork with what I'm guessing was concealer. Next, she went for a complete respray with what I think was foundation. To finish off the paint job, the finishing touches were applied with what looked like lipstick, mascara, blusher and eyeliner.

What happened next truly shocked me. Having spotted something in the mirror she was holding, she reached into her bag for another piece of apparatus. Suddenly, she popped open the bonnet and got to work cleaning the engine. Okay, maybe I've gone a bit overboard with the MOT analogy here, but she basically started brushing her teeth.

Brushing her teeth. On a train! Not just on a train, but in her seat, opposite other passengers! I've seen people flossing before, but full-on teeth-brushing was a new commuting low. Or so I thought. Having already made me gag twice, firstly as her nail dust entered my nasal cavity and secondly with the sight of her gnarly teeth, she then decided to test my gag reflex to the full. She opted for a two-pronged attack, applying hairspray and perfume almost simultaneously.

As the tiny particles hit the back of my throat and I started to feel like I was losing consciousness, I couldn't help feeling that she was some sort of foreign spy, sent on a mission to stop me completing my book.

I desperately searched for some clues as to why she might be doing all this as I felt my breath getting shallower, and I finally found the answer I was looking for on the ID card attached to her laptop.

Her name was Linda and she worked in marketing.

Wednesday 17th July 2013

I've always enjoyed people-watching, but it's time to admit that my people-watching has got out of hand. I can no longer consider myself simply a people-watcher, and as hard as it is for me to come out and say it, I've realised that I need to be true to myself and just admit it.

Ladies and gentlemen, I am officially a nosey bastard.

To be a good people-watcher you have to blend in; you need to take everything in without looking like you're taking anything in. Believe it or not, a great way of people-watching is to ditch the watching altogether and simply listen. I see people do it all the time on the train when they close their eyes to make it look like they're sleeping, whereas in fact they're simply lulling the talkers into a false sense of security. Often the subject matter will become far less guarded if the talkers believe people around them are asleep. I'll often be in a situation at home where I think my wife has drifted off so I reach for the remote, only to be told quite aggressively that "I was watching that!"

I can be confident in admitting that I am officially a nosey bastard and no longer a people-watcher because I've lost the ability to be covert. Either that or I simply don't care if I get caught; either way, instead of sitting back and taking it in, I now find myself leaning forward, craning my neck and on some occasions even moving closer to the action.

For the last three months I've been closely monitoring the movements of a guy on my train. He gets on my carriage a couple of stops after me and immediately heads for the toilet. He then proceeds to spend fifteen to twenty minutes in there (on every single journey) before coming out and standing in the vestibule. He'll get on with reading his book, checking his phone or reading a paper, and then ten minutes before arriving at Cannon Street, he'll go back into the toilet and stay there until we pull into the station.

At first it intrigued me. I watched with interest as he went about his strange routine. Day after day he did exactly the same thing and I felt like I was immersed in the remake of Groundhog Day. It wasn't long though before it started to annoy me. It annoyed me because once he was locked inside that toilet I had no idea what he was up to. I've never really been interested in what strangers get up to in the toilet – for the most part it's pretty self-explanatory and I've never felt the need to explore it any further, but this guy was definitely up to something.

He couldn't need the toilet that badly, could he? He surely hasn't been able to fine-tune his bodily functions to that degree. What if the train was late? What if the toilet was occupied? And what is it with the second visit fifteen minutes after the first?

Finally, today, I was able to work it out. Normally, after his first visit he scurries off to the vestibule area as there aren't any available seats, but this morning there was a seat available right opposite me. He sat down, placed his bag on the floor, and started to read his book. Suddenly, there they were: two tell-tale clues which were to help me solve the riddle.

Having removed his book from his bag and placed the bag on the floor, he had inadvertently left it open and facing me. Staring at me were two spent wrappers and a rolled-up ball of tin foil. Then clue number two revealed itself. As he made himself comfortable in his chair and buried his head deeper into his book, his right hand started to make a move towards his mouth. Success! He had managed to pick the bit of food from his teeth, and I was able to finally confirm that he spends ten minutes in the train toilet every day eating his breakfast.

Let's all just take a moment to let that sink in.

HE SPENDS TEN MINUTES IN THE TRAIN TOILET EVERY DAY EATING HIS BREAKFAST!

If someone asked me to compile a list of the 100 places I wouldn't want to eat my breakfast, I'm pretty sure the train toilet would be second only to prison.

The only thing worse than the thought of him eating breakfast in the train toilet every day is the thought of what he does during his second visit…

Monday 22nd July 2013

Whatever happened to the slogan 'Keep Britain Tidy'? During the eighties and nineties you couldn't go anywhere without being reminded to dispose of your detritus responsibly as the slogan was plastered across billboards, TV and even on your rubbish itself.

Looking around, the litter problems don't seem to have got any worse, so I'm tempted to say that either the advertising campaign was a huge success and has stuck with us and been passed down through the generations, or it was a complete waste of time and money as we're in a similar situation now, even without the constant reminders.

I actually think it's neither of those two. I think that the litter problem has got a lot worse, but the difference now is that there are more people employed to pick it up. I think rather than spending millions on a campaign making people aware, the government and councils just started spending the money on employing people to pick it up.

It kind of makes sense – they're spending the same amount of money while also tackling the issue of unemployment. If there were to be a slogan today, it would probably read something like this: 'We're keeping Britain tidy. Fancy helping us out?'

I remember at school that if anyone was caught dropping litter, they were put on litter duty, meaning they had to spend a lunchtime clearing up litter. It's a fantastic idea because not only does it tackle the litter problem head-on, while also teaching the litterer a valuable lesson, it also rubs their nose in it by making them pick up the litter of all of the people who got away with it. It's like punishing a failed bank robber by making him count all the money the last lot got away with.

I'm not sure that schools are allowed to do it anymore, most likely down to some sort of health and safety issue because little Jonny might hurt his back bending over. If that is the case, I'd still theme the punishment around the crime. I'd insist that they make a bin for their metalwork assignment, I'd confiscate their school bag and make them walk around with a black bin liner, and if that didn't have the necessary effect I'd make them do their work experience with the council's refuse-collection team.

Maybe the true reason for the demise of the 'Keep Britain Tidy' slogan is that no-one really understands where to put their rubbish anymore. It's ok telling us to bin our rubbish, but with so many different bins available these days, they need to create a whole new campaign in order to educate us on exactly where we should bin it. Nowadays we have black bins, brown bins, green bins, blue bins, orange bins, bins for glass, bins for paper, bins for garden waste, bins for food waste and even special bins for dog poo.

Every few months our local council has to send out a twenty-page brochure just to try to explain the bin collection process, in which we get fed nonsense such as "Black bins will be collected every Monday, with the Mixed Recycling bins and Garden Waste bins being collected on alternate Mondays, except bank holidays, when they will be collected on Tuesdays."

I'm now so confused that I've had to resort to creeping around in my pants at midnight checking out my neighbours' bins. I'd like to add that the pants are a by-product of me getting comfortable in the evening and are not specifically selected for the mission in hand.

Wednesday 24th July 2013

I found out today that a gift I had lovingly and thoughtfully bought for my wife for her birthday had expired.

If I'm being completely honest, it wasn't so much a loving and thoughtful gift, it was more of a desperate and last-minute one. I did what everyone does in a last-minute panic and started Googling 'gift experiences'. Having run out of both time and ideas, the 'Pampering day for two' seemed the perfect gift as my wife had been going through a tough spell at work, and I figured there was a slight chance I might just be asked to be the 'plus one'.

We all know that the best present you can buy someone is a present which can end up benefiting you too. Everyone does it. My parents were responsible for one of the most outrageous "Here's a present we bought for you, but in fact it's for us" purchases back in 1990. My brother and I have birthdays which are very close together, and it's been that way as long as I can remember. My brother's falls on the 7th of August and mine falls on the 22nd. It was the weekend before my brother's birthday and my parents announced that after months of discussing it, we were finally going to get a puppy. After driving to the animal rescue centre and picking out a beautiful little scrawny black and fawn mongrel, my parents simply announced "Happy Birthday, you two!"

That was it. A puppy purchased and two birthdays catered for. As much as I loved that dog, I couldn't help but be a little bit disappointed – not only was I celebrating my birthday two weeks early, I was having to share my present with everyone in my family. As if to prove I wasn't the only one who was unhappy with the current arrangement, our newly-named puppy Brandy went and pooed all over our cream sofa.

I've thought about using the same technique with our daughter, but my wife has insisted that she definitely wouldn't appreciate a birthday which consisted of a round of golf in the morning followed by a trip to watch Watford play in the afternoon. "That's a shame," I said. "What a waste of the golf lessons I bought her last Christmas!"

It seems however that 'Gift experiences' are not the perfect desperate last-minute solution they purport to be. My wife is pregnant and wanted to use the experience in the latter stages of her pregnancy in order to relax and unwind before the big day, but I've learned today that these items have a specific 'use by' date and just like milk which has gone beyond its date, they're worthless.

How can an experience you've purchased expire? It was purchased with cold, hard cash and the last time I checked cash does not have an expiry date. Imagine how ridiculous it would be if you purchased this book on Kindle and after a week of not being read, it suddenly deleted itself. Maybe that's not such a good example because I have the Kindle app on my iPhone and thanks to me not bothering to download the latest software, I find that books are regularly deleting themselves.

The only possible reason to have such a ridiculous policy is to increase profitability, because companies know that a certain number of vouchers end up sitting on the mantelpiece gathering dust. I imagine that by ensuring there's a 'use by' date, it means the companies can then work out the percentage of unused vouchers and can therefore bring down the cost of the experience to make it more affordable for everyone. While this practice might make perfect sense on a spreadsheet, it doesn't make it any easier for me to have to tell my wife that while she can't go on her pampering day, she has in fact ensured that other people can do so for less than they thought it might cost!

Thursday 25th July 2013

There aren't many times you can walk into work and say "Sorry I'm late, boss, but I was up all night trying to catch a bat!" Well, that's my excuse this morning and I'm sticking to it.

We have a simple bedtime routine where my wife uses the bathroom first, while I do manly things like turning the complicated electrical items off and making sure the windows and doors are shut. It's a routine that works, and it has the pleasant side-effect of allowing me a little extra time to finish watching that documentary on the attempted assassination of Ronald Reagan, while still making me look like a gentleman.

Last night, just five minutes from the end of the aforementioned documentary, my wife ran into the living room (quite a sight when your wife is six months pregnant and naked) and declared that there was a bat flying around our bedroom.

Now, it's been particularly hot the last couple of weeks so we've had to have the windows open, and an unfortunate side-effect is having a lot of night-time visitors, namely moths.

"Are you sure it's not a big moth?" I asked, knowing that moths are particularly fond of lights and lamps, often casting strange shadows.

"Unless there's a type of moth that's jet black and has massive ears, then yes, I'm pretty sure. Can you get rid of it?" she asked.

"You stay here," I said, making sure not to answer her question directly, because in truth I had no idea whether I could. As I slowly crept up the stairs, one at a time, I heard a theme tune slowly entering my head. It was the theme tune to Mission Impossible, but I felt that the title was a little negative, so I forced another one into my head to accompany me on the journey to my nemesis.

Da na na na na na na na – Batman!

Much better.

The bat was flying around the room in circles, confused, wondering why the world had suddenly got so much smaller. I was surprised at just how calm I was, and I took a few moments to take in its beauty. That feeling of calm lasted around twenty seconds and beauty quickly turned into the beast as it brushed my head on more than one occasion. In order to ensure that the bat didn't escape into other parts of the house, I had decided to close the door as I entered the room, and there's something slightly disconcerting about being trapped in a room with a wild animal. Ok, it might have only been a bat, but bats can have rabies and I don't think many people would be queuing up to be locked in a room with a rabid animal.

How the hell was I going to get rid of a bat? It was flying at head-height and had absolutely no interest in flying anywhere near the open window. It was looking tired so I turned off the light, left the room and closed the door, hoping that at best it might find its own way out of the window and at worst it might be able to land and get some rest.

My wife phoned the RSPCA and the advice on the recorded line told us to turn off the light and open a window. "Ok, I've done that; what next?" I asked. "If that doesn't work, we need to call environmental health," she said. "Ok, so let's do that," I replied. "They don't open until the morning," she said. "Bugger," I said.

So what next? I did what anyone in the same situation would have done. I posted a status update on Facebook.

"Does anyone know how to get rid of a bat?"

The replies I received were mixed. I received helpful advice such as leaving fruit on the window ledge, and unhelpful advice like being told to call Batman.

After another three unsuccessful attempts at coaxing the bat out by waving my arms, I resorted to grabbing our daughter's fishing net from the shed. Using very slow, careful movements I was able to manoeuvre myself under the bat's flight path and raise the net just as he flew into it. I took the net straight outside and very carefully turned it over and the bat flew away very happily. Ironic really that the first thing we have ever caught in a fishing net is a bat.

I've since been told that I should not have attempted to catch the bat and that bats are protected species and should only be handled by those who hold a bat licence. I apologise unreservedly to anyone who is upset with my actions, but I was in the difficult position of having to deal with one bat or face the wrath of another.

Friday 26th July 2013

With only a few months until our new baby meets its makers, (I'm aware that's a strange phrase to use) we've been busy trying to make decisions. I'd completely forgotten just how many decisions there are to be made, and I'm travelling in this morning completely exhausted, still wondering if we were right to choose a Moses basket over a crib and whether we'd chosen the right sterilising kit or not.

The fact we've decided not to find out what we're having is making things a little trickier. It means that even when we have finally made a decision, we then have to agree on a colour which is suitably unisex. The problem with unisex colours is that they tend to be very boring, and you end up with a nursery decked out in a dazzling array of creams, browns and yellows, resulting in a room which looks ready to go to war in the Middle East.

Inevitably we got onto the subject of pushchairs and prams. Actually, let me just correct that: couples no longer discuss pushchairs and prams, they discuss 'travel systems'. In a time when the world has gone gadget-crazy, the world of baby transportation has also received a technological facelift. 'Travel systems' are designed to take care of your baby's transportation needs from new born baby to toddler, and will inevitably consist of a pram which is able to turn into a pushchair, (think Transformers for Mums) while some others will also include a car seat which clips onto the frame.

Buying a 'travel system' these days is much like buying a car – you consider things like luggage space, brakes and even bloody suspension. At one stage, I thought I was going to have to compare the fuel consumption, tax brackets and insurance groups.

After a lot of in-depth research consisting of randomly typing things into Google, my wife decided that she wanted one of the most expensive ones, the Bugaboo. The first time around we were persuaded to purchase one of the shop's own brands after an impressive demonstration from the guy working the shop floor and also assurance that it was their best seller. That it may have been, but we soon found out that it was also almost certainly the heaviest 'travel system' on earth, and the pram absolutely did not and definitely would not go completely flat as we were led to believe. Still, at least we're not bitter about it.

Wednesday 31st July 2013

This morning I found out the answer to a question I had never previously considered.

The answer was five times.

The question was "How many times do you have to make eye-contact with a stranger before it becomes unbearably uncomfortable?"

It was a strange journey this morning. There was a weird atmosphere about the train, one of frustration and tension, brought on no doubt by both the predictable delays and the unpredictable weather. Seats were scarce as usual and the guy who managed to grab the prized seat opposite me almost had to physically fight off the competition (a woman in her fifties who simply never stood a chance). He sat there like a lion after a kill, panting wildly, beaming with pride over his acquisition. He was looking around for a nod of appreciation, a raised eyebrow with which to acknowledge his achievement, some sort of recognition that he was the alpha male.

I just scowled back, meeting his gaze, trying to look unimpressed and non confrontational; I wanted him to know that while I was willing to stare at him, I wasn't willing to start on him. The look continued for an uncomfortable five or six seconds until he finally looked away.

Andy Leeks 1 – 0 Lion King

There was something about him that I didn't like. It could have been his bullishness, it may have been his smug demeanour and, who knows, it might just have been his ghastly tie. Whatever it was, I was unable to look away and busy myself with my writing. My unmoving stare meant that whenever he looked up, he was met by yours truly scowling at him again. To his credit, he didn't shy away and was able to give as good as he got, until eventually I had to look away.

Andy Leeks 1 – 1 Lion King

This ridiculous charade carried on another couple of times, with each of us claiming victory, tying the score at two each.

Andy Leeks 2 – 2 Lion King

With only five minutes left until the train was due to pull into the station I started to play a little tactically in an effort to swing things in my favour. I was aware that the next point would ultimately seal victory, so I started to rub my eyes and blink, trying to increase the moisture, allowing for a far longer stare. I tried to imagine that the guy opposite had done something far more serious than simply barge his way into the seat opposite me. Suddenly this guy was responsible for me failing my first driving test, he was the reason I had to wear braces for five years at school, and he was the guy on eBay who gave me negative feedback even though I explained in detail that the item did have a few scratches.

Twenty seconds in and I could sense that he was giving up. I could see small movements in the corner of his eyes, his nose was lightly twitching and then it happened – he took the coward's way out. He delved into his pocket to answer a phone call; only it wasn't a phone call, it was a fake phone call. Having had to perform many fake phone calls myself while walking the streets of London, (in order to avoid people in coloured tops wielding clip-boards) I knew all of the tell-tale signs to look out for, such as the lack of a ringtone, a blank caller display and garbled conversation which made no sense. In fact, thinking about it, back in my drinking days most of my phone calls must have been fake phone calls.

Anyway, I'm claiming it.

Andy Leeks 3 – 2 Lion King, final score.

Thursday 1st August 2013

This morning I experienced something amazing. Now, when you read the word amazing, I'm sure most of you assume that amazing means good. Kind of like if you were to say (and I'm not trying to put any words in your mouth here) "Have you read As They Slept (The comical tales of a London commuter) by Andy Leeks? You haven't? You should, it's amazing!"

Well, today, by amazing I mean startling, puzzling and entertaining, all rolled into one. Kind of like if you were to say "Have you seen Lady Gaga's wardrobe? You haven't? You should, it's amazing!"

I was on the final leg of my morning commute and the train was a distant memory as I completed the last few hundred yards on foot. Suddenly and without warning the rain came down thick and fast, and without an umbrella there was nothing I could do but carry on and get wet. I remember being envious of the lady in front of me as she confidently unfurled her tiny telescopic umbrella, opening it above her with a one-handed flourish.

I happened to notice that one of the spokes of the umbrella was broken, which made the umbrella look like a giant bat with a huge broken wing, flapping in the wind. I guessed that she was on the phone to a friend at the time, using some sort of hands-free device, as I could hear her talking and she was gesticulating wildly.

One of the annoying side-effects of hands-free communication is that it ensures the person using it, in the minds of all onlookers at least, is without doubt a complete lunatic. I'm not exactly sure why they call it hands-free, because as soon as the hands are free from the restrictions of a handset, they seem to go on a quest of their own. I've been punched in the face by a hands-free communicator on more than one occasion and I've been tempted in the past to throw money at them, certain that they are some sort of busking mime act.

Suddenly, as I drew up alongside the lady, desperate to overtake, (see chapter on pedestrian racing – Tuesday 5th February) the wind blew her umbrella inside-out and with it, broke another spoke. She screamed at the top of her voice and it was at this point that I realised she wasn't on the phone – she was in fact having some sort of mini breakdown. Clearly fed up with the broken umbrella, she stood motionless for a second before shouting at the top of her voice (I apologise for the language you're about to read, but I feel it's absolutely necessary to quote exactly what she shouted):

"FUCK! THE FUCKING FUCKER'S FUCKED!"

And to think, people say that the English language is complicated!

Friday 2nd August 2013

As a commuter, I've had to learn to cope with disappointment. One of the first disappointments you experience as a commuter is finding out the gold card you are issued with is not in fact real gold, (as the price would lead you to believe) it is in fact a piece of yellow card which fades after two weeks and stops working after four.

You seem to spend your life trying to convince the conductor on the train that your ticket is valid. "It's the 24th July," you say confidently, knowing full well that he doesn't believe you and neither would you if the situation were reversed. Worse still is when the ticket has faded AND stopped working. It makes for some very awkward and angry exchanges at the ticket barrier as you plead your innocence while being physically and verbally abused by the people behind. There's a certain skill to staying calm while being accused of being both a liar and an arsehole.

When I first started commuting, I was travelling in from Watford and often had to catch three trains to get to work. That meant six barriers, and journeys to and from work meant that my ticket found its way through twelve barriers each day. Being a lot younger back then, I was often out in the evenings and at weekends too, so in some weeks, my ticket went through as many as seventy or eighty barriers. That's a lot of wear and tear on a little piece of card, and I found that I regularly had to replace it. During one replacement ticket request I was told that I would have to pay a charge to have it replaced.

"Why?" I asked, confused.

"I can see that this is the third one we've issued this year, and while we're happy to replace cards which stop working due to wear and tear, we charge a small administration fee for those which are damaged due to negligence," he said authoritatively.

"How can using my ticket be classed as negligence?" I asked, genuinely bemused.

"This has clearly gone through the wash, sir; we get it a lot. We charge a small fee in order to cover our administration costs, and it has the added benefit of ensuring you're more careful next time," he said accusingly.

"But it hasn't," I said incredulously. "The trousers I keep my pass in haven't been washed for weeks," I stated, probably giving away more than I should have. In my defence, I lived at home with my parents at the time and my Mum had a very simple rule: "I will happily wash your clothes, but you've got to put them in the basket by the washing machine," she would say. But because the washing machine was in the utility room, which was downstairs, and my trousers would be taken off upstairs, this very rarely happened.

I argued for longer than I should have, the effort and the stress certainly outweighing the £2 which was being demanded, but I just couldn't let it go. How could they be accusing me of negligence when it was their poor-quality tickets and their over-zealous machines which had caused the damage?

"Sniff it," I said, totally serious. "If it had been through the wash it would smell of Persil Non Bio, but I'm confident it will in fact smell like my sweaty back pocket," I went on.

"Really, sir, that's not... "

"SNIFF MY CARD!" I demanded, and to my amazement, he did.

"Well, I certainly can't smell any washing powder," he said, "and as you seem adamant, I'm prepared to waive the fee this time, but please be more careful in future."

I skipped away happy, not because I had saved £2, but because I was the moral victor. I had done nothing wrong and I had proved it, by asking a stranger in a uniform to sniff something that had been housed inches from my backside for the past eight weeks. Not the greatest of moral victories, but a victory all the same.

Less than a week later, however, my Mum, fed up of my laid-back attitude towards clothes-washing, decided to wash my trousers and with it my newly acquired card. Still, I suppose a clean pair of trousers was worth the £2 in the end. It would have cost more at the dry cleaners.

Monday 5th August 2013

My wife has constantly been complaining of memory loss in recent weeks, and although I do my best to keep her calm, telling her that it's probably down to the pregnancy and the extra hormones, she's been adamant that she has an actual, recognised condition.

"You do have an actual, recognised condition," I said. "It's called hypochondriasis."

"What's hypochondriasis?" she replied, and just to wind her up, I said "I told you last week; you must have forgotten!"

So I was genuinely shocked when my wife called me the other day to confirm that she had been diagnosed with CRAFT syndrome.

"I was speaking to Amy next door and she said she used to have it, and that was when it all made perfect sense to me."

"What are the symptoms?" I asked, desperate to find out more.

"Just general forgetfulness during pregnancy," she calmly explained.

"Is it permanent? Will it go away after pregnancy?" I asked.

"Who knows?" she said nonchalantly. "I could be stuck with it forever."

"Is there anything you can do, or maybe I can do, to make it better?" I asked, getting more and more worried by the minute.

"No, not really, we'll just have to both learn to live with it," she said.

My life had been turned upside-down. There I was joking that my wife was a hypochondriac, and now here she was confirming my worst fears – she was in fact suffering from a condition from which she might never recover.

"When did you see the Doctor?" I asked.

"Oh, I didn't need to. Amy knew what it was straight away and it made perfect sense," she said.

"CRAFT syndrome," I said out loud. "Is that an acronym of some kind?"

"Yes," she said. "It stands for Can't Remember A Fucking Thing; most pregnant women get it," she said, trying and failing to hold back a laugh.

I couldn't believe I'd been taken in; I genuinely thought my wife might have an incurable illness.

"Let it be," I said.

"Bless. Thank you; it's nice to see you can take a joke," she said.

"No, LETITBE," I said. "Last ever time I try being empathetic!"

Now, while my wife's brain is constantly trying and failing to come up with the necessary information, it seems that my brain is doing the opposite. My brain seems intent on supplying information without any forethought at all. This afternoon, while paying for my lunch at the self-service till, going through the rigmarole of scanning, weighing, swearing, re-scanning and then bagging, a guy went up to the manned till next to me and asked for a packet of cigarettes. I won't mention the brand because I'm not sure if it constitutes a violation of the advertising rules on tobacco products. Let's just say that he asked for something like a packet of Satin Slice.

As the lady went to grab the cigarettes, he said "Oh, and a lighter, I've bloody gone and lost mine again."

As she selected a lighter the man suddenly interjected "A red one please; red is my lucky colour," to which I replied without thinking "It's clearly not that lucky if you keep bloody losing them!"

I don't quite know why I said it. It's the kind of thing most people would think, but not say, yet I was more than happy to bypass the area of the brain responsible for vetting speech, and let it escape.

Sarcasm is often deemed the lowest form of wit, but let me tell you, sarcasm with a stranger sits even lower down on the scale, and the look he gave me absolutely confirmed that fact.

Tuesday 6th August 2013

One of the few perks you get as a commuter is the huge choice of free reading material on offer. Every morning you can pick up a free copy of the Metro, every evening you can take a free copy of the Evening Standard, and throughout the week you're forcefully offered countless other papers and supplements.

What I'll never understand though are the people who sit quietly, like a cat ready to pounce, waiting for a paper to be put down. There's one in every carriage, eyeing every single paper, waiting for the opportunity to launch their attack. The paper will be placed on an empty seat or table and it will be snatched away as if the person's life depended on it.

There's a paper-cat on my train this morning. I can see her eyeing all of the papers around her. Not content with trying to read over everyone's shoulder, she's now actively seeking out a paper for herself. If she's so desperate to read a paper, why didn't she pick one up on the way to the station? As far as I'm aware they're available free of charge at every station. Don't get me wrong, I'm all for sharing. In fact if everyone shared a newspaper, I dare say it would make quite a difference to both the environment and the economy, but I just find paper-sharing with strangers a little bit weird.

Call me a fussy old sod, but I see a discarded paper as litter and unless I was on paid litter duty, you wouldn't ever see me picking up someone else's paper. For me, it would be the same as picking up someone's ice cream wrapper and licking it. That paper has been read by its owner; the pages have been folded, creased and turned, often by licked thumbs and fingers. There's probably more DNA on that paper than the average crime scene, so why would I ever want to expose myself to that?

I remember watching a guy a couple of months ago absolutely going to town on his morning paper. When I say going to town, I mean that he was flapping it, flicking it and folding it as if it were going out of fashion, while all the time coughing, sneezing and licking his thumbs to his heart's content. He tossed it on his seat upon getting off at London Bridge and then I watched in astonishment as the person who had sat next to him, who had just watched the episode of CSI Origami unfold in front of him, not only went on to read the paper, but happily licked his thumbs while doing it.

Having spent the last forty minutes desperately seeking out a paper, the cat finally managed to get her hand on one. Rather than looking pleased, she seemed nonplussed, and after only thirty seconds or so had folded the paper up and put it between her head and the window and closed her eyes.

So, it seems that she wasn't looking for reading material at all; she was simply looking for something to rest her head on. Surely there has got to be something more comfortable than a folded up newspaper; something with far less DNA from random strangers. Maybe she could bring her pillow in with her? That said, by the look of her, while that might satisfy the first criterion, I'm not sure it does the second.

Wednesday 7th August 2013

I think it's about time somebody highlighted the issue of train rage. Road rage has hogged the headlines for far too long and it's time other rages had their moments in the spotlight.

Once again we were subjected to cancellations and delays last night, owing to a track-side failure in the Charing Cross area. Having had to give up trying to get a train from Cannon Street, I made my way to London Bridge on foot and arrived both hot and bothered. The station was alive with a swarm of angry commuters, and as I surveyed the scene I could see swathes of shaking heads, gesticulating arms and sweary phone calls taking place.

I used to be one of those people. I could shake my head and gesticulate with the best of them and you only need to ask my wife to find out how sweary my phone calls home could get. In recent months, however, I've managed to calm down considerably. Strangely, the more frequent the cancellations and delays are, the calmer I've become. There now seems to be such an inevitability to it all that I'm able to prepare myself for the worst before I even arrive at the station. I've found that if I expect there to be delays and cancellations before I arrive at the station, then anything else is a bonus. Incidentally, I started employing a similar attitude towards birthdays from when I was about thirteen.

So as I sat down on the station concourse to cool down, I watched the angry scene play out in front of me. Every single emotion was represented as I scanned left to right. In the middle of the concourse there were tantrums, tears and tiffs, but on the outer edges there was a calmer air of acceptance, with people sitting and watching the entertainment unfolding in front of them. It was almost as if we were the spectators in the Colosseum and the people in the middle were charged with tackling the lions.

Unbelievably, my thoughts of ancient battles nearly became a reality as two men suddenly squared up to each other.

"Why don't you watch where you're going?" said the guy in his mid-to-late fifties, wearing a very nice suit which was unfortunately let down by the tatty old rucksack slung over his left shoulder.

"Why don't you fuck off?" said the rather blunt man in his early forties.

The rucksack was then placed on the floor and the two men, both clearly old enough to know better danced around it in pretty circles, pretending to throw punches at each other. Cue further swearing and a very good rendition of the Benny Hill theme tune from the gentleman next to me.

"You should be old enough to know better," shouted a lady in the distance.

"Why don't you grow up?" shouted another.

The guy doing the theme tune stopped, certain she was talking to him, but upon realising that she wasn't, picked up where he'd left off.

In a few seconds it was all over, finishing with the guy with the rucksack calling the guy without the rucksack a little prick, which then led to the guy without the rucksack kicking the guy with rucksack's rucksack.

I watched them storm off in opposite directions, huffing, puffing and snarling, bright red with rage and embarrassment. Suddenly they both stopped to check the departure boards and, upon realising there were delays, proceeded to stand less than ten paces apart. The next twenty minutes were more excruciating to watch than the preceding two, as each of them tried and failed to avoid eye-contact. As each of them calmed down, I couldn't help thinking how silly they must have felt and how weird it must have been to be thinking "There is a stranger whose bag I have publicly kicked standing less than fifteen feet away from me."

As I said at the beginning of this chapter, it's about time other rages had their moment in the spotlight. Never have I witnessed a road rage incident where the two drivers got back in their cars, only to drive ten metres down the road and park next to each other.

Monday 12th August 2013

I was in the unfortunate situation yesterday where I made my child cry. It was completely avoidable and I am 100% to blame, which makes it all the more difficult to admit to and even more difficult to do in writing. However, I would ask that you do not contact social services, at least until the end of the chapter, so as to give me a chance to explain.

We were enjoying a pleasant afternoon in the garden, and my daughter had grown bored of playing with her sand and blowing bubbles (I'd like to point out that those are two separate activities; I like to think that she's clever, but she's not that clever). I asked her what she'd like to do, and she elected to do some drawing.

"Bring the paper and pens out here," I said, keen to keep her outside in the fresh air.

I could see that she had become distracted on the way back out into the garden as she'd remembered the paper, but instead of pens, she had in her right hand a selection of animals from her farm.

"How are we going to do some drawing if we don't have anything to draw with?" I asked.

"Aeroplane!" she shouted, distracted once again, as she looked towards the sky, pointing.

Suddenly, I had an idea. "Would you like Daddy to make you an aeroplane?" I asked, convinced that I was about to earn some serious cool points.

"Yes," she said eagerly. "Can I fly in it?"

"No, I said," convinced I'd just lost the cool points. "It's one made of paper that you can throw."

"Oh…" she said, turning her attention back to the two chickens and a cow which were still in her clutches.

Thanks in part to the lukewarm response, I went on to make the best paper aeroplane that I can ever remember making. It was streamlined, aerodynamic and folded to perfection.

"Watch this!" I shouted as the plane took flight. My daughter looked on in amazement as it speedily made its way from one end of the garden to the other. I was relieved to see that it was heading harmlessly towards the hedge; that is, until it caught a sudden gust of wind and changed trajectory. Suddenly, instead of heading harmlessly towards a hedge it was heading harmfully towards my daughter's head and, as if in slow motion, it made contact with the corner of her eye.

I ran towards her as fast as I could, dodging the two chickens and a cow which had been launched on impact, and managed to calm her down. Luckily the plane had missed her eye by millimetres and crash-landed into her temple. As she screamed in pain, my daughter uttered six words which made my heart sink.

"Daddy, don't ever hurt me again!"

I felt awful because as a Daddy I'm meant to be the one protecting her, not the one hurting her. I had a similar heart-sinking moment a few weeks ago, when another child at nursery had said something to my daughter and I was sure she was being picked on. "Daddy, a girl called me a dog today!" she had said. I couldn't believe that children could be so cruel at such a young age.

"Why did she call you a dog?" I asked, not quite believing what I was hearing.

"Because I'm always picking up sticks," she said, matter-of-factly.

I shouldn't have jumped to conclusions, and I should have made the connection myself because she had somehow amassed a huge collection of sticks in the previous few weeks. It's still her favourite thing to do and if ever we're outside and running out of traditional entertainment, we can always fall back on the tried and trusted "Let's see if we can find some sticks" game.

When I think about it, I don't know why I work so bloody hard, because I think my daughter would be more than happy living the simple life. Her favourite food is bread, her favourite drink is water and all she wants to do is collect wood. She would have been better off born in the bloody 1500s.

Tuesday 13th August 2013

I'm not a fan of drunks as a general rule. It's difficult to converse with someone who is rude, argumentative and irrational, and it's for that same reason that I very rarely speak to traffic wardens.

As a child I remember being around my fair share of drunks. I remember being confused at family gatherings, wondering what was so bloody funny all the time, and why the hell Uncle Steve was asleep on the front lawn. Of course I remember the good things about those family get-togethers too; I remember the extra pocket-money from my distant relatives, the abundance of unhealthy snack food and my personal favourite, the extended bedtime hours. More often than not, however, those extended bedtime hours were less to do with the party atmosphere and more to do with the fact that Uncle Steve had moved from the front lawn to my bed!

This evening I encountered another kind of drunk, and it's one I like. On the train this evening, we have the polite drunk. Dressed impeccably, save for the off-centre tie and his wine-stained teeth, there's nothing this man is not intent on apologising for.

He is clearly aware that he's had one or two too many at the 'strategy lunch', and is now overcompensating on a monumental scale, in a futile attempt to come across as sober.

He has apologetically advised us that he'll be getting off soon, apologised that his feet might be in people's way, and apologised about his phone going off, before fumbling around for the mute button. In fact, the one thing he hasn't apologised for thus far is the smell of his breath. There's no pulling the wool over my eyes though, because even if I hadn't spied his wine-stained teeth and been subjected to his toxic breath, I had already seen the yearning look on his face as the drinks trolley made its way past.

I'm glad to say, as the train pulled into his stop, he didn't let me down. Having already apologised profusely to everyone in the carriage for having to get up from his seat, his phone began to ring, for which he apologised to everyone once again.

"I thought I had put it on mute," he announced as he stepped off the train.

Just as the doors were closing he answered his phone, and the only words I managed to catch were…

"I'm sorry…"

I'm guessing he'll need to say it a few more times this evening before he's forgiven!

Wednesday 14th August 2013

I'm fairly confident that everyone, at one stage or another, has been told off. Even Snotty Simon the school prefect would have been told off at some point in his life, whether by his father, the choir master or even his bridge partner. I am confident there will always be someone who has been affected adversely by your actions and who is more than happy to tell you about it.

I wasn't a particularly naughty child, but I do remember being told off from time to time. I always found it incredibly hard to deal with, primarily because it was forbidden to answer back. Whether it was my parents, my teachers or even crazy Mr Johnson from number 42, I just stood there and took it.

The reason for me covering the subject of tellings-off this evening is because less than fifteen minutes ago I was told off. While it was an incredibly humiliating experience, it's important to note that the advantage of being told off as an adult is that you can argue back, and in my case argue back with vigour.

My wife had reminded me this morning to bring home a paper, not because she was particularly interested in catching up with the day's news, but because we're moving and the paper comes in handy when wrapping up delicate items.

I very rarely read a paper nowadays, thanks mainly to this book, but I have been known to bring home a paper in the winter, as they come in extremely handy when lighting our open fire.

With my wife's words fresh in my mind as I strolled back to the station from a hard day's work, I glanced at the huge stack of papers outside Cannon Street station and decided to grab a handful. What could be the harm? The papers are free, they'll come in extremely handy for our move, and they'll be recycled responsibly once used.

"You can't do that," came a voice from behind me.

I looked behind, fully expecting to witness someone doing something they shouldn't be doing. Was it the guy crossing the road without waiting for the green man? Was it the guy walking up the steps with white socks and black shoes on?

"Why are you taking so many?" said the voice from behind me.

I'd like to say at this point that I came back with something incredibly witty, something like "Excuse me, Madame, I can't talk now – I've got too many papers to deliver," or "I'm in training for the world origami championships," but I actually just said "What's it got to do with you?"

Clearly up for an argument, she went on to say "It's one paper per person."

"I'm sorry," I said. "I forgot to check out the rules."

"Just because they're free, it doesn't mean you can just help yourself," she said, and this is where she was wrong. I absolutely could and indeed did help myself. In fact, had I so de-sired, I could have hired a truck and travelled around the city, systematically relieving London of all its free papers and I wouldn't have broken a single law. (Assuming of course that I had paid the bloody congestion charge) Often when free samples are given away, or there are 'buy one get one free' offers, there are limits as to how many one can have, but with free papers I'm certain it's a case of take what you want and when they're gone, they're gone.

The woman tutted as if her life depended on it before reaching around me to pick up her own paper.

"You could have had one of mine," I said. "I've got plenty!"

She carried on up the steps with a final flurry of tuts and I thought no more about it, until I took my seat on the train and, lo and behold, saw someone familiar opposite me.

I was expecting a tut, but she surprised me with a huff instead and busily went about reading her precious paper. With my bag full of papers safely stowed in the overhead compartment, I busied myself with writing this very chapter. After around twenty minutes, she put her paper down on the table between us and sat back and closed her eyes.

After a few minutes, once I was sure she was asleep, I decided to make my move.

"Excuse me, do you mind if I read your paper?"

Of course I had no intention of reading it, and I'm ashamed to admit that my sole purpose was to get under her skin, as she had managed to get under mine. As it turns out, it's a good job I had no intention of reading it as she simply looked me up and down and said "I think you've got enough of your own," and promptly folded it up and sat on it.

"Here, you can have mine," came a voice from behind. "Some people can be so bloody rude!"

Thursday 15th August 2013

Ever since the smoking ban came into force in July 2007, we have had to put up with publicans complaining about the declining trade.

While I'm sympathetic to the position they find themselves in, I can't help feel that more could be done to attract a wider audience. I haven't once visited a pub that has managed to provide all that's required to please everyone, because to please everyone it would need to have good food, a great atmosphere, a collection of elderly drunks, a collection of offensive drunks, a darts team, a jukebox, a dance floor, a play room, a pool table, a big screen and of course a topless waitress or two. No pub is ever going to be able to manage all that. In fact some pubs can't even cover the basics, which I consider to be beer mats and toilet seats. I see it as my right as a paying customer to expect to be able to rest both my beer and my arse on something.

While pubs insist on doing nothing to encourage new customers, it does beg the question of where all the customers are going. They can't be going to other pubs, because they all seem to be in the same mess, so they must be going somewhere else. I thought most people must have either cut down their drinking altogether, or simply have started drinking more at home, but this evening I found out that there's another group of drinkers, keen to carry on drinking, but clearly happy to be doing so on their own terms.

This evening, as I made my way to the station, I saw a group of young men and women gathered around a couple of benches, each with a drink in their hand. I'd guess there were ten or so people of varying ages, some stood up chatting, others casually sat on the benches and the grass surrounding them. A few of the guys had cans of Stella in their hands, another couple of guys had what looked like bottles of pear cider, and there were a couple of girls pouring miniature bottles of wine into plastic cups. They all looked happy and relaxed, enjoying the evening sun, and I can't help feeling they were almost certainly having a much nicer time there than they would in some dark and dingy pub. I dare say they saved a fair few quid too. In fact the only downside I could think of (aside from the fact that drinking in a public place is probably illegal) is that there were no toilet facilities. Where are these rebellious few going to empty their bladders?

While on the subject, I have a story about needing the toilet which I'm a little ashamed to relate. I will though. I apologise for what you're about to read, but I feel I need to get it off my chest in order to get over it and get on with my life. I remember the exact date it happened, partly because I'm still mentally scarred, but mainly because it's a date that's very difficult to forget. It was December 31st 1999.

I was twenty years old and had an active and happy social life. Most of my friends had returned from university for Christmas and we'd all arranged to meet up in London to enjoy the Millennium celebrations. There was a party atmosphere, and the police had turned a blind eye to the fact that almost everybody was drinking alcohol. My friends and I were no different, and we had stopped at a shop on the way and stocked up on three carrier bags full of beer. At around 11pm we made our way to Trafalgar Square, and it was at this point that things started to get serious.

Suddenly, in a matter of minutes, people started piling into Trafalgar Square and we got totally stuck in the middle with nowhere to go. It got so crowded that we could no longer move and I remember my chest feeling tight as more and more people piled in. I remember saying at one point that we needed to get out, but my friends were right when they simply said "How?"

We all stopped drinking at that point, not through choice, but simply because there was not enough room to raise our hands to our mouths. We were effectively sardines, and as I started to think about sardines and the sea, I realised just how much I needed the toilet.

HELP! How was I going to get out of this one?

I'll tell you exactly how I got out of that one: I used my initiative. I remembered that earlier on, having finished the last of one of the bags of beers, I'd stuffed the carrier bag into my coat pocket. Without a moment's thought I reached for the bag, unzipped my flies and started weeing. Absolutely no-one but me knew that I was having a wee, because we were so tightly packed in. The relief was incredible as I finished and tied up the bag. I had no idea what to do with the bag and so spent the next hour just holding it until the crowd finally started to disperse.

Once there was enough room to move, my friends and I started to walk towards Euston station. We figured the tubes would be packed and, after being squeezed in so tightly for the last hour, thought it would be nice to stretch our legs. Before long I was nonchalantly walking along, swinging my bag back and forth, until my friend Gary suddenly shouted "Andy, be careful, it looks like one of your beers has spilt!"

It was then that I remembered I was holding a bag full of wee and not a bag of beers. Only it wasn't a bag full of wee, it was a bag half full of wee, and I was happily leaving a trail all the way back to Trafalgar Square. I feel confident that had the police needed to track me down that evening, they could have dispensed with the tracker dogs completely and simply used their own noses.

Worse was to come. A friend of mine, having taken a turn for the worse earlier on in the evening, had suddenly recovered enough to want to carry on drinking.

"Andy, you didn't tell me you still had some beers left! I'll help you out if you're struggling!"

"No, it's alright," I said as I made my way to the nearest bin. "This stuff tastes like piss!"

So how these bench drinkers were going to relieve themselves I had no idea, but I did smile when I saw there were a couple of carrier bags amongst them.

Friday 16th August 2013

As I made way down the steps at Cannon Street station this morning, ready to complete my daily fifteen-minute walk to work, I was confronted by the usual handful of people keen to thrust things upon me. I remember a time in London when the only people you ever encountered were people who were keen to take something off you, namely your wallet or watch; yet nowadays all anyone seems to want to do is give you stuff. Fridays seem to be the busiest days, and because of this I've started to call it 'Freebie Friday'. I honestly think there's enough free stuff being given away at train stations these days that you could conceivably survive being marooned there, penniless and naked, for weeks at a time.

This morning there were a team of enthusiastic youngsters handing out drink samples, there was a man giving away copies of City AM, there was a man giving away copies of Sport, and there was a middle-aged woman giving out what looked like business cards of some kind. Everyone went straight for the free drink of course, with one or two people accepting the free papers, but the poor woman was being completely ignored.

She looked sad and dejected, wondering how her tiny little cards could ever match up to a free drink or paper, so I thought I would brighten up her day and relieve her of one of her business cards. I think the reason people rarely accept business cards on the street is because it's impossible to tell what you're accepting until it has found its way into your hand, and there's nothing worse than being stuck with a business card which says "Tits-out Tuesday! 50% off drinks and private dances when you present this card."

I've been in the tricky situation of being in possession of one of these cards before, and it's never an easy one to explain. I was perfectly innocent and had a perfectly reasonable excuse, but that didn't stop me feeling as guilty as hell. I had been on a stag weekend down in Bournemouth, and at various stages of the night you get handed cards and flyers for various pubs, clubs and inevitably, 'late-night establishments'.

I realised as soon as it was handed to me that it wouldn't be required, but you can't simply hand it back, and putting it straight into a bin is just plain rude. I made a mental note to dispose of it when out of sight, but of course the beer started to flow and in my pocket it remained, until my wife found it five days later when doing the washing.

You see, darling, I told you that was what it was doing in my pocket all along.

Phew. Moving on...

As I approached the middle-aged lady, I had a terrible feeling I would be frantically looking for a bin as soon as I got round the corner, but I was pleasantly surprised to see a very respectable-looking company on the card, so I accepted it with glee.

Even better was the bold lettering on the front of the card stating:

25% PREFERENTIAL SAVINGS.

"Ha ha, suckers!" I thought as I continued to read the card. "You can take your free drink and your free bloody paper..."

Oh, bugger! As I read the rest of the card, I realised what my preferential offer was for.

Davy's - a family-owned Wine Merchants since 1870.

As good as the offer might be, it's no bloody good to a guy who's teetotal and whose wife is nearly seven months pregnant!

Monday 19th August 2013

After two full weeks of pleading and begging, I finally gave in to my wife, on the proviso that what we were about to do would count as both our anniversary and her birthday present. While those with a filthy mind may well be conjuring up rude images, I regret to inform you that anything of that nature would almost certainly require me to trade in an anniversary, birthday, Easter, Christmas, and a sizeable down-payment on shoes.

What I had in fact agreed to was an evening of Shakespeare. I'd booked tickets to see an outdoor performance of Romeo and Juliet in the grounds of a nearby medieval castle. "Wonderful!" I'm sure many of you are thinking, but for me it wasn't "Wonderful!" It was a pain in the arse. I have voiced my dislike for Shakespeare ever since we were made to dissect it line by line at school, and my feelings certainly haven't mellowed as I've got older.

I can certainly appreciate the talent, and I dare say if Ant, Dec and Simon Cowell had been around in the 1600s, William Shakespeare may well have been performing at Ye Olde Royal Variety Performance, but for me it's all a bit much. In my eyes William Shakespeare suffered from terrible verbal diarrhoea, and his work reminds me of my school English assignments, full of unnecessary padding.

Don't worry, I do appreciate the irony of me criticising Shakespeare's work. It's like my Dad giving Tiger Woods advice on his swing. And in many ways my book is an example of just how diverse the English language can be. One the one hand you have a man who spent decades with a quill and a pot of ink, carefully crafting stories of love and heartache, and then here I am tapping away on an iPad, talking about free newspapers and weeing into plastic bags.

After my initial scepticism, I was encouraged to see that amongst the props were foot-balls, football rattles and football scarves. Unfortunately it was short-lived, as the props were simply to help warm up the crowd and to distinguish between the characters. What followed was just under four hours of unabated Shakespearian dialogue. Pure joy for my wife and absolute hell for me. I tried my best to get into it, but I couldn't help thinking "Just get to the point, man." I eventually ended up entertaining myself by trying to guess the names and professions of the people in the audience – a completely pointless task as I would never be able to find out the answers. I was however genuinely surprised to see so many Richards in attendance, and who would have thought there were so many taxidermists living locally?

I suppose one of the main issues I had is that I felt very uncomfortable in the surroundings. I come from a fairly working-class background and I'm used to going to the football, surrounded by the smell of meat pies and the sound of 20,000 grown men enquiring as to who the wanker in the black is. So imagine how out of place I felt when the smell of meat pies had been replaced by the gentle whiff of smoked salmon, and the only sounds were the gentle pop of champagne corks.

Whatever my thoughts on Shakespeare, I have to give credit to the actors, who did an amazing job. There were times when I was so in awe of their ability to remember all those lines that I very nearly choked on my couscous.

Tuesday 20th August 2013

It was at exactly 12.38pm yesterday when I realised. I can be that specific because it was at precisely 12.38pm when I received a text message from my Mum, wishing me a happy anniversary.

"Bugger!" I thought.

I leave the house at 6:45 each morning and while I would like to give my wife a passionate and proper goodbye each day, I'm usually running a few minutes late and she's more often than not completely sound asleep. Yesterday I think I elected for a peck on the forehead.

Wait. Hang on. No, yesterday morning my wife woke up! She woke up! I remember now, I kissed her on the forehead and she woke up and met my gaze, wishing me a safe journey.

Up until I started to write this chapter I'd assumed that although I'd forgotten, my wife was none the wiser, but now that I've re-traced my steps, we definitely engaged in conversation in the morning. Now I come to think of it, she did have a look of "Haven't you got something to tell me?" in her eyes. That said, eyes aren't easy to read in the morning, what with the black rings and the copious amounts of sleep.

Maybe I got away with it? Maybe she forgot too?

The thing is, even if she had forgotten for that brief moment while she was coming to, she certainly would have already bought and written a card, something I'm ashamed to say I hadn't done. The first clue that it was my anniversary (and as clues go, it was a fairly good one) was the message from my Mum wishing me a happy one.

"Thanks, you too! X" I replied, clearly panicked.

I remember being rather smug when we originally set the date. The 19th August is just three days before my birthday, and I remember thinking at the time that it would be almost impossible to forget the anniversary when it's so close to my birthday. All I'd have to do would be to realise that my birthday was coming up, and that would be an instant reminder to buy an anniversary card. The problem is that I don't really make a big fuss about my birthday and have never had the need to buy myself a bloody card, so I never give it a moment's thought. I realise now that we should have got married on the 26th August, then I would have had the perfect visual reminder – seeing a row of cards on the mantelpiece for four days leading up to the event.

In a way I think anniversaries are unfair on us men. It's not in our nature to do complex and unnatural things like remembering dates and buying cards. I've never quite worked out if women enjoy taking care of marking the calendar and buying the cards, or whether they do it simply because they know that we won't. If the latter is the case, then surely we should be given a little bit of slack?

A friend of mine came up with an interesting way of remembering his anniversary. He realised that every year he got an email from Pizza Express wishing him a happy birthday, so he decided to add his details to their mailing list again, only this time using a different email address. Instead of inputting his date of birth, he changed it to the date of his anniversary, and he put his first name as "Don'tForget" and his surname as "YourAnniversary". Every year he receives an email a few days before his anniversary with the words "Don'tForget YourAnniversary" in the title, which is his cue to go and get a card. Ingenious!

This year marks seven years since we were married, and I am reliably informed that we're now entering a phase known as the seven-year itch. The seven-year itch is the period in which people have been known to take stock of their relationship and decide whether or not it's worth sticking with. I'm sorry, but I can't imagine anyone taking seven years to work out whether or not they can get on. It rarely takes me longer than seven seconds. I only need to overhear someone on the train use phrases like "manage expectations" or "touch base" and I immediately feel compelled to poison their coffee.

As if to prove that I haven't been affected by the itch, I wrote the following words in my wife's card.

Dearest Wife

Happy Anniversary

Seven years and not the slightest itch!

Lots of love

Andy

Reading it back now, I can appreciate why she was a little upset at the wording...

Wednesday 21st August 2013

I was just about to make a start on today's chapter when I noticed that the guy opposite me, who was no older than 25, was getting stuck into a crossword. "That's not unusual," I hear you say. "A lot of people have a crack at the crossword when they're reading the paper." I agree, but this guy was heavily engrossed in what my Nan would call a 'Puzzler'. It's essentially a thick book of crosswords with a generic smiley woman with big hair and massive white teeth on the front. I've never seen one of these books in the possession of anyone under 65. In fact, I'm not sure I've ever seen one of these books outside of a WH Smiths, an old people's home or a hospital. Without a second thought, I took a photo and put it straight on Facebook with the following comment:

"I have a lot of respect for this chap. Never mind iPads or iPhones, where's my book of crosswords? His Nan must be so proud!"

While I was happy to mock this poor young chap, I wasn't prepared to ridicule him, so I edited the photo to blur out his face. (How very thoughtful of me). I was quite proud of my observation and so made no effort to hide what I was doing, meaning the woman next to me had a perfect view of my iPad, and the status update I was just about to post. I proudly pressed the post button and gave her a "Wasn't that funny?" kind of a look, and she gave me a knowing nod and a roll of the eyes in return.

Mission completed, I started to formulate a plan for today's chapter. It was impossible to get going though, because every few seconds I was disturbed by someone either liking or commenting on my post. Every time a comment came through, the whole screen was filled once again by the photo of the guy opposite, and I had to quickly alter the angle so as not to get caught by him. Each time I did so, I made sure to gesture to the woman next to me in a kind of "That was a lucky escape" way.

Then it just happened. The woman next to me put down her book, looked at me, then looked at the guy opposite and said seven simple words. "So darling, how was your day to-day?"

"Aaaaaaaaaggggghhhh!"

Right then I thought I was about to receive a few words of my own, but to her credit she didn't say anything. I turned off my iPad and sat there motionless, looking straight ahead. I was so embarrassed. Luckily for me, they got off at the very next stop. Lucky because it meant that the awkwardness was kept to a minimum, but also lucky because it left me enough time to finish this chapter.

Thursday 22nd August 2013

It's my birthday today, and it's the first time I have ever worked on my birthday! Even as a child I avoided having to go to school due to the date it fell on, and as I crept into adulthood I always managed to find an excuse to take the day off. "My wife's booked a surprise for me," I would say as I handed in the holiday request form, knowing full well I had nothing more planned than sitting in my pants all day eating chocolate cake.

I always felt sorry for the kids at school who had to come in on their birthdays. Birthdays are the one day a year when you're allowed to be spoilt; twenty-four hours of pure unadulterated selfishness. By going to school or work, you're shortening that already extremely small window considerably.

I asked my boss this morning that as this was the first time I'd ever worked on my birthday, was there any chance I could treat it a little differently?

"How do you mean?" he asked, puzzled.

"Put my feet up and take it easy," I said.

"I thought you wanted to treat it differently," he replied.

Charming!

Another good reason for not going to work on my birthday is that I miss out on having to buy the cakes! Call me a grump, but why the hell should I buy cakes for everybody when it's MY bloody birthday? Surely birthdays are the one day a year when you can sit back and let other people buy things for you. Not once have I woken up on my birthday and thought "Never mind me, everyone, here's a couple of hundred quid – why don't you go out and treat yourselves?" The tradition must have started somewhere. I imagine it started with the office junior one year. Fed up of sending him to fetch tartan paint and left-handed screw-drivers, someone somewhere told the office junior that when it's his birthday he has to buy the cakes, and this whole stupid birthday cake-buying nonsense was born.

I'm on the evening train home now, looking forward to seeing my wife and child, but I can't help feeling that I've been cheated. By insisting on sleeping for the first seven hours and then spending the next twelve hours at work, I've reduced my twenty-four hours of unadulterated selfishness to just five, and that's if I make it to midnight without falling asleep!

So, seven months pregnant or not, my wife's got her work cut out this evening as she only has five hours to squeeze in a three-course meal cooked from scratch and a luxurious massage followed by a perfectly run bath, all while providing some insightful and interesting chat about Watford's chances of lifting the title this year.

No? Well, a man can dream...

Tuesday 27th August 2013

After working on my birthday for the first time ever last Thursday, I decided I needed to take a day off to get over the shock of it all, so I took the following day off. It was a bank holiday weekend so it had the added advantage of turning a long weekend into a four-day break! We checked the weather forecast on Thursday evening, and as soon as we realised Friday was going to be warm and pleasant, we decided it would be nice to spend the day at the beach. I say beach because no-one seems to call it the "seaside" anymore. I suppose calling it the seaside when you're an adult seems a bit silly, and maybe calling it the beach feels that little bit more grown up. In fact, that makes perfect sense, because when you become a grandparent, the name gets changed again. Instead of the seaside or the beach, as soon as you get to retirement age, you start to call it the coast!

I grew up in Watford, and with the nearest beach being an hour and a half away, we only ever really saw the sea when we went on holiday each year. I remember as a child being in awe of the local children and being so jealous that they lived so close and could just pop to the beach whenever they wanted. My earliest childhood memories are of visiting places like Camber Sands, Folkestone, Hastings and Dymchurch, and I can still remember that feeling of excitement as we packed up the car, ready to spend a week in the land of sea gulls and sea shells. For me, one of the fantastic things about moving to Kent was the proximity of the beaches. We're now only about half an hour's drive away from a selection of beautiful sandy beaches, and as we packed up our things for our day out, I could feel my inner child itching to get out.

"Can I get an ice cream when we get there?" I asked as I started to pack the car.

"You can do what you like, darling, you're 34!" she said, looking at me like I'd just regressed a full 25 years.

"I meant shall we all have an ice cream when we get there! I wasn't asking for permission; I was purely asking if we should all get an ice cream when we get there, or whether we should maybe wait until after lunch..."

"Whatever you say," she said, smirking as she got into the car.

I couldn't decide whether I was more annoyed with my wife for trying to humiliate me, or with the fact that it had just dawned on me that I was 34, courtesy of the previous day's festivities. We drove on in silence for a few miles until our daughter shattered the peace by uttering the five dreaded words:

"Are we nearly there yet?"

My daughter has been on many long car journeys in the past, including Scotland, Wales and Devon to name but a few, and never once has she uttered those five words, yet here we were ten minutes into a trip to the beach and suddenly here they are. I can only surmise that the words "Are we nearly there yet?" have nothing to do with the length of journey and everything to do with the type of journey. We did what every parent does in the same situation and simply said "Nearly," knowing full well we had barely left. Not to disappoint, my daughter then proceeded to do what every other three-and-a-half-year-old would do and repeated those words every two to three minutes.

Just as we were expecting our daughter to ask us for the eighth time if we were nearly there yet, she surprised us with the words "Stop it!" Our daughter has started to talk to her imaginary friends of late, so it's not unusual to hear her barking out random instructions, so we left her to it.

"Stop it"

"Don't!"

"Stop doing that!"

And then finally:

"Mummy, tell it to stop!"

My wife and I looked at each other, puzzled. We had tried in the past to get involved with her imaginary arguments and had been told very matter-of-factly "Shh, I'm talking to my imaginary friends," so we were surprised that we'd been invited to intervene.

"What is it?" my wife asked, trying her best to turn around in her seat, but failing miserably due to a combination of a seatbelt with a hair-trigger locking mechanism, and a seven-month bump.

"The window, it keeps copying me. Tell it to stop!"

Unsurprisingly, the window didn't stop copying her, despite the sternest of words from my wife, and luckily for us we arrived just before being asked if we were "Nearly there yet" for the ninth time. We had decided on Dymchurch, swayed by the promise of unspoilt sandy beaches and donkey rides for the little one, but as we pulled into the car park I was at a loss as to whether we were in the right place. The sat nav was very confident that we were, proudly declaring that we had "Reached our destination," yet all I could see was a line of parked cars, a large grassy bank, and a pay and display machine. I decided to look for the vital clues, scanning the sky for seagulls, the car park for children carrying buckets, and the benches for flat caps and blue rinses.

I was delighted to see that all were present, so paid the £6.00 parking fee and scaled the grassy bank to be greeted by our first views of the sea. I wasn't disappointed. The sun was out, the beach looked clean and, although busy, there was plenty of space to settle down to enjoy a peaceful lunch. Our daughter started happily digging in the sand as we unpacked our things. We had a lot of things... We had a blanket, a couple of chairs, buckets, spades, flags, beach balls, sun cream, sunglasses, hats, towels, drinks, crisps and sandwiches. Finally, we were unpacked and settled and I had just taken a bite of my sandwich when it struck me that the sea seemed a lot closer than I remembered when we first arrived. By my second bite I was certain that it was getting closer and by my third bite I'd started packing up our things. We had a lot of things! We had a blanket, a couple of chairs, buckets, spades, flags, beach balls, sun cream, sunglasses, hats, towels, drinks, crisps and bits of sandwiches.

What I hadn't realised is that although Dymchurch has a lovely sandy beach, for approximately four hours a day the whole of that sandy beach is swallowed up by the tide, meaning that visitors to Dymchurch are restricted to sitting on the concrete sea wall. It was just our luck that those four hours happened to coincide with the four hours we'd intended on spending at the beach. It's ironic to think that I spend all week worrying about and checking train timetables only to be scuppered on my day off for not checking the bloody tide timetable.

While kids may say the funniest things, I can't help feeling that they get some things absolutely spot on. As I sat on the sea wall, with no beach in sight, I declared there and then that until I'm retired, the area where sea meets land will only ever be referred to as the seaside.

Wednesday 28th August 2013

As I look around the carriage this morning, I can see a real mix of people. It's a nice reminder that commuters come in many forms, and very rarely fit the stereotype of smart suits and broadsheet newspapers. I would say that only around half of the people in my carriage this morning are wearing typical business attire, while the other half are adorned with a colourful array of casual clothes.

So as a tribute to commuters everywhere, and in the hope that you all recognise a few of the people mentioned, I've decided to present my latest poem. Ahem-hem.

There's not one person that makes a commuter,

Some sit quietly and work on their computer.

Others use the time to apply their make up,

While others look depressed over their latest break-up.

Then there are those who talk on the phone,

And others who can't leave their privates alone.

Of course there's always a noisy eater,

And you always sit next to the broken heater.

There's always a train guard who looks like Yoda,

And a guy in the corner with questionable odour.

There's always someone tapping their feet,

And here comes fatty with his huge broadsheet.

There's always an old guy who should have retired,

And a person who's ticket has just expired.

The guy with the braces, who's starting to snore,

And the one with the glasses, the office bore.

The hungover guy, collapsed in a heap,

Five or six others fast asleep.

But always be careful and make sure you look

For the guy by the toilets, who's writing a book...

Friday 30th August 2013

It's been two years since we moved to Kent. Two years isn't a particularly long time, but it's long enough for us to realise that it's the place where we want to grow old. As much as I enjoyed growing up living in a busy town, village life just seems to suit my grumpy personality far better. Where I used to moan about the traffic lights, I now moan about the tractors. Where I used to moan about the youth of today, I now have to deal with the elderly. Where I used to moan about the dog poo littering the pavements, I now find myself moaning about the faeces of dog, cow, sheep and bloody horse. So basically there's still just as much to moan about, but the surroundings help me recover from my outbursts far quicker. All in all, it's a much quieter lifestyle and one that I very much enjoy. Who knows, if it wasn't for the longer commute I've found myself having to take, perhaps this book would never have been written. Maybe I'd still be staring blankly around the carriage, wondering why everyone was asleep.

One thing I haven't enjoyed about living in Kent is the fact that we're renting. When we originally moved to Kent, we needed to settle quickly as my wife was starting work at a new school, and we needed to find a child-minder for our daughter. We decided that the best way would be to start renting, with a view to buying in a couple of years. We knew we'd be good tenants, so picked a rental property we liked and settled back, safe in the knowledge we'd found our home for the next couple of years. Well, this weekend we're just about to move house for the third time. Three house moves in two years, with the latest one falling when my wife is seven months pregnant.

While renting may offer extra flexibility, it also offers less security, in that you can be served notice at any time after the initial tenancy period has expired. In both cases the landlord's circumstances had changed and so, although frustrating, it was totally understandable that we were required to move out. We've found it quite hard to explain to our daughter, and even now she hasn't quite got it.

"Can I take this to the new house?" she asked, holding out her right hand to reveal a small fluffy teddy.

"Yes, darling, we can take everything. In fact it's a fundamental requirement that we do, otherwise we'll be short of possessions and it's likely we won't get our deposit back."

"Oh," she said, looking around thoughtfully.

"Can I take this to the new house?" she asked, holding out her right hand to reveal a wooden figure.

"Yes, we're going to take everything. Everything you can see, we'll be taking to the new house."

"The stairs?" she pondered.

I was just about to lose my temper when I remembered a conversation we'd had earlier in the day, in which I was explaining to her that we were moving into a bungalow and so there wouldn't be any stairs. Maybe she genuinely thought that we could just move the stairs into the new place and that would solve the issue of being restricted to just the ground floor. Just as I was about to give her a thoughtful, sensible answer she asked:

"Are we taking the garden?"

Monday 2nd September 2013

I am writing today's chapter covered in scratches and having had just a few hours sleep. It is with genuine sadness that I must say that's the first time I've ever been able to stake that claim. After an exhausting weekend, we've finally completed the move to our new house, and now we have the unpleasant task of unpacking everything. Some people say that the unpacking part of the move is the fun part, as your new house becomes a blank canvas, allowing you to start afresh. Things you have grown bored of can be thrown out, things you had forgotten about can be put back out, and partners who interfere can apparently be told to get out!

While it might seem like the perfect opportunity to clear out the clutter, I believe it only truly works if you live on your own. I have lost count of the times that either my wife or I have said the words "but it might come in handy", "all it needs is a new battery" or "well you got to keep your golf clubs". Before we had children, we used to have a running joke where anything which didn't quite fit the other's taste would "look perfect in the spare room," but now we don't have a spare room we've each found ourselves trying to convince the other that the ideal place for that decorative floral picture frame / piece of Watford FC memorabilia is the garage. My wife's pregnancy has exacerbated the issue because it's meant that I've been responsible for a lot of the packing. I'm happy to admit that I am terrible at packing. When asked at the supermarket if I need any help with packing, I always say no, only to end up being told to "Give it here, I'll do it" by the check-out operator.

I'm also ashamed to admit that at 34 years old, I've only ever packed my own suitcase once, and that was only because I was taking part in a charity cross-country 'challenge' and the preparation notes had stated that "If you do not pack the right kit you could die". I was happy to be packing my own bag for the first time, because I was looking forward to the challenge. Only the word 'challenge' turned out to have been used in lieu of the word 'race'. What I had assumed would be a gentle jaunt from the East to the West coast of Scotland very quickly turned into a race by bike, boat and foot, and with the change of word came the change in my mood.

I love a challenge. The word challenge conjures up lovely childhood memories of arm wrestles in the park and trying to fit fourteen gobstoppers into your mouth. The word race, however, conjures up horrendous childhood memories of finishing second-last, ahead of only smelly Steven, in the egg and spoon race and seeing the genuine disappointment in my Dad's eyes for the very first time. (A look I would soon have to get used to).

The word challenge evokes a sit-up-straight, slap-the-desk-and-let's-get-this-done response, while the word race causes an involuntary shudder followed by a backing-away-and-sitting-down kind of response. Now I'm fully aware that there are people out there who love to race. In a weird kind of a way, I do too. In the right circumstances, racing to beat someone else is fun. I used to race my brother to see who could finish our milkshake first. See what I mean? Fun! Win or lose, it doesn't matter. Fun!

In the two weeks leading up to the 'race' I packed and re-packed my bag approximately twelve times. The equipment list had been checked, re-checked and then checked again. There were more ticks present on that one sheet than I had acquired in seventeen years of schooling. Thermals, First Aid kits, torches, waterproofs, maps, lists, list of lists, lists with maps, maps of lists. If I thought for one second that I could have fitted in my own defibrillator, it would have been packed.

While my bag-packing on that occasion could be considered a success, measured purely by the lack of death and not race position, it is my only success to date. But leading up to this weekend I'd been responsible for a lot of the packing, which, much like the supermarket, involved me picking up random items and putting them in bags until said bags were full. Again, much like the food shopping, the problem then comes when it's time to unpack and, in order to put things away, you end up having to keep retracing your steps from one place to another. Fine if you're a bald, slightly overweight, but ultimately healthy 34-year-old, but not fine if you're a hormonal, irrational, somewhere-in-her-mid-thirties-year-old.

Friday 6th September 2013

As you can see from the title of today's chapter, it's Friday, and if I'm totally honest, I feel a little cheated.

Normally on a Friday I have an extra spring in my step, a warm feeling inside and an altogether happier outlook on life. I am reliably informed that this feeling is commonly referred to as the 'Friday Feeling'. Now, if you believe everything they say in the adverts then you can easily re-create this feeling simply by purchasing and devouring a Cadbury's Crunchie, although I can categorically confirm that there is no amount of chocolate covered honeycomb that could have recreated that 'Friday Feeling' on a cold and wet Monday morning back in the days when I liked a Sunday-evening tipple.

This morning I feel cheated because although it's Friday, the feeling is nowhere to be found. The spring in my step has been replaced by a lead weight, the feeling inside can be best described as tepid, and my outlook on life right now is "What life?"

The problem I have is that, not for the first time this year, my body clock has been tricked. By having a couple of days off to sort out our new house, I've inadvertently re-set my weekly clock and my body is suddenly back on Monday mode. All day today I've had an uncontrollable urge to be irrational and grumpy with everyone I speak to, I've felt compelled to ask people what they have been up to over the past couple of days, and I've been feeling guilty all day for not calling my mum. It's not fair; I should be able to enjoy having the odd day off during the week, without the worry of having to return to a Monday mood. My brain seems to be a permanent let-down; not only is it constantly being tricked, it's always forgetting things too. I'm always finding myself saying things like "Darling, don't forget to remind me to…" and "Oh, I mustn't forget to…" before both my wife and I go on to completely forget whatever it was we were meant to do.

I've heard stories of people tying string around their fingers in order to help them re-member things, but that still relies on the person being able to actually remember what the thing was.

Hang on a minute – I've got it! Next time I have time off during the week I'm going to introduce my own version of the string technique. I'm going to tie some string in a big loop around my neck and hang a Crunchie from it. Even if it doesn't work, at least I'll have something nice to eat on the train on the way home!

Monday 9th September 2013

Having recently moved, we decided to attend the obligatory car-boot sale this weekend. Preparing for a car-boot sale for most people is easy; it usually involves sorting possessions into three categories.

1) Stuff that you want to keep because one day it might be useful.

2) Stuff that you want to sell.

3) Stuff that in an ideal world you would love to sell, but you reluctantly agree to throw away. Things such as broken crockery, old toilet brushes, etc.

There you have it – three simple categories.

We had nine, and they went like this.

1) Stuff that I wanted to keep, but my wife wanted to throw away.

2) Stuff that my wife wanted to keep, but I wanted to throw away.

3) Stuff that I wanted to sell but my wife wanted to keep.

4) Stuff that my wife wanted to sell but I wanted to keep.

5) Stuff that we both agreed should be kept.

6) Stuff that we both agreed should be thrown away.

7) Stuff that we both agreed should be sold.

8) Stuff that we didn't know we had, meaning we were not 100 percent sure whether it was ours or not, which meant we couldn't commit to throwing it away or selling it.

9) Stuff that we daren't even look at for fear of creating more categories, which mainly consisted of big boxes simply labelled 'Spare room'.

There should be a simple rule when clearing out a garage – the number of categories should be equal to or less than the number of corners available, and as my garage is not a nonagon, (something with nine sides – I had to Google it) I found myself having to improvise.

"Right, we'll put everything that's being thrown away over there by the tools, and every-thing that's being sold over there by my golf clubs. Hang on, that doesn't work – we might end up throwing away the tools and selling my golf clubs..."

Three hours later we had more categories than eBay and more piles than the average doctor has to deal with in a year.

Having only ever bought at a car boot sale, I was totally unaware of the stress involved in actually selling the stuff. I'd assumed that the three hours of arguing, swearing, categorising and sub-categorising were the only stressful parts of the process; the selling part was meant to be the part were we reclined our chairs and waited for the suckers to start throwing money at us.

Not so, because the stuff that my wife and I had only a few hours previously described as "ugly" and "tatty" were now being dressed up as "quirky" and "dependable". Like a seasoned estate agent, I was revelling in finding the tiniest selling point in the crappiest of crap. At one point I told someone that what they were buying was better off without the original box, as it's one less thing to worry about losing! I really don't know whom I was trying to fool because if anyone ever described themselves in a lonely hearts ad as "quirky" and "dependable", you would immediately know that they were ugly and boring.

I was amazed at how defensive I became too. Let's remember that the previous night I was happily tossing items twenty feet across my garage, boldly declaring "That's another piece of crap we can sell!" Yet faced with even the slightest disapproving look from anyone wearing corduroys and I was ready to pick a fight. I lost count of the amount of times I felt like shouting "Oi, it might be crap, but it's my crap!"

So having spent the afternoon being bartered down from 50p to 30p by a stream of less than enthusiastic octogenarians, I can finally declare that we made a grand total of £33.25. Not bad you might think. £33.25 for what was essentially a load of old junk.

Unfortunately, we did spend £7.00 on the pitch, £9.00 on food and drink, and £4.00 on the tea-cup ride to entertain our little one, so we made a grand total of £13.25 profit. Having spent three hours in the garage and four hours at the boot fair, that works out an hourly rate of about £1.89. Add in the fact that our marriage was very nearly brought to a premature end on more than one occasion, and I can safely say that we won't be doing another car-boot sale any time soon.

Tuesday 10th September 2013

This morning I have once again witnessed the same half a dozen people running as if their lives depended on it to get this train. Laden with heavy bags, laptops, umbrellas, coffees and awkward shoes, they charge down the road, puffing and panting and leaving a cloud of dust in their wake.

From where I stand on the platform, I can see them approaching from a hundred yards away, and it's a constant source of amusement for me to pick a winner each morning. It isn't as easy as it seems, because I often have to make quick decisions based on a complex set of variables. I'll often find myself weighing up head-starts, the number of bags, and the various types of footwear, and there's no greater satisfaction than picking the guy at the back based on his sporty trainers and lack of bags, and seeing him overtake the entire field to claim victory.

In horse racing they have a handicapping system where they give the highest rated horses additional weight to carry, and having seen the handicapping system in action in humans, I think they should most definitely consider it for the 100 metres at the Olympics. Let's be honest, it's getting a bit boring at the moment, what with Usain Bolt winning everything in sight. Who wouldn't want to watch Usain Bolt trying to snatch glory in a pair of winkle-pickers while all the time trying not to spill his coffee? To be honest, he's that good at the moment that he could probably manage it. In fact, he could probably drink the coffee and still win.

Having watched the commuting version of Wacky Races play out in front of me every morning for the last year or so, I think I've finally come up with a solution. I've come up with a way to ensure that these poor souls no longer have to risk their health or their coffees in order to make the train each morning. It's a radical piece of thinking and it's an idea I'm happy to share with the world for free. Are you ready? Right, here it is – the perfect solution to ensure that never again will people have to run for the train each morning:

GET UP EARLIER!

There it is, I think you'll agree that the many long nights I've spent trying to tackle this thorny issue were time well spent. I've also come up with radical solutions for weight loss, (eat less and exercise more) drug addiction, (don't take it) and STDs (stay celibate).

Wednesday 11th September 2013

Every so often I'm reminded of just how stupid people can be. This morning, upon entering a public toilet, I was confronted by what looked like an unattended laptop bag. At first I just froze. I had no idea what to do. A few years ago, I would have simply picked it up and taken it to the lost-property desk, but we live in an age now where an unattended bag in central London can be a fairly serious security threat. If I'm completely honest, the constant warnings of 'threats to our security' seem a little over the top at times, but I do understand why we need to be so aware. So instead of picking it up and marching off towards the lost property desk, I just stared at it. Could I be the unwitting participant in a hidden camera show? Were there cameras watching my every step, waiting for me to make my move?

Suddenly there was a noise from one of the cubicles. I'd assumed I was alone, so it came as a bit of a fright when the flush sounded and a well-dressed man emerged and wandered towards the bag. He looked at me and nodded, and while I tried to give him my best "Seriously, mate! Why the hell did you leave your laptop there?" look, all I actually mustered was a simple nod in return. Just seconds later he had washed and dried his hands and left the toilet with the bag slung over his left shoulder.

Who in their right mind thinks "I could bring this valuable item into the cubicle with me, but no, I think I'll leave it outside, creating an easy opportunity for any thief, while also generating a massive bomb threat at the same time?" When does a little extra space when taking a crap ever outweigh the chance of being responsible for a bomb threat? Even if we ignore the bomb threat for a second, this guy seems to have an unbelievably relaxed approach to his possessions. Any would-be thief entering that toilet would have thought all of their Christmases had come at once. Not only is there an unattended laptop, but he also has a ten-foot head-start with the added bonus of the victim not only being behind a locked door, but also naked from the waist down. You hear of crimes taking place where in order for the thief to get away, he orders the victims to back away, lock the door, and even remove items of clothing; well this guy seems intent on doing the thief's work for him!

I spent so long standing in amazement at the stupidity of the man that people had filed in behind me and taken the two spaces at the urinal, so I was left to use his recently vacated cubicle. Once there I was presented with a crime far worse than any laptop theft and far more explosive than any potential bomb threat.

Ladies and gentlemen, we have a floater!

Thursday 12th September 2013

There's been talk over the last few days of wipe-clean plastic bank notes being introduced by the Bank of England by 2016. Currently, Bank of England bank notes are made from cotton fibre and linen rag, and the reason for the proposal is that the new notes will be cleaner, more secure and ultimately more durable. Made from a thin and flexible material called polypropylene, the new notes will have a longer life-cycle, meaning they will be more environmentally friendly – it's been reported that some of the current notes only last around a year. I'm assuming those notes are the lower denominations and not the higher ones. I can't imagine a £50 note will ever get worn out because they are totally impossible to spend.

"I can't take this," the person in the shop will say, before looking at you as if you're the one being unreasonable.

"It's real!" you say, trying your best not to sound like a criminal.

"There are counterfeit notes in circulation and we just can't take the risk," comes the reply.

"Surely you can just palm it off onto the next paying customer," you say, now sounding exactly like a criminal.

Eventually, after a ten-minute stalemate, the manager of the pound shop will ask you to leave, and while you find yourself still in possession of the big pink note, you have to make do without the family pack of Haribo.

While the idea of copying other nations by creating notes which are cleaner, more secure and more durable, while all the time being more environmentally friendly, is a good one, why not go one step further and come up with a world-first? Why not get rid of bank notes altogether? Why should we have notes at all – we have the technology to be able to transfer money back and forth instantly, so why couldn't we create a system where we can do this efficiently and easily while on the move, to anybody that we wish. I know it's a crazy suggestion and one that no doubt will attract huge criticism, but in my view paper money seems to be a huge part of the problem when it comes to crimes such as money-laundering and drug-dealing. Surely wipe-clean, super-durable notes are just going to play into the hands of the criminals? But can you really see drug dealers on street corners accepting payments straight into their bank accounts via a chip and pin device? "There you go, sir, if you'd just like to pop in your number. Don't worry, I'll look away. I specialise in drugs, not financial crime!"

In fact, having thought the idea through in great detail, (in the time it's taken for the train to travel from Tonbridge to London Bridge) I can confidently state that by getting rid of bank notes we will solve all crime, we will eradicate all UK national debt and we will ensure that no-one will ever be in a situation where they can't buy a pack of Haribo. The only losers in my new paperless money system are those who liked the show 'Million Pound Drop' and anyone who still receives money from relatives at Christmas.

Tuesday 17th September 2013

I've worked in the City of London for just over ten years, and up until this morning I had never once seen anyone wearing a bowler hat. Growing up, I was fed dated images of City workers trotting off to work in a pinstriped suit, complete with umbrella and bowler hat, and before working in London myself, I'd assumed that London was still awash with these eccentric toffs.

I can't deny that I was mildly disappointed when I first witnessed the reality: a bunch of arrogant idiots dressed in a range of cheap mismatched high-street suits. And lest you think I'm being unfair, I include myself in that. I'd assumed that I would stick out like a sore thumb, and that as soon as my first pay-cheque had cleared I would be making a visit to Messrs Johnson & Co. to purchase my very own Charlie Chaplain fancy-dress outfit. It wasn't necessary however, as I blended in perfectly. I was so disappointed. Times had obviously moved on, and pinstriped suits and bowler hats were no longer the uniform of the successful city worker.

I remember the initial excitement and then ultimate disappointment of non school uniform days at school. It was only fifteen minutes into woodwork, with my favourite jumper covered in sawdust and wood glue, when I realised what a terrible idea it was. A blazer might be an annoying, old-fashioned accessory for most, but I truly loved my blazer. I was able to travel incredibly light thanks to the multiple pockets, and it served as a perfect umbrella when pulled over my head, thanks mainly to its shiny material, gained from months of not being washed. Even when not being worn it served a vital purpose as a makeshift goalpost.

So while walking to my office this morning, I was pleasantly surprised to see a man wearing a bowler hat. While his suit wasn't pinstriped, it was certainly an upgrade on the normal mismatched offerings, and he walked with genuine pride and purpose. While some might view him as an eccentric idiot, I was happy to applaud him for trying to keep hold of the old traditions. That was at least until I saw him lift his hat and bow his head to an attractive lady on the other side of the road.

I reserve the right to change my mind. Ban the bowler for good.

Wednesday 18th September 2013

A year ago today I posted an angry rant on Facebook, proudly declaring that "Sleeping on trains is a waste of time!"

Little did I know at the time that those words were to become the inspiration for this series of books. I'll be forever grateful to the friends who stuck up for the sleepers, because were it not for them, this series of books would never had existed. Had they simply said "Too right Andy, I'm with you 100% there!" rather than what they did go onto say, which when paraphrased goes as follows "Andy, you are an idiot, everyone sleeps on trains, so just pipe down and join them!" then 'As They Slept' would only ever have been a phrase uttered after the words "and murdered his neighbours..."

So much has happened to me in the last year, and much of it I've shared through these books. In a way, writing on such a regular basis has become a sort of therapy. Whereas in the past I might have bottled certain things up, resulting in feeling stressed and emotional, these books have allowed me to discuss my feelings and to air my frustrations.

While writing down everything that pisses you off and then allowing the world to read about it may be a little extreme for some, I can't help feeling that if more people took the time to keep a diary, the world could be a far happier and harmonious place. It would also serve as fantastic reading material in many years' time, when you'd look back at the time in your life when you were genuinely pissed off just because your partner kept coming to bed late, especially as you approach the years when just making it to bed each night is a genuine bonus.

I've learned a hell of a lot in the last year too. I've learned that I'm far grumpier than I ever gave myself credit for. It seems that there's nothing I'm not prepared to grumble about, but while that may be the case, I've also learned that by writing about it, I became far more accepting of it.

I've also learned that family time is precious and that children grow up so fast. Again, by writing about the experiences we've had as a family, I feel that I've appreciated them so much more. (The trip to Cyprus aside – writing about that will never be able to turn those sad memories into happy ones).

It's been a year of change too. My wife gave up work in February as she was finding that working as a full-time teacher and being a mother didn't go hand-in-hand, so she decided to take a step back and consider her career options while being able to spend more time with our daughter. As it turns out, it was the perfect decision, because after trying to conceive for over 18 months, my wife fell pregnant just a few weeks after saying goodbye to her class. That's the stress teachers are under nowadays.

Fittingly, this week sees a big change for me too. With my wife due to give birth in a matter of weeks, my employers have been fantastic in offering me the option to work from home until the new arrival is settled. My wife had an emergency caesarean section last time around, and the thought of being at least two hours away should the worst happen was a scary one. But my employers were able to provide me with everything necessary for me to work from home on a full-time basis. I really can't thank them enough for that.

It does however mean that this really is the end of the line for this series of books (pardon the pun). I've been asked by numerous people to keep on writing, but I've always been certain that a year is enough. The challenge was to write for a year, and that's what I've done. The fact that I won't be commuting for the next three months is another clear sign that the challenge has reached a natural conclusion.

So there we have it, Dean Mason, I did it. I wrote a chapter on every commute for a year, and I did it "As They Slept"

Special Thanks

Emma, Charlotte and our newest addition Sophie – For your constant support and happy smiles.

Euan Davidson – For being a truly great editor and answering all of my stupid questions.

Steve Lawson – For providing the design and expertise required to make this book look as good as it does.

Dean Mason – For providing the inspiration for the book and an honest if not altogether positive foreword.

My Mum and Dad – Everyone thanks their Mum and Dad don't they?